THE MONTROSE & BERVIE RAILWAY

The Last Train, coming out of the tunnel under North Esk Road in Montrose. This is now the route of the Montrose bypass. *Author*

Class 'J37' No. 64608 at Inverbervie with an unusually long train for Montrose on 22nd February 1964. Two brake vans were provided to carry an Aberdeen Transport Society party, most of whom actually travelled in the cab! *Norris Forrest*

To my mother,
Margaret Young,
for her love and encouragement.

The Montrose & Bervie Railway

A Study of Transport in South-East Kincardineshire 1770–1966

Mike Mitchell

Lightmoor Press & the Caledonian Railway Association

The 12.44 train from Bervie calls at Johnshaven on 1st September 1948. *J.L. Stevenson*

Contents

Acknowledgements		6
Introduction		7
Chapter 1	The Setting	9
Chapter 2	Early Roads	11
Chapter 3	The Bervie Turnpike Road	15
Chapter 4	The Stagecoach Age	21
Chapter 5	Coastal Shipping and Canals	25
Chapter 6	The Railways	27
Chapter 7	The Bervie Railway	33
Chapter 8	Operating the Bervie Railway	45
Chapter 9	The Montrose & Bervie Railway Company in Retrospect	53
Chapter 10	A North British Branch Line	55
Chapter 11	The L&NER Years	63
Chapter 12	British Railways and Closure	69
Chapter 13	A Summer Holiday on the Bervie Line	81
Appendices		
1	Turnpike Road Finances	91
2	Railway Infrastructure	95
3	Signalling and Operations	113
4	SNER-M&BR Working Agreement	125
5	Montrose & Bervie Accounts 1865-1881	127
6	The Amalgamation Bill Proceedings	129
7	Coaches, Carriers, Omnibuses and Buses Running through Bervie 1837-1950	133
8	Bervie Line Fares – 1st May 1913	135
9	Known Bervie Line Station Agents 1866-1966	137
10	Montrose & Bervie Railway Company Directors and Principal Shareholders	139
11	The Stonehaven Extension	145
Bibliography		149
Index		151
About the Author		152

Published by LIGHTMOOR PRESS in conjunction with the CALEDONIAN RAILWAY ASSOCIATION
© Mike Mitchell, Lightmoor Press and the Caledonian Railway Association 2015
Designed by Nigel Nicholson

British Library Cataloguing-in-Publication Data. A catalogue record for this book is available from the British Library
ISBN 9781 89988996 9
All rights reserved. No part of this publication may be reproduced, stored in a retrieval system or transmitted in any form or by any means, electronic, mechanical, photocopying, recording or otherwise, without the written permission of the publisher

LIGHTMOOR PRESS
Unit 144B, Lydney Trading Estate, Harbour Road, Lydney, Gloucestershire GL15 5EJ
www.lightmoor.co.uk
Lightmoor Press is an imprint of Black Dwarf Lightmoor Publications Ltd
Printed by Berforts Information Press, Eynsham, Oxford

Acknowledgements

Thanks are due to the staff of the National Records of Scotland, Edinburgh; The National Archive at Kew; the National Portrait Gallery; the Libraries, Leisure and Culture Department, Dundee; Aberdeenshire Archives at Old Aberdeen, and the Inverbervie Library, especially Margaret Gray who helped with many of the illustrations from her personal collection. The contractor drawings are reproduced courtesy of Blyth & Blyth of Edinburgh, the successor company of the original contractor. Most of the newspaper references were found using the British Newspaper Archive; researching this work would have taken far longer, and might even have proved impracticable without this excellent resource.

I would also like to record my gratitude to the many people who helped with photographs and illustrations, especially the late Michael Mensing who allowed me to use his beautiful views of the branch in its latter days. Illustrations are individually credited in the captions, but I would particularly like to thank Hamish Stevenson for allowing the use of the photographs by his father, J.L. Stevenson. Thanks also to John E. Adams of St. Cyrus; Mike Cooper of the Great North of Scotland Railway Association; Andrew Kennedy of the Caledonian Railway, Brechin; Allen Smith of the Benholm & Johnshaven Heritage Society; The Montrose Air Station Heritage Centre, and Allan Rodgers for their assistance in locating interesting views. I am grateful to Allan Rodgers for many of the plans and drawings in Appendix 2, for permission to quote extensively from his 1999 article in the *North British Railway Study Group Magazine*, together with the map of the branch. I am also grateful to Gordon Casely for permission to use part of his obituary of Mary Officer, and to Robert Kennedy for permission to reproduce his feature article on the closure in 1966.

Walter Blakeman of Laurencekirk generously gave me the use of his collection of Scott family memorabilia, and it is to him that I owe the discovery of the photograph of Hercules Scott. Unfortunately the painting by Lorimer to celebrate Scott's tenure as Chairman of the Montrose & Bervie Railway has not been located. Thanks are also due to the staff of Lathallan School, which is now based in Scott's former home, Brotherton Castle. Care has been taken to trace and gain permission for the use of illustrations, but for any wrongly credited, I apologise.

Keith Jones, Allan Rodgers and Alistair Nisbet gave invaluable support in checking the text for errors and omissions, as well as providing constructive criticism. Both Allan and Alistair have written magazine articles on the Bervie Branch, and these are listed in the bibliography. I would also like to thank my sister, Irene, for proof-reading the text. However any errors which remain are entirely my responsibility. Finally, I would like to thank the Caledonian Railway Association for helping bring this project to publication.

Prices are quoted in the original currency of pounds, shillings and pence. For readers who are not used to these units, £1 = 20s and 1s = 12d. The rate of exchange at the time of conversion was 1 shilling : 5 new pence.

Dr Mike Mitchell
Huddersfield

The return freight from Bervie to Montrose approaches Den Finella Viaduct at 3.35pm on 6th July 1964. This was the highest viaduct on the line, though that fact is hidden by the vegetation on the west side. The locomotive is ex-North British Railway Class 'J37' No. 64558. *Michael Mensing*

Introduction

Inverbervie is a very small town, and never was a place of any consequence. It was erected into a royal burgh by David the Second, in 1362, on occasion of his being shipwrecked there, and kindly received by the inhabitants. It has no harbour, and no natural advantages of any kind, and it possesses neither trade nor manufactures.[1]

So did the Commission on the Municipal Corporations in Scotland dismiss the place in 1835. In fact the Commission got it wrong – Bervie was already a manufacturing centre, with a linen spinning mill in operation since 1787, a flax spinning business commencing six years later[2] and some inshore fishing. It was also the location of a weekly market and a stop on the mail coach services to Aberdeen and Edinburgh.

Bervie (as it was officially named until 1926 when the name was changed to Inverbervie) is the largest of the villages on the north-east coast of Scotland between the former Kincardineshire county town of Stonehaven and Montrose in Angus. Stonehaven (population 3,009 in 1861) is fifteen miles south of Aberdeen, while the much larger town of Montrose (population 14,563 in 1861) is about thirty-five miles north of Dundee. Of the others, Gourdon and Johnshaven are small fishing villages, while St. Cyrus is a small settlement clustered around the Montrose–Aberdeen road, itself replacing an earlier fishing village at Milton of Mathers which was washed away by the sea around 1790.[3]

As the Commission acknowledged, Bervie is an ancient town, recognized as a Royal Burgh in 1362, when David II was shipwrecked there. It predates most of the settlements on the coast, including much of Stonehaven, and can trace its documented history back almost as far as Aberdeen.[4]

The Bervie Branch was unusual in being operated by two of the major Scottish railway companies, first the Caledonian Railway and then the North British, and in having services provided by both for a short time. This book, generously supported by the Caledonian Railway Association, examines the development of this part of south Kincardineshire from the late eighteenth century in the context of road transport improvements and then the introduction of the railway. It then goes on to establish whether the railway was a successful investment for the original local owners, and analyses the reasons for the railway's decline and closure.

Notes

1. *Local Reports of the Commissioners on the Municipal Corporations in Scotland* (London, 1835). The Bervie section was written by James Campbell.
2. D. Bremner, *Industries of Scotland: Their Rise, Progress and Present Condition* (Edinburgh, 1869) states that the first mill for spinning linen yarn was established on the Haughs of Bervie in 1787 by Sime & Thorn; it was reputedly the first in Scotland to use machinery for this process. See also I.J. Burness, *The Flax-spinning Industry of Inverbervie & District 1787-1992* (Inverbervie, 1994). An account of the jute industry published in the *Dundee, Perth and Cupar Advertiser* [*DPCA*] on 16th April 1850 (p. 3) gave the start date for the Thom & Co. flax spinning mill as 1793, but went on to recount that '*as the preparing machinery was defective, the quality of the yarn produced was of an*

Bervie about 1880. This is looking north along King Street. The carriage on the left by the church gates is the only traffic. *Margaret Gray*

ABOVE: This very early, and surprisingly rural, photograph shows the Haughs of Bervie and some of the textile mills in operation in the mid-nineteenth century. The gas works in the foreground was opened in 1845. The building in the middle is the Old Mill; how old it actually was is not known, but there is a reference to a spinning mill in the Haughs in the Sessions Rolls of 1838. In the distance, on the left is the Upper Mill, while to its right (on the Bervie Water by the Clay Braes) was the first spinning mill in Scotland. The group of buildings in the right distance is the Pitcarry Mill. The steep track in the foreground was called the Gassie Brae at that time, while the more easily graded track to the mills was the Middle Brae. *Margaret Gray*

inferior description.' Within ten years or so flax spinning mills had been established at Montrose and Dundee, presumably producing better quality yarn.

3. South Kincardineshire is also known as the Mearns (the inland part round Laurencekirk usually known as the 'Howe of the Mearns').
4. Aberdeen's charter dates back to the reign of David I (1124-53). However, it is a much older settlement, with reference to it as 'Devana' on Ptolemy's map of 146AD and evidence of human habitation much further back. According to *Fermfolk and Fisherfolk*, J.D. Smith and D. Steven (Aberdeen, 1989), the coastal villages date from 1600-1700, and Stonehaven from 1500-1600. This is clearly wrong, as Stonehaven is mentioned on a thirteenth-century map and was established as a settlement by the fifth century. It remained '*an insignificant settlement*' (J.J. Waterman, *Aberdeen and the Fishing Industry in the Eighteen Seventies*, Aberdeen, nd, p. 35) until about the beginning of the seventeenth century. In 1655 Thomas Tucker described Stonehaven as '*a little fisher town where goods have formerly been brought in, but not of late, because hindered from doing so by the neighbourhood and privileges of Montrose*'. The new town of Stonehaven, however, is much more recent, dating from the late eighteenth century, when it was laid out on a grid pattern by Barclay of Ury on the Arduthie Links, following his purchase of the area in 1759. Many of the streets are named after his relatives.

Robert Barclay of Ury (1731-97) was one of the most prominent of the improving landlords of the eighteenth century. He invested so heavily in his estates that on his death a series of economies had to be implemented at Ury.

Chapter 1

The Setting

Kincardineshire Agriculture in the Eighteenth Century

To understand the development of this part of north-east Scotland, it is necessary to look at the landholdings in the area, and the nature of its agriculture and industry.

Robertson's *General View of Kincardineshire*[1] described the coast south of Stonehaven in the following terms:

This territory extends about 18 or 20 miles in length, along the shore, from Stonehaven to the Northesk, and might have been included in one division with the preceding [north of Stonehaven to Aberdeen], were it not that the soil, composed of different materials, and that the general aspect of the surface, more inviting to the eye, shew a marked distinction in nature. It rises in general, with a bold rocky shore, from 100 to 300 feet in height, and expands into plain fields, many of which are in high cultivation; but laid out in every direction, according as the several rivulets or deep ravines bend their course from the conterminous hills to the ocean. Some of these hills (and generally the most barren) approach close to the sea; but the greater part are in the back ground, and although very numerous are not lofty; none exceeding 500 feet in height. The soil in the lower parts, is of every description from the most worthless, to the most valuable. But it is oddly intermixed; entire wastes, in some places lying contiguous to the most fertile fields. The greater proportion, however, is of the latter description; some of the lands near the shore being as productive perhaps, as any in Britain, bearing the most luxuriant crops of beans, wheat, clover, &c. This tract, stretching inland from 4 to 5 miles, may comprehend about 85 square miles, or 54,400 acres; of which one half is in cultivation. It extends through the southern part of the parish of Fetteresso, and comprehends the entire parishes of Dunnottar and Kinneff, the greater part of Arbuthnott, together with the whole of Garvock, Bervie, Benholm, and St. Cyrus.

The agricultural improvement movement in the late eighteenth century is traditionally held to have been responsible for a great increase in the productivity of the land, though at the expense of uprooting the traditional small farms and their replacement by larger units. Features of the improvement usually involved removal of stones (and their use in building dykes to enclose fields) and the introduction of a crop rotation system to improve yields. The agricultural improvement movement was well-established in the area; the earliest and most notable of the improving landlords was Robert Barclay of Ury, Stonehaven, who began to improve his estates from 1760.

On the death of his father in 1760, he worked for nearly 40 years to improve the quality of his land. This was achieved by draining and levelling large areas. Construction of dykes and ditches and the adoption of many farming techniques which were widely adopted in the surrounding area. In all over 2,000 acres of arable land was cultivated by him in this way, and 1,500 acres of wood planted. It is he we have to thank for the development of the Mearns as the foremost agricultural county it is today.[2]

In the parish of Ecclesgrieg (St. Cyrus) a number of landowners such as Robert Scott, William Graham of Morphie and Sir Alexander Ramsay of Balmain introduced techniques such as liming, turnip cropping and enclosure of moorland, but a map of 1774 showed a relatively small area enclosed. Fraser, in *Portrait of a Parish*, a history of St. Cyrus, noted that:

when Robert Scott began his improvements, 10s-15s was considered a high rent per acre for farmland, and tenants were by no means easy to find. By 1790 the price had risen to anything between 20s and 40s. By 1807 the best land in the Mearns was being let at as much as £5 per acre and there was no trouble at all in finding tenants.[3]

The impetus for this change was economic, reflecting a desire to see better returns from their landholdings by landowners, but was also a response to declining crop yields since 1707, following a surge in the seventeenth century. By 1820 production had reached its seventeenth-century performance, and had grown by 58% by 1850. However, production of food failed to keep pace with population growth, and grain imports were increasing, leading to higher prices and therefore an incentive to farmers to increase domestic production. Proponents of the enclosure and improvement movement have argued that rental values doubled or even trebled as a result of improvement, and a primary reason for the Statistical Account of Scotland published between 1791 and 1799, as well as the New Statistical Account published in the 1830s, was to chart the progress of 'progressive' agriculture. However, a recent study[4] demonstrated that the difference in productivity between enclosed and unenclosed parishes was about 20%, reflecting the fact that some improvements in agricultural methods (such as the use of fertiliser or the growing of turnips) were not dependent on enclosure. The productivity growth was more than enough to warrant investment in the land, but less spectacular than has been claimed.

These developments had a direct effect on the population which could be supported in the area. Table 1 shows population movements at forty-year intervals from 1755 in the five seaside parishes south of Stonehaven.

Table 1: Population Movements in East Kincardineshire 1755-1871				
Parish	**1755**	**1791**	**1831**	**1871**
Dunnottar	1,570	1,906	1,852	2,102
Kinneff	858	1,000	1,029	1,062
Bervie	655	985	1,137	1,561
Benholm	1,367	1,560	1,484	1,569
St. Cyrus	1,271	1,763	1,598	1,552

While the population growth was not significant – except in Bervie, where the development of flax and jute mills drove the population increase – none of the parishes suffered significant losses. A minor exception was Johnshaven (in Benholm parish) which suffered from British Naval press-gang depredations during the Napoleonic Wars, and later from a decline in the fishing industry as Aberdeen began to dominate that activity. In contrast to the coastal parishes, Garvock suffered nearly a 50% reduction in its population between 1755 and 1791 as farms were consolidated. However, even here the population fluctuated greatly as activity in the quarries changed.

Table 2: The Principal Estates in 1810			
Village	Estate	Extent	Owner
Bervie	Hallgreen	1,489 acres	James Farquhar MP
Johnshaven	Brotherton	2,650 acres	Lt-Col Hercules Scott
St. Cyrus	Laurieston	3,336 acres	John Brand

Improving access

Robertson[5] noted that Lt-Col Scott of Brotherton, near Johnshaven, had '*subscribed liberally*' to making a good road from Johnshaven inland to the Howe of the Mearns, and had also devoted a great deal of effort to improve his lands. All the major landowners were investing in their properties at this time, but this appears to be the first recorded instance of transport improvement being seen as part of the overall drive to develop landholdings.

While improvements in agricultural practices could make a difference to the value of landholdings, the main impediments to progress were the lack of access to wider markets and the limited ability to bring materials in. The general state of access to the Montrose–Stonehaven coast was poor in the later eighteenth century and this restricted trade; Robertson noted both Gourdon and Johnshaven harbours as unsatisfactory, and the main road variable at best. He described Gourdon, the sea-port for Bervie, as having '*remarkably bad access*', rendering it '*very inconvenient for trade*', while at Johnshaven, '*The harbour … is even less frequented; owing chiefly to the want of good roads of communication*'.[6]

Although the tiny harbour at Bervie had been improved by Telford in 1819, it suffered from continual build-up of shingle at the mouth of the River Bervie and was abandoned by 1830, the few salmon boats simply being winched up onto the beach and the rest of the fleet moving to Gourdon.

Notes

1. G. Robertson, *A general view of Kincardineshire; or the Mearns; Drawn Up and Published by Order of the Board of Agriculture* (London, 1810).
2. Stonehaven, *Still Thriving*, at www.Mearns.org.uk
3. D. Fraser, *Portrait of a Parish* (Montrose, 1970).
4. C. Douglas, 'Enclosure and Agricultural Development in Scotland', in *Economic History Society Conference Booklet*, 2004 (at http://www.ehs.org.uk/events/ehs-annual-conference-archive.html), pp. 10-15.
5. G. Robertson, op. cit., p. 200.
6. *Ibid.*, p. 200.

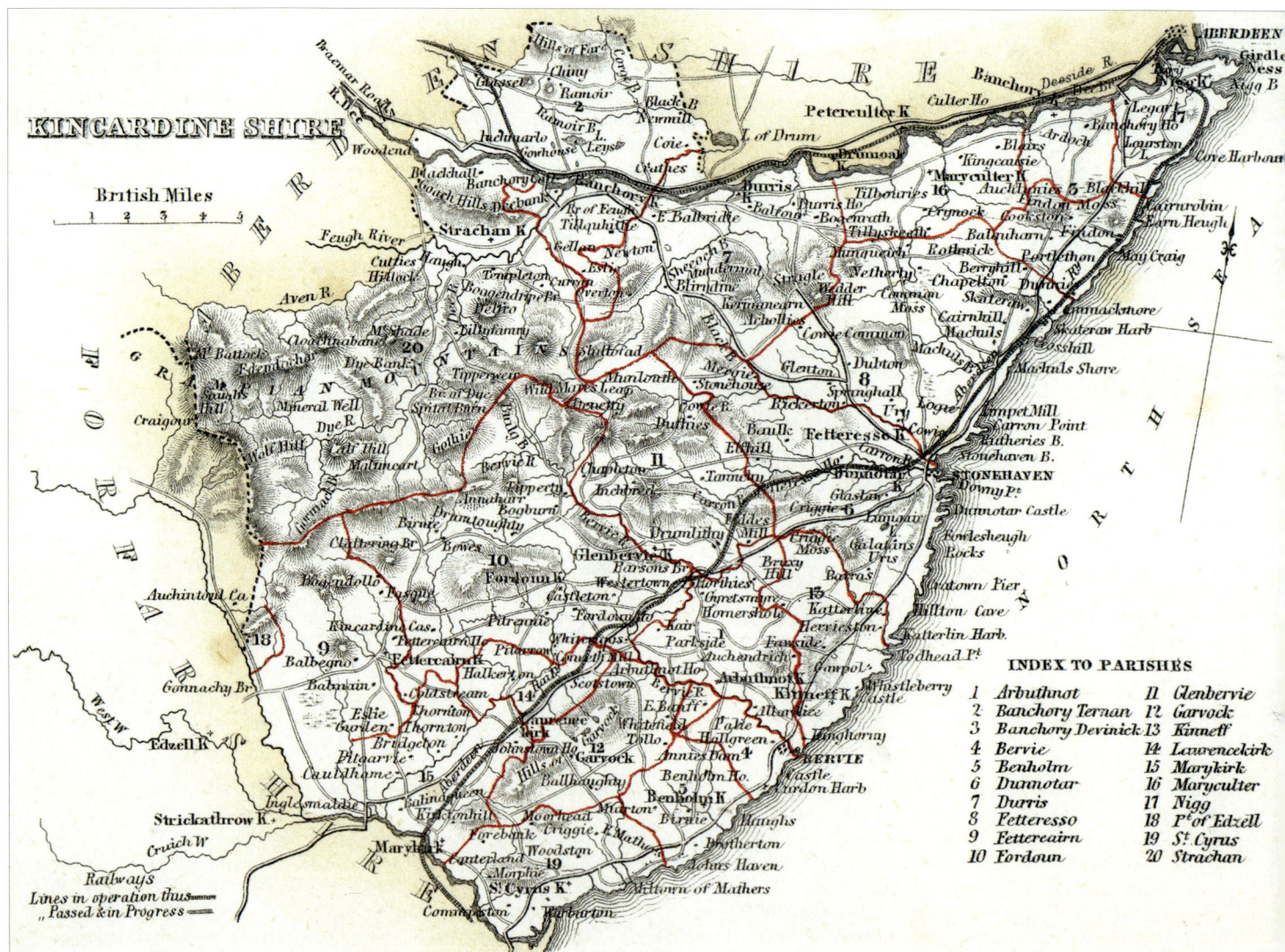

Map 1 1860 Fullarton map showing Kincardineshire and its parish boundaries. The Aberdeen Railway is shown, but the Montrose and Bervie has yet to be built. It passed through the three south-eastern coastal parishes of St. Cyrus (Ecclesgreig), Benholm and Bervie.   *Author's collection*

Chapter 2

Early Roads

Roads in Kincardineshire before the Kincardineshire Roads Act 1796

In his 1992 doctoral thesis Thomas Day describes how the roads before the middle of the eighteenth century in the area would:

if compared to the worst-made, rutted farm road of today, be considered unfavourably. To call them roads is in effect a misnomer. As there was no wheeled transport, they were more likely to be narrow crooked tracks, avoiding major obstacles. … All merchandise and bulk goods were carried in packs and creels on the backs of men and beasts.[1]

Until the passage of the Kincardineshire Roads Act in 1796, the responsibility for road maintenance and construction lay with the Justices of the Peace and Commissioners of Supply.

The Royal Commission on Roads in Scotland noted that:

There appears to have been no general legislative provision on the subject of roads in Scotland, until the beginning of the seventeenth century, when the Act 1617, chap. 8, gave power to Justices of the Peace to mend highways and passages to or from any market town or seaport, and to punish those who injure such, and declared that the breadth of highways to market towns should be 20 feet at the least, and that those of larger breadth should remain unaltered, and be maintained by the Justices of the Peace, as well as all other ways from any town to the parish church, with power to report to the council where new roads are required, and also to punish such as refuse to mend highways and passages.

This Act was renewed in the same terms by the Act 1661, cap. 38, and appears to have been the only existing provision for the construction or maintenance of public roads till the year 1669, when a statute was passed (1669, cap. 16), which for the first time introduced the system of personal service or labour on the roads, which was termed Statute Labour.[2]

Under the 1669 Act there were powers to levy highway rates of 10s per £100 of rentable value and to summon all cottars and tenants to carry out unpaid labour on the roads for six days per year; this obligation could be 'commuted' by the payment of 3d per day missed. However the system was not working; even where work was done on the roads, it was done poorly and unwillingly. The Revd James Scott, describing the situation in Benholm, the parish to the north of St. Cyrus, said:

From the nature of the soil, and the difficulty of bringing gravel from the shore, the high way has hitherto been deep in winter. Nor are the cross roads in a better state. The statute labour is insufficient, and is performed with reluctancy.[3]

The incessant wars in the eighteenth century – between 1702 and 1815 Britain was at war with France for sixty-four years, not to mention two major rebellions in 1715 and 1745 – meant that transport was given a low priority, except where it was seen as necessary for the rapid movement of troops. One of the effects of the 1745 Rebellion was to promote a system of military roads connecting garrison forts and built under the supervision of General Wade. However, none of these roads was built in north-east Scotland. Sea transport was made more hazardous because of the actions of foreign privateers and British Naval press-gangs, while the need to move troops quickly around Scotland also provided an incentive to improve the roads.[4]

A volunteer in the Duke of Cumberland's army described his journey through Kincardineshire thus:

After leaving Montrose about a Mile, I came to the North Esk, where there is a small Ferry for Foot Passengers, but the Horse fords it when there is little Fresh in the River, which runs with a strong currant; however my Horse being heavy, I got very well over, by keeping up against the Stream, after which I cross'd over eight Miles of the most wretched Country to Bervie; the Road being excessive bad, I lost a Shoe from my Horse; it likewise rain'd and blew hard, which much fatigued me.[5]

The sequestration of estates from landowners who had supported the Jacobites in the 1745 Rebellion brought an opportunity to fund some improvements. The Montrose magistrates submitted a 'memorial' to the Commissioners of Annexed Estates on 25th April 1769, and the Minutes of the Commissioners' meeting on 3rd July 1769 recorded a submission to King George III asking for £500 to be granted to assist with funding a new bridge over the North Esk. This was agreed, and the Commissioners noted on 6th August the following year that *'work is now begun, and carrying on with all Diligence'*. Notwithstanding this, a further petition was submitted in June 1773 asking for more money. It stated that the foundations were laid for the eight-arch, seven hundred feet long bridge in October 1770. The architect was John Adam and the contractors were Andrew Barrie and Patrick Brown, who had quoted a total price of £6,000 sterling for the work. However, the magistrates were approximately £1,000 short. The petition noted that work was expected to be completed later in the summer of 1773 but that additional expenditure had been incurred; not only had they the cost of getting James Smeaton, the canal engineer, to survey the river, but Mr Fullerton of Kinnaber had submitted a claim for £220 for his ferryboat. Also, no allowance had been made for the earthworks and land acquisition costs of the approach roads. The alternatives to additional funding were the stopping of work, or the imposition of a toll. The amount asked for was left vague, and the magistrates merely prayed that the Commissioners would *'take their case into consideration and grant them some further aid'*. In the end the bridge cost £6,500 and they raised the money largely through collections in parish churches. It opened on 18th October 1775.

The bridges at Benholm and Bervie also sought to benefit from the Annexed Estates fund; an undated Memorial from the Kincardineshire Commissioners of Supply asked for £100 to complete the new bridge at Benholm, which had fallen down in March 1773, and £120 was granted towards the cost of the new Bervie Bridge in 1778.[6]

While the improvement of the bridges was a major advance, the state of the intervening roads remained variable. The ministers writing in the Old Statistical Account gave widely varying descriptions of the roads in their parishes. The roads in the parish of Fettercairn were described as being *'in excellent condition'* because the principal heritor had *'paid much attention to these matters'*,[7] while the Revd William Walker wrote of the roads in his parish (Ecclesgreig, or St. Cyrus):

So late as 35 years ago, to travel from Montrose to Bervie (which is only 13 miles), in a carriage, was a dangerous journey.

There was a rough, and often an unsafe ford, to pass through the North Esk; then a steep water-worn path to climb up to the common level of St. Cyrus parish; and then 3 dens [ravines] to pass, without bridges, by narrow and winding paths down their steep sides, without one foot of made road all the way. … Now indeed, these inconveniences are in a great measure remedied, by the bridges thrown over the North Esk and Den Fenel, the Burn of Woodston, and the Den of Laurieston; and it is with pleasure that the author of this narrative is informed, that government have lately granted 100l [£100] to heighten the Bridge of Laurieston, which is now the most difficult pass in this parish.[8]

In his *General View of the Agriculture and Rural Economy of the County of Aberdeen* (1794), James Anderson pointed out that because the current roads had been established when wheeled traffic was almost unknown, and:

As bogs had originally been the most dreaded obstructions, to avoid these, the roads had been, in general, carried along the high grounds where they could be come at; so that, in many cases, they carried a considerable way about, to shun the vale and get up a hill.

The resulting gradients were '*very inconvenient*' for wheeled traffic and this, coupled with a poor surface, meant that the roads were:

in such a miserable state, that unless it be for a few months in the summer, it is impossible to drive a carriage upon them with more than half an ordinary load. Indeed, through the greatest part of the year it is more difficult to drag an empty cart along these roads, than it would be to draw one fully loaded, were they in a proper state of repair.[9]

So long as the economy of the area was little above subsistence level, and with what little trade there was being handled by sea, the improvement of the roads was not seen as important, but it became evident to the landowners that the value of their properties was being held back by the primitive state of land transport.

The effect of poor roads meant that only settlements close to coastal ports could import lime or coal, or could export manufactured goods or agricultural produce, since wheeled traffic was so restricted. A set of returns of wheeled vehicles subject to 'wheel carriage tax' which survives in the National Records of Scotland in Edinburgh lists the carriages with two and four wheels which existed between 1785 and 1797 in Kincardineshire, while a parallel series lists carts. In the coastal parishes south of Stonehaven there were only two recorded carriages in 1785, while even by the end of the century this number had only increased to five. Unsurprisingly, one of the carriages in 1785 belonged to James Scott of Brotherton, while the others were largely owned by neighbouring landowners. There were two carriages for hire in Stonehaven in 1785 and twelve in Montrose, but it seems likely that these did not venture far outside the town boundaries.[10]

The Development of Royal Mail Services

One of the measures of how isolated an area was is the extent to which postal services reached it; postal communication was necessary to enable contracts to be exchanged, and to establish whether goods were available or had arrived. Without a postal service it was only possible to carry out trade by immediate bargain, with payment in cash or goods being made locally.

According to Bremner's *Industries of Scotland* (published in 1869), the first public coaches in Scotland ran between Edinburgh and Leith in 1610, when Henry Anderson, improbably a native of Stralsund in Pomerania, obtained a Royal Patent giving him exclusive rights for fifteen years on the route. He imported coaches, wagons, horses and staff from Stralsund and charged 2d for each passenger.[11]

Although Aberdeen is noted as having a 'common post' as early as 1595,[12] and in 1674 a regular Post Office mail service from Edinburgh was instituted[13] replacing

Minute of meeting of Montrose Town Council agreeing to apply to the Commissioners of the Annexed Estates for £500 towards the new North Water Bridge, 6th August 1770.
National Records of Scotland, E727/34

Survey of the Rates and Duties on Wheel Carriages ... in the Shire of Kincardine for ... commencing the 5th July 1784 & ending the 5th April 1785 by William ... Surveyor

Wheel Carriage Tax.

Date of Survey.	Masters and Mistresses Names and Designations.	Actual Number	Carriages with 2 Wheels, Duty L. 3 : 10 s. each.	Carriages with 4 Wheels, Duty L. 7. each.	Duty		
1785	Benholm Parish						
	David Scott of Nether Benholm Esq	1		1	£	5	5
	James Scott of Brotherton Esq	1		1		5	5
	Totall	2		2		10	10
	Dunnottar Parish						
	John Milne in Mills of Stonehaven	2		2		10	10
	Fetteresso Parish						
	Vice Admiral Robert Duff	1		1	£	5	5
	Robert Barclay of Ury Esq	1		1		5	5
	Totall	2		2		10	10
	Marykirk Parish						
	James Irvine of Kingcausie Esq	1		1	£	5	5
	John Menzies of Pitfoddels Esq	1		1		5	5
	Totall	2		2		10	10

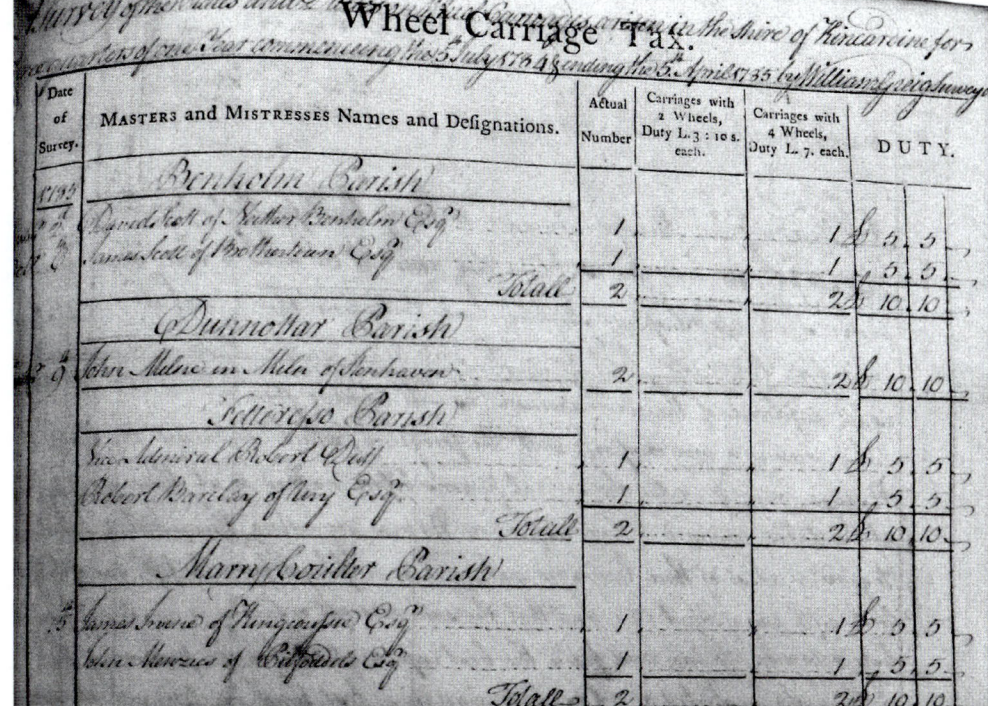

Part of the 1784-85 Wheel Carriage Tax Returns for Kincardineshire. There were only a couple of carriages licensed in each parish, with those in Benholm being registered to David and James Scott.

Crown Copyright, National Records of Scotland, E326/8/1

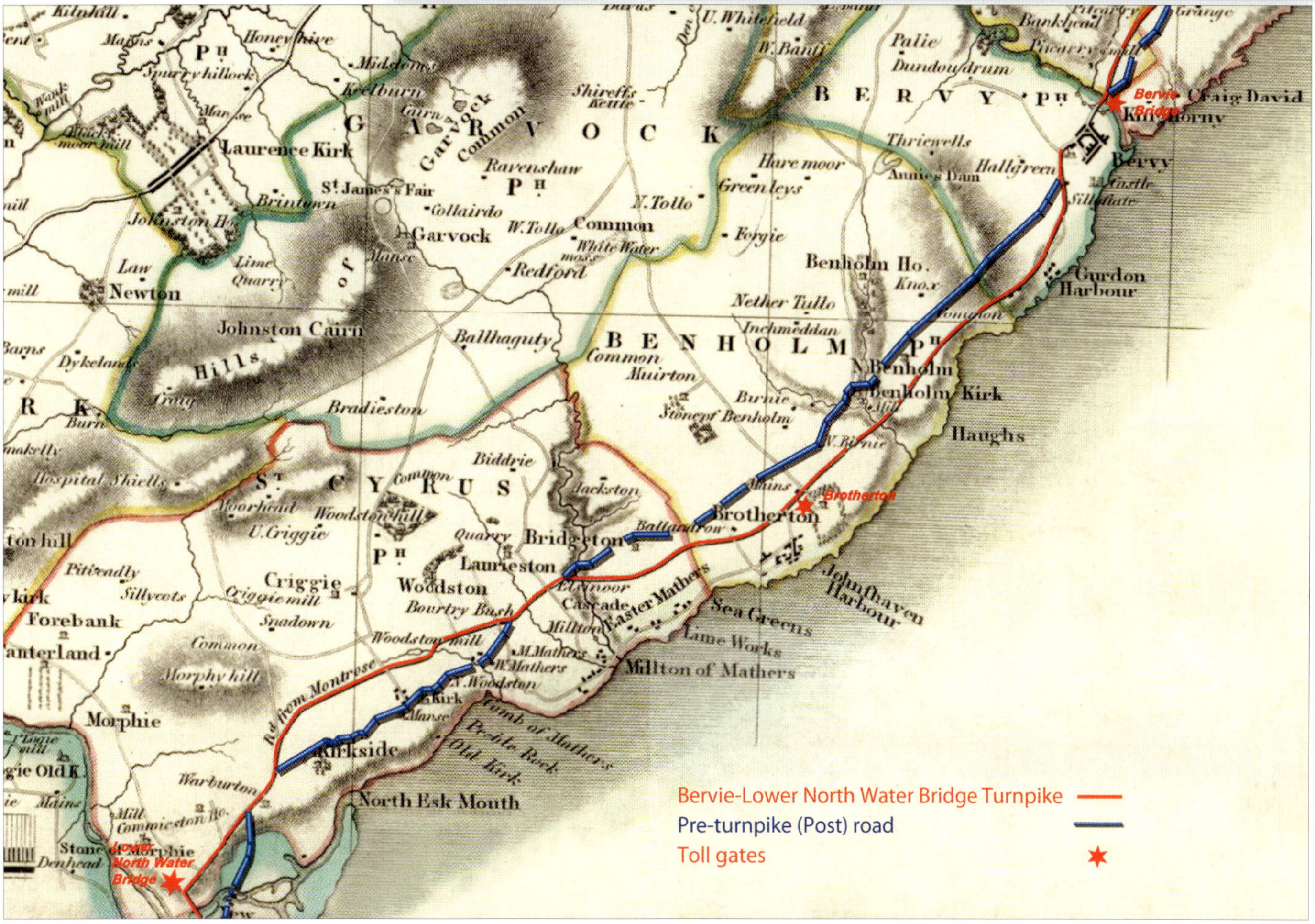

Map 2 This map (based on Taylor's *Atlas of Scotland*) shows the different line taken by the Bervie–Lower North Water Bridge turnpike compared with the previous coach road, and perhaps explains why it took so long to build. The villages of Benholm and Woodston were bypassed by the new coastal alignment, while Brotherton and St. Cyrus (not shown on the map, but on the turnpike south of Woodston Mill) were placed on the main transport route. The modern A92 road follows the turnpike route. The exact location of the Brotherton toll gate is not known for certain.

By permission of the National Library of Scotland

an earlier unofficial foot post, it remained impossible to convey mails by other than 'runners' until much later because of the condition of the roads. A 'memorial' written in the reign of Queen Anne (1702-14) informs us that three foot posts or carriers went weekly from Edinburgh to Aberdeen via Cupar (Fife), Dundee, Montrose, Bervie and Stonehaven, for which they were allowed 6s 8d each, plus 1s 6d for the ferries.[14] A proposal by the Aberdeen postmaster that runners should be replaced by horses on the Edinburgh mail in 1716 was turned down because the cost was felt to be excessive,[15] though by the middle of the eighteenth century horses were in use on a three-stage system which was a great improvement in terms of speed.[16] The introduction of wheeled vehicles to carry the mail had, however, to await the improvement of the roads north of the Tay.

Postal services were also very expensive; William Maitland's 1753 *History of Edinburgh* quoted rates for Edinburgh to Bervie and Aberdeen of 3d for each sheet of paper, or 1s for a one-ounce letter.[17]

Just how hazardous the journeys faced by the post riders could be was illustrated on the evening of 6th November 1779, when the Aberdeen–Edinburgh post was:

stopt about four miles south [of Aberdeen], and the mail carried off by a person who appeared to be a tall middle-aged man. … He threatened to take the post-boy's life, if he did not go forward to Stonehaven. The boy went forward till he came to Causeport, about a mile south of the place where he was stopt; and, having got men to escort him, he returned directly back to Aberdeen, from whence parties of the South Fencibles, now lying there, were immediately sent out in search of the robber, and the post-boy was again dispatched south.[18]

A reward of £50 (equivalent to £7,500 now) was offered in an age when such robberies were routinely punished by the death penalty. Nor was the occasional robbery the only hazard faced by the post-boys. On 24th September 1785, when:

John Christie, post-rider, an old man, had arrived at the western bank of the Elliot on his customary journey from Dundee to Arbroath with the mail bags. It was a wild night. There was a great storm of wind and rain, and the usually small stream had been converted into a roaring torrent. The post-rider was an old sailor, who had served in the fleet more than thirty-seven years, and he seems to have thought that the Elliot, formidable as it then appeared, was not such an obstruction as should delay his journey. He accordingly headed his horse to the ford, but he was swept away by the torrent and drowned, the horse alone reaching the further side in safety.[19]

The following year the councils of Arbroath town and Forfar county built a bridge over the Elliot stream.

In February 1792, the postal surveyor, Ronaldson, was still just noting a *'general desire'* to extend the posts to Aberdeen – still, he believed, impracticable because of the condition of the roads, although that had not deterred the Edinburgh & Aberdeen Fly coach, which by that time had been running for over ten years.[20] At last, in October 1796 the Postmaster General announced that a Royal Mail coach was to be instituted between Edinburgh and Montrose on 5th May 1797, the roads that far having been sufficiently improved.[21] The Aberdeen extension commenced on 1st August the following year,[22] though it is not known what improvements in the roads further north had allowed this development. However, it is clear from other public announcements at the time that privately operated stagecoaches had also started running over both the Dundee–Brechin–Laurencekirk–Stonehaven–Aberdeen routes and the coast route through Montrose and Bervie by the time the first through mail coaches started.

Notes

1. Thomas Day, 'Studies of the development of the turnpike roads and their associated engineering infrastructure in north-east Scotland 1780-1880' (unpublished PhD thesis, Aberdeen, 1992), section 1.1 Introduction.
2. *Report of the Commissioners for Inquiring into Matters Relating to Public Roads in Scotland*, 1859 Report, pp. xi-xviii (hereinafter referred to as *'Royal Commission on Roads'*).
3. *Old Statistical Account, Vol. XIV, Kincardineshire [OSA]*, p. 237.
4. There is evidence that the hazards of attacks on shipping off the north-east coast of Scotland encouraged the building of the Aberdeen–Banff turnpike – see J. McIntosh and A. Small, 'Road Development in the North-East of Scotland 1746-1815: the Maritime Connection', in *Scottish Geographical Magazine*, Vol. 111, No. 3, pp. 159-67 (1995). The construction of roads in Scotland by General Wade after the 1745 Rebellion mainly affected the Highlands, but the state of roads in Kincardineshire did impede the passage of Cumberland's troops as the next quotation shows.
5. J. Ray, *A Compleat History of the Rebellion from the First Rise, in 1745 to its Total Suppression at the Glorious Battle of Culloden in April 1746* (Bristol, 1752), p. 290.
6. *Caledonian Mercury [CM]*, 30th Nov. 1774, p. 3, carried a letter saying that now the North Esk Bridge had been opened for carriages 'at last', the *'dangerous and often impassable river of North Esk may now be crossed without danger or expense.'* It had been open as a temporary footbridge since September 1773 (*CM*, 29th Sep. 1773, p. 3), but as late as January 1774 carts were still fording the river (John Forbes fell off his cart and drowned on 12th January 1774 [*CM*, 19th Jan. 1774, p. 2]). Interestingly, the work on the Benholm Bridge was supervised by Scott of Nether Benholm, and the Revd Young of Benholm Parish, reflecting the wide responsibilities assumed by probably one of the few educated men in the area. It was 1798 before the Bervie Bridge was finished. Papers on all three bridges are in National Records of Scotland [NRS], E727-34 and E728-29 files.
7. *OSA*, p. 105.
8. *OSA*, p. 96. The new bridge across the Den of Benholm was started in 1775 (*CM*, 14th Jun. 1775, p. 2).
9. J. Anderson, *A General View of the Agriculture and Rural Economy of the County of Aberdeen (etc)* (Edinburgh, 1794), pp. 22-23.
10. Wheel Carriage Tax Returns, NRS, ref. E326.
11. D. Bremner, *The Industries of Scotland: Their Rise, Progress and Present Condition* (Edinburgh, 1869) – Coachmaking.
12. A.R.B. Haldane, *Three Centuries of Scottish Posts* (Edinburgh, 1971), p. 16.
13. *Ibid.*, p. 25.
14. S. Cowan, *Perth, the Ancient Capital of Scotland: the Story of Perth from the Invasion of Agricola to the Passing of the Reform Bill* (Perth, 1904).
15. Haldane, op. cit., p. 40.
16. *Ibid.*, p. 56.
17. A. Smail, 'The Scottish Postal System in 1753 and 1759', in *Scots Magazine*, 1st Nov. 1899, p. 472.
18. *CM*, 24th Nov. 1779, p. 4.
19. G. Hay, *A History of Arbroath to the Present Time* (Arbroath, 1876), p. 361.
20. Haldane, op. cit., p. 79.
21. W. Alexander, *Northern Rural Life* (Aberdeen, 1879).
22. Public announcement in *Aberdeen Journal [AJ]*, 24th Jul. 1798, p. 1.

Chapter 3

The Bervie Turnpike Road

The Kincardineshire Roads Act 1796

Up to the end of the eighteenth century, the responsibility for upkeep of roads in each county lay with the Justices of the Peace and the Commissioners of Supply (county councils). This was done by a system of levies on landowners and the imposition of demands for free labour (or latterly a money payment) from local tenants – the so-called commutation system.

Powers to take tolls at bridges, causeways and ferries had existed since the 1669 Act of the Scottish Parliament and the first Scottish turnpike, in Midlothian, was completed in 1714.[1] By 1788 there were seventeen trusts in Scotland but none covered roads north of Perth.[2] Trusts were controlled by the local landowners, and they had the powers to impose tolls, raise subscriptions and borrow money. At the same time, local Acts of Parliament gave powers to the Commissioners of Supply to form Commutation Road Trusts. These replaced the unpopular system of statute labour with a local tax for road repair, and this too was overseen by local landowners. In Kincardineshire, most commutation and turnpike roads were authorised by the Kincardineshire Roads Act of 1795[3] which led to the establishment of two 'road districts' covering the main roads through the county. The First District covered the north of the county, and the Second District the two main routes from Stonehaven southwards to the River Esk, the county boundary. By a further Act of 1817[4] the Second District was permitted to divide itself into two subdivisions, covering the Stonehaven–Laurencekirk–Upper North Water Bridge (Forfar) road and the Stonehaven–Bervie–Lower North Water Bridge (Montrose) road,[5] although in fact subdivisions had been established unofficially at the meeting of the Second District Trustees on 30th May 1796.[6]

The Aberdeen–Stonehaven road was soon under construction, though even at this stage there was some dispute over the exact line to be followed. The Bridge of Dee (Aberdeen) to Stonehaven road was said to have been determined according to the surveyor's plans in the Act, but the two roads south of Stonehaven were not clearly defined. As a result it was decided to have Charles Abercrombie,[7] who had conducted the original survey and produced the plans for the Act, also survey those routes. An alternative plan submitted by a small party of landowners was thrown out:

Mr Logie observed ... that the County at a most numerous meeting having approved of and adopted Mr Abercrombie's line of road, considered itself as pledged to the public for it; and for that reason when the Town of Aberdeen under a different set of Trustees forming the first district, agreed to make the Road from Bridge of Dee to Stonehaven, the County conditioned that it should be done by Mr Abercrombie's plan. As to what was called Mr Innes's plan it was treated with silent contempt, and virtually departed from at the last Meeting when Mr Abercromby's [sic] line of road from Stonehaven to Laurencekirk was adopted.[8]

However, the two competing plans for the Bervie road were still contentious. It was agreed that the Stonehaven–Bervie road should follow Abercrombie's plan, and from Bervie to the North Esk river (the Lower North Water Bridge) that by Innes. George Robertson Scott of Benholm said that the Act was based on the Abercrombie plan, despite what the last meeting had agreed. Innes's plan for the Bervie–North Water Bridge section was not suitable, he said, as '*it runs for four miles with the sea on one side and a precipice on the other.*'[9]

In August 1796 it was reported that the contractors were now working on the Aberdeen–Stonehaven road and the four miles nearest Stonehaven on the Bervie road. However, the Trustees were clearly having trouble getting money out of the subscribers, some of whom were using non-payment as a way of ensuring their own local road was built first. On the section from Stonehaven to Drumlithie road end, for example, Viscount Arbuthnott was to be prosecuted for non-payment and Scott of Dunninald was to be pursued for £500 due. In June 1798 the Clerk reported that the Viscount was fighting his payment and Scott of Dunninald had placed money at the bank in Montrose to be used on the express condition that it be used only:

for the purpose of making and repairing that part of the line of Road directly North from Bervie, approved of by the Trustees, beginning at the bridge now building at that place.[10]

The Trustees decided not to allow anybody to impose such conditions on their payments and to take legal action if necessary to recover the money. In the event, they did not have to because Scott paid up. There is no record of further action against the Viscount, so presumably he paid up as well.

The four miles of the Bervie–Stonehaven road nearest Bervie was advertised for contract in November 1799, but the contract had to be re-let the following August because of the death of the contractor, Andrew Brown. The opportunity was also taken to invite tenders for a new toll-house at the north-east corner of the Bervie bridge.[11]

Construction of the first sub-division road (from Stonehaven to Drumlithie road end) was started in late 1797 and by April 1798 the second sub-division road (from Drumlithie road end to Laurencekirk) was under way. The road between Stonehaven and the Upper North Water Bridge (south of Laurencekirk) opened throughout later that year, and by 1800, when two years' experience of operating the toll gates had been achieved, it was decided to put the operations out to tender for one year from 15th November 1800, the toll revenues to be shown to the bidders for guidance.[12]

On the Bervie road, the new bridge over the Bervie Water was completed in 1801, and a sub-committee produced a list of competing roads which were to be stopped up, an important power possessed by the Trustees to maximize the toll income. The Stonehaven–Bervie road opened in late 1801, with the tolls at Invercarron (Stonehaven) to be let on 5th November that year.[13] In the event, however, no suitable tender was received, and the Trustees decided to run it themselves for a further year.[14]

Progress on the Bervie–Lower North Water Bridge section was much slower. By 1806[15] it was reported that only about seven miles of the road had been constructed; this seems to have been the result of a problem with the availability of funds[16] as well as the continuing dispute over the route south of Bervie.

By August 1811 the Trustees were able to report that:

The Road from Bervie towards Lower North Water Bridge being now finished as far as Ballandro loan, the Meeting resolved immediately to collect Toll duty at the Bar erected at Bridge of Brotherton.

The Meeting further considering that there will be in the course of a few weeks a sufficient extent of road made to the North of the North Water Bridge to authorize the trustees to erect a Bar at the said Bridge, resolved to erect a Bar accordingly, and, as soon as the surveyor shall certify that that part of the road contracted for by Alexander Brown is finished in terms of his contract, to collect Toll duty, by employing a person for that purpose, in the same manner and upon the same terms before mentioned as to the Bar at Bridge of Brotherton.

While George Robertson, in his *General View of Kincardineshire* of 1810, acknowledged that the road from Bervie northwards to Stonehaven was 'one of the best roads imaginable, and is upheld by turnpike', he was still complaining that:

from Bervie south to Montrose, through a hill and dale country, it is not merely up and down hill, but also kept in miserable order, having no funds to support it but the commutation money, which is altogether inadequate to a road so much used as this. It has long been in contemplation to alter its course, and to make it turnpike. But the coterminous proprietors have never yet been able to agree on the plan to be adopted for this purpose.

However, he added in a footnote:

since writing the above, measures have been adopted, and are now putting in execution, to alter this road into an almost entire new line, and to complete it in the best manner.[17]

The line of road was very important, as whether a community was on the turnpike road would make the difference between it thriving or becoming a backwater. This was not an issue on the fourth sub-division (Stonehaven–Bervie), where the landowners agreed that the line should run through the village of Kinneff, but south of Bervie on the fifth sub-division it was an altogether different matter.[18] A bitter feud erupted between two landowners in the Benholm area, about three miles south of Bervie. Colonel James Scott of Brotherton and George Robertson Scott of Benholm argued that the road should pass through their respective properties. At a Trustees' meeting on 30th April 1808, George Scott reported that sufficient funds were now available to make the Bervie–Lower North Water Bridge road, and that the 'most agreeable' line was the line laid down in the Kincardineshire Roads Act, with a deviation to take it through the village of Benholm and his lands. In December 1808 advertisements appeared inviting tenders for the remaining work, which was to be completed by 1st June 1809.[19] However, at the meeting of 7th August 1809 a furious argument broke out between George Scott and Colonel James Scott over the line to take. George Scott had sought to pre-empt the decision by instructing a contractor to start work on his 'deviation' and a mile of this had already been constructed. Colonel Scott referred to the eight-year-old dispute which had held up progress. George Scott protested that:

the alteration is unjust in so far as the line of road through the parish of Benholm ... was central and runs near to the Church and therefore renders any other parallel commutation road unnecessary and gives accommodation to those proprietors and individuals who have for time immemorial had the benefit of the vicinity of the public road – whereas by this [the Colonel Scott] alteration a line is adopted running at the extremity of the parish at a distance from the Church and of those who have hitherto enjoyed the benefit of the public road so as to render necessary a parallel commutation road through the whole of the parish and thus that interest of the parish and of those who formerly enjoyed the public road is sacrificed to the interest of one individual who grasps at a new advantage for himself at the expense of his neighbour – That for this injustice no adequate degree of public advantage can be assigned as a reason since it has been ascertained that the whole length of deviation from Abercrombie line is two miles and a quarter – That the line of this deviation can be made for two-thirds of this length at an elevation not exceeding one foot in a hundred and for the remainder not exceeding one foot in forty two – That it adds to the length of the whole line only two hundred yards which to a cart travelling at the rate of three miles per hour occasions a delay of two minutes – That by avoiding an expensive Bridge ... at the den of Brotherton and by its vicinity to materials it can be executed with a saving of £400 – And by affording a facility of keeping up four miles of the old road where it is perfectly level it affords an opportunity an additional saving of £2,000 taking into account the saving of surface damages – That this line is therefore in every respect the most eligible.

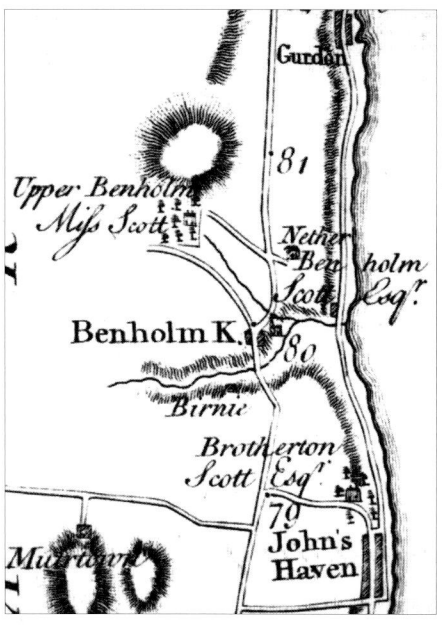

This portion of Taylor & Skinner's 1776 map shows the old road from Bervie through Benholm towards Johnshaven and the south. Benholm village was centred on the road network prior to the making of the turnpike, which took a line about half a mile to the east.

By permission of the National Library of Scotland

Despite his objections, Colonel Scott's line won the day, and a form of peace was restored by the Trustees agreeing at their 3rd October 1809 meeting that George Scott should be reimbursed for the cost of the mile of road he had built, and be repaid his advances to the Trust. This might have been the end of it, but for years afterwards George Scott took every opportunity to obstruct the progress of the road.[20] It may be that George Scott managed to by-pass the new road for a time as the old road through Benholm village was still passable. However, the Trust had powers to close alternative routes bypassing the toll gates, and a sub-committee reported in May 1816 that the old road through Benholm should be closed when the new road opened.[21]

When Colonel Scott proposed at the Trustees' meeting on 2nd September that year that the report should be implemented, now that a completion certificate had been issued for the new road, George Scott objected, saying the Benholm road was 'a useful high road and not a bye road' – but he was outvoted and the road was closed. Benholm today is a sleepy village about a mile off the A92, and has probably fewer dwellings than it had at the beginning of the nineteenth century.

Another example of the effect on a community was the diversion of the turnpike between St. Cyrus and the Lower North Water Bridge. The old post road had taken a line down along the banks of the North Esk River through Milton of Mathers to a ford about half a mile downstream from the new bridge; the turnpike kept to the higher ground through the village of Ecclesgreig (now St. Cyrus) and to the east of Kirkside estate before descending slightly to join the bridge. Milton has almost completely disappeared, while St. Cyrus was, and is, a thriving community. Happily in this case the landowners agreed on the line and there was no dispute over the new route.

Toll evasion was a problem at some locations, despite the action

CHAPTER 3: THE BERVIE TURNPIKE ROAD

Bervie Bridge circa 1880 not long after the abolition of tolls; the toll-house can still be seen on the left, with its schedule of charges displayed on the wall, and the tollgate posts and gates at the entrance to the bridge. The toll-house was demolished to make way for the Jubilee Bridge in the 1930s. In the background can be seen (on the left) Bridgend House before its third storey was added, and in the distance, to the left of the church, the King's Arms Inn, where stagecoach horses were changed. It later became the school and was extended at the rear.
Margaret Gray

taken to stop-up the competing roads. When the tolls were let at Invercarron for 1804-5, for example, the incumbent toll-keeper, a Mr Steel, complained that travellers were avoiding the toll gate and asked the Trustees to erect a wall and a railing to close off by-pass routes.[22] These measures did not solve the problem, however, as Steel complained two years later that the:

carravan which runs twixt Aberdeen and Montrose, had passed the Invercarron bar without paying toll as usual, or producing pass Tickets, for the period from 9th February to 14 November 1805.[23]

The First and Second districts were amalgamated into the Kincardineshire Consolidated Turnpike Trust in 1838. This covered the main road from Aberdeen to Stonehaven, and the coast road to the Lower North Water Bridge, as well as the Laurencekirk road to the Upper North Water Bridge, but not the South Deeside, Slug or Netherley turnpikes. The opening debt was £12,000, and the Trustees set about improving the roads in the Consolidated District: average spend on road and bridge repairs between 1839 and 1847 was just under £1,600, after which it fell back to £652 over the next nine years. Nevertheless, toll revenue was buoyant (until the Aberdeen Railway and then the Bervie Railway dramatically reduced it), enabling the Trust to pay off its debts by 1849 just in time to beat the opening of the railway. In 1858 the cash reserves stood at £3,647:

Another portion of Taylor & Skinner's 1776 map showing the new North Water Bridge and the old road over the Kinnaber House ford.
By permission of the National Library of Scotland

and the Trustees are of opinion that in the course of a few years, if they could legally do so, they should be in a position to abolish all the tolls on these roads, and maintain both them and the statute labour roads from the statute labour assessment in the parishes and the interest of the accumulated capital.[24]

By 1863, despite the immediate effects of railway competition, the Trust had investments of £3,565 and a cash balance of £897, allowing it to carry out repairs on all the Commutation Roads as well as its own, and to receive an income from one of the other trusts in the county.

The Kincardineshire Consolidated Turnpike Trust was financially very successful, in marked contrast to those elsewhere in Scotland, or indeed in the rest of Kincardineshire. In Aberdeenshire, for example, the turnpikes were almost universally in poor financial (and physical) condition, and the situation in Forfarshire (Angus) was little better. The much better position of the Kincardineshire Consolidated Trust was achieved partly through careful control of contracts, by a close attention to the repaying of loans and by a well-established system of tendering (or 'rouping') the toll bars, so that the Trustees had guaranteed income. The toll-keepers took the risk of a shortfall (as well as the chance of a gain), though they could supplement their income by selling liquor to the drivers, a practice finally banned in 1853.[25] Although the stagecoaches paid a commuted rate, they were a very important element of the revenue of the Trusts, right up until the opening of the railways caused the coaches to be withdrawn.[26] At the meeting of 1st May 1837 Colonel Scott could report that the debt for all five districts of the Trust had been reduced to £7,655 14s 1¾d and that the debt on the Stonehaven–Bervie–Lower North Water Bridge had been cleared. As a result, the toll bar at Brotherton was to be removed from 26th May 1837.[27] The Trustees had also made a shrewd bargain with the new Aberdeen Railway Company. In return for not objecting to the Railway Bill, the railway agreed to guarantee the tolls at £3,000 a year for ten years. If the debt were extinguished before the end of the ten years, the railway would be entitled to any surpluses. Within twelve years the debt had been completely extinguished, just two years before the opening of the Aberdeen Railway, but this deal ensured that even if the railway had opened earlier, the Trustees would have been protected. The fact that most of the Trustees were also investors in the new railway no doubt eased matters, but it was clear, even after the opening of the Aberdeen Railway, that the Trustees were managing their operation prudently.[28] Colonel James Scott's nephew, Hercules Scott, was a leading Trustee for most of the period between the opening of the Aberdeen Railway and the abolition of the trusts in 1878.[29] He campaigned throughout for the abolition of the tolls, arguing that the Trust had sufficient reserves for the road maintenance to be funded without them. Giving evidence to the Royal Commission in June 1859, Hercules Scott outlined his position:

I have for some time taken an active interest in road matters in the county of Kincardine, and am one of the Road Board, who are appointed by the general body of Trustees to attend to business connected specially with the turnpike roads. Besides the commutation roads, I am especially connected with those turnpikes which are comprised under the Consolidated Trust. There has lately been a scheme in operation, under which the Turnpike Trustees have employed the Commutation Trustees to expend the amount specially voted for the turnpike roads, in the proportion applicable to the parts of those roads passing through the several parishes. This scheme has been undertaken with the view of simplifying the conduct of the repairs of the turnpike road, and establishing one settlement and set of accounts.

I hold that the accumulations of funds which have taken place in the Consolidated Trust are both illegal and unjust, as I conceive that the Trustees are not justified in raising from tolls a larger sum annually than necessary for the maintenance and repair of the roads; and that the present generation are in this way made to pay for posterity. As yet, the tolls that have been removed are mostly those in the central part of the county, and least remunerative, whilst those on the confines have been continued – the effect of which has been to lay the burden of maintaining the whole roads principally upon the parties who have to pay the frontier tolls.

Part of a turnpike map showing the network round Stonehaven. The turnpikes to Aberdeen, Netherley, Laurencekirk and Bervie can be seen, as well as the Slug Road Turnpike and the toll-houses at Invercarron (Bervie and Laurencekirk), Redcloak (Slug), Polbare (Netherley) and Cowie (Aberdeen).

CHAPTER 3: THE BERVIE TURNPIKE ROAD

The best-preserved relic of the Bervie Turnpike is the double toll-house at Invercarron, Stonehaven. The Laurencekirk road is to the right, and the former main road to Bervie on the left. *Author*

I am myself an advocate for the abolition of tolls; and as a substitute I see nothing that would be fairer than an assessment on lands and heritages. The expense of collection by means of tolls I consider out of all proportion to the advantages derived from them. I assume that a tollkeeper must have an average profit of £33. Some of the bars in this county let for not more than £50 or £60.

I am also of opinion that, under any system of assessment, the tenants should have a voice in the management. At present, the community who pay the tolls are practically unrepresented in all matters regarding the turnpike roads and the rates of tolls.

I think there would be a great advantage in this county from the roads being under one surveyor; and, from the alteration of the traffic, I see no reason why the turnpike and commutation roads should be managed separately.

If the Commissioners wish it, I can forward them a report of the proceedings which took place in our County Road Meeting on 30th April, when a series of resolutions, condemnatory of the system adopted by the Consolidated Trust, was moved by me, and elicited much discussion. In the course of the argument, the whole of the pros and cons, statistics, etc., were fully brought out, which might be useful.

I think, in the event of a measure passing through Parliament abolishing the present obsolete distinction between the two classes of roads the existing organization employed in connection with commutation roads might advantageously be extended to the entire road system. Individually, I should be in favour of district management and application of funds in preference to application, etc., by parishes but I find a very strong feeling against any such withdrawal of local control over funds locally raised ….

The Commissioners having wished me to submit the queries put to me to D. Scott, Esq. of Brotherton, my father, I am instructed by him to state it is his decided opinion that the land must eventually keep up the roads, and that proprietors may just lay their account for it. He believes, even if tenants be nominally assessable, they will give so much less rent, and thus fling back the charge on their landlord. In general, he concurs with the replies I have made, and is especially convinced of the necessity of abolishing tolls.

However tolls remained until abolished by the 1878 Act.

THE IMPACT OF THE TURNPIKES

While the Kincardineshire Consolidated Trust turnpikes were financially successful, it had never been the aim of the Trustees to maximise profit from them. The aim was to improve communication with the wider world, and to abolish tolls where this could be done as debts were paid off. Several of the Kincardineshire toll bars were removed by the 1830s, and the only reason tolls remained until 1878 was the suspicion of some trustees that they would be giving an advantage to 'outsiders'. The effect on the area was profound, however, and it was not long before the advantage of being near the turnpikes was mentioned in sales documents.[30]

A more tangible measure may lie in the effect on population levels and valuations of estates. Between 1801 and 1851, the year after the opening of the Aberdeen Railway, the total population of Kincardineshire rose from 26,349 to 34,598, an increase of 31%, but the effect on the coast was quite patchy, with Bervie Parish increasing quite rapidly because of the development of new jute mills there, but St. Cyrus and the Johnshaven remaining static.[31] A rather better indicator is the analysis of occupations in the villages. Over a different timescale, from 1837 to 1867, there was a considerable increase in the number of trades being offered in the villages, with Bervie and all the villages along the coast to St. Cyrus recording large increases in the number of shopkeepers and tradesmen.[32]

NOTES

1. Authorised by an Act of Queen Anne (12th Anne) in 1713. *An Act for Upholding and Repairing the Bridges and Highways in the County of Edinburgh.* This Act was continued (in 1750) by 24 Geo II, c. 35. Most turnpike Acts were passed in the period 1770-1800; unlike in England where the first call on revenues was payment of interest, in Scotland the first call was maintenance of the roads. This was to lead to many trusts building very high debt levels.
2. J. Patrick, *The Coming of Turnpikes to Aberdeenshire* (Aberdeen, nd) p. 7.
3. 36 Geo III.

4. The Kincardineshire Roads Act 1817, 57 Geo III, c. 52.
5. The qualifications of ordinary trustees were as follows. First District: proprietors of land in Fetteresso, Banchory-Devenick, Maryculter and Nigg, with a rental value above £400 Scots; the eldest sons and heirs apparent of such heritors; one guardian or trustee of any minor qualifying. Second District: proprietors of land in the County of Kincardine with a rental value at or above £100 Scots; the eldest sons of such persons; the guardian or trustee of each minor possessed of land to that extent. To these were added the Provost and magistrates of Aberdeen, the Sheriff-Depute of the County, the Members of Parliament for the town and county, and sundry others. These two Districts operated in tandem until they were amalgamated in 1838 when a Consolidated Trust was established. £1 Scots was 1s 8d sterling.
6. The first meeting of the Second District Trustees took place on 30th April 1796. At the following meeting, on 30th May, it was decided to establish five subdivisions, these were: 1st-3rd on the Stonehaven–Laurencekirk–Upper North Water Bridge, the 4th covering the stretch from Stonehaven to Bervie Bridge, and the 5th thence to the Lower North Water Bridge.
7. Charles Abercrombie (1751-1817) was an eminent civil engineer and native of St. Cyrus who designed among other things the alignment of Union Street, Aberdeen.
8. Trustees' Meeting, 1st July 1796.
9. Trustees' Meeting, 2nd August 1796.
10. Trustees' Meeting, 5th June 1798.
11. *AJ*, 18th Nov. 1799, p. 1, and 11th Aug. 1800, p. 1.
12. Trustees' Meeting, 5th August 1800.
13. Trustees' Meeting, 6th October 1801.
14. In fact the tolls at Invercarron and Bervie Bridge were successfully let in July 1802 (Trustees' Meeting, 1st July 1802).
15. Trustees' Meeting, 30th September 1806.
16. At the Trustees' Meeting of 30th April 1808, it was reported that sufficient funds were now available to construct the road.
17. G. Robertson, op. cit., p. 406.
18. At the Trustees' Meeting on 30th August 1796, a motion by Allardyce of Dunottar that the Bervie–Stonehaven road should run as follows was passed unanimously: '*To begin at the Bridge of Bervie and be conducted by an equal elevation along the east side of the hollow of Pitcarry to the Cottage house of Largie, from thence turning round through a hollow towards the moor below the house of Falside where it may fall into the old road, and proceeding nearly along it near to the Bridge of Uras, to run as nearly as conveniently can be from thence to Stonehaven in the line laid down by Mr. Abercromby [sic].*'
19. *AJ*, 21st Dec. 1808, p. 1.
20. When the contract for the Bridges on the Bervie-Lower North Water Bridge road was let, it was found that the only suitable stone was from quarries owned by George Scott. He insisted that only his own labour could be used to extract the stone (Trustees' Meeting, 30th April 1810). At the meeting on 1st October 1811, he complained that toll bars had been erected irregularly at the Bridge of Brotherton and the North Water Bridge. A sub-committee was appointed to look into it. He then moved that there was no right to collect tolls until four miles of the six miles nearest Bervie had been completed. However this motion was deferred until after the sub-committee had reported. Finally, at the meeting on 30th April 1812, George Scott said he would move that no toll should be charged unless the traveller had travelled two hundred yards before the gate.
21. Meeting of Second Division Trustees, 11th May 1816. The sub-committee reported that they '*were of opinion that between Sillyflatt and the Farm House of Knox the old road is now useless and should be shut up; that from the junction with the Johnshaven and Garvock road southwards to the Bridge over Den Finella the old road will when the new turnpike road is finished and opened be rendered useless and ought then to be shut up accepting always such access as may be necessary for enabling Mr. Scott of Brotherton's Tenants to pass to the Mill and Kirk of Benholme; and that from the Bridge of Den Finella southward to its junction with the new turnpike road the old road should be narrowed to the dimensions of eighteen feet wide and kept open to that extent for the accommodation of the neighbourhood.*'
22. Trustees' Meeting, 23rd October 1804.
23. Trustees' Meeting, 30th September 1806.
24. Statement to *Royal Commission on Roads*, 1859 (report, p. cix). The other Kincardineshire turnpikes were in a less fortunate position. The others were: the Slug Turnpike (15¾ miles from Stonehaven to Banchory, established 1800) which had outstanding debt of £9,089 – £2,025 of which was owned by the Consolidated Trust; the South Deeside Turnpike (14 miles from Aberdeen to Banchory owned by the South Deeside road established 1837) which had £17,308 of debt, and the Netherley Turnpike (11 miles from Stonehaven to Maryculter, established 1820) which had £1,083 of debt. There were also two bridge trusts: the Marykirk Bridge (1811, debt £6,969), and the Wellington Bridge in Aberdeen (1829, debt £9,815) which also included the 4½ mile link to the Stonehaven road at Charleston.
25. The Act for the Better Regulation of Public Houses in Scotland (1853) prohibited toll-houses from selling wines and spirits unless they were more than six miles from a public house.
26. From 1839 to 1850 the Kincardineshire Consolidated Trust received an average of £1,551 per annum from coaches; the equivalent receipt from all other tolls was £1,895. The coaches therefore accounted for 45% of toll revenue in this period. After 1850 coach revenue rapidly disappeared as all long-distance coaches were withdrawn in the area.
At the meeting of 6th October 1835, there was a petition from '*the lately established stage coach called the "Braes of Fordoun" running in the daytime between Brechin and Aberdeen by Fettercairn and Auchinblae.*' It was granted a 66% reduction on normal rates. A petition was also received from the 'Swift' coach which was now running in daytime between Stonehaven and Bervie. It was granted a 50% reduction on the Stonehaven–Lower North Water Bridge section and the same rate as the 'New Times' coach on the Aberdeen–Stonehaven section. However a petition from the 'Union' coach to pay same as the 'Defiance' coach was refused. At the same meeting a petition from William Cruickshank (a Stonehaven innkeeper or 'vintner') for a proposed coach service to Aberdeen was agreed at the same rate as the other stagecoaches on the road.
27. At maximum there were twelve toll bars on the Kincardineshire Consolidated Trust roads, including a double gate at Invercarron, south of Stonehaven, one for each of the Bervie and Laurencekirk roads. They were (starting from Aberdeen) Bridge of Dee, Jellybands (Cammachmore), Bridge of Cowie, Invercarron (Laurencekirk Road), Bridge of Mondynes, Laurencekirk, Inglismaldie (Upper North Water Bridge), Invercarron (Bervie Road), Fawside (Kinneff), Bervie Bridge (north end), Brotherton and Lower North Water Bridge. By 1878 this had been reduced to seven gates, the others having been removed as follows: Fawside (1824), Brotherton (1837), Bridge of Cowie (1851), Bridge of Mondynes (1857) and Jellybands (1859).
28. Meeting of 30th June 1852 received a report from a sub-committee which recommended that '*in respect of altered circumstances by the opening of the Railway, and the consequent decrease of traffic, the Surveyor be instructed to reduce the outlay in repairs, exercising for that end the best of his discretion, and, as far as practicable, limiting the annual outlay on the several portions of the roads, so that it shall not exceed the sums following:- From Bridge of Dee to Bourtreebush, £75; from Bourtreebush to Stonehaven £55; from Stonehaven to Bervie £60; from Bervie to Bush of St. Cyrus £50; from Bush of St. Cyrus to Lower Northwater Bridge £55; from Invercarron Tollbar to Bridge of Mondines [sic] £45; from thence to Laurencekirk £30; and from thence to Upper Northwater Bridge £40.*' The subsequent financial returns (see Appendix 1) demonstrate that these instructions were largely adhered to.
29. The Roads and Bridges (Scotland) Act 1878 abolished turnpike trusts in all counties which had not already abolished them. Kincardineshire had waited, as it did not wish to have the expense of getting its own Act. Responsibility for roads was then taken over by Kincardine County Council, established under the Local Government (Scotland) Act 1889. Maintenance of roads was devolved to the County Road Board and to district bodies based on the pre-1890 districts (Aberdeenshire Archives, files KC2/7 and KC2/8). These continued in operation until 1930, when the Local Government (Scotland) Act 1929 required county councils to divide their county into districts, each with its own district council, composed of one or more electoral divisions. To these district councils were delegated a number of duties, including road maintenance. This system remained in operation until the establishment of the regions in Scotland in 1975 under the Local Government (Scotland) Act 1974. The area previously covered by Kincardine County Council was taken over by Grampian Region.
30. In 1805 Ballandro Farm adjacent to the Brotherton estate was advertised for sale and the proposed new Bervie–Montrose turnpike was mentioned as a sales point. '*Lands of Balandro for sale ... are intersected by the present road, as well as by the intended turnpike between these towns ... The town of Johnshaven contains upwards of 200 dwelling houses, and 1300 inhabitants; and as it is the nearest sea-port in the How [sic] of the Mearns, with which it is intended to make a better communication by new roads, it will soon increase*' (*AJ*, 27th Nov. 1805, p. 2).
31. Data from decennial census.
32. Pigot (1837) and Slater (1867) directories.

Chapter 4

The Stagecoach Age

Development of Stagecoach Services

The first public passenger road transport on the road south of Aberdeen seems to have been provided by William Driver, a Montrose hotelier, in 1775, when he advertised that *'one or two post chaises'* were to be stationed at Provost Christie's hotel in Bervie so that travellers could get a service to Stonehaven.[1] This was shortly after the completion of the North Water Bridge in September 1774, so it was odd that he was offering a service only between Bervie and Stonehaven, rather than from Montrose, though the better road north of Bervie with fewer deep ravines may also have had a bearing. This was an 'on demand' service with no fixed timetable, and it is not recorded for how long it ran.[2] On 14th June the same year, Driver announced a similar service from Montrose to Bervie.[3] The idea was resurrected in 1803 when it was announced in the *Aberdeen Journal* that:

> It having of late years been found a great inconveniency to the public in general, and travellers in particular, that the communication betwixt Montrose and Stonehaven by the post road on the coast side, had been much impeded

Above: Royal Mail coach ticket dated 1817 for a journey from Aberdeen to Stonehaven. The fare was 5 shillings.

Top: *Caledonian Mercury – Saturday 4th March 1775. Image © The British Library Board. All rights reserved. Included with permission of The British Newspaper Archive (www.britishnewspaperarchive.co.uk)*

> and often interrupted from no POST CHAISES having been kept at BERVIE, the intermediate stage betwixt Montrose and Stonehaven; they are respectfully acquainted, that a Company has been formed at Montrose and Stonehaven, who have resolved to keep neat Post Chaises, and careful Drivers, at Bervie, which are now put in there, and ready for the accommodation of the public on the shortest notice, upon being applied for at any of the Inns, or the stables of Tweedale and Milne, who think it their duty to mention to the public, that this road betwixt Montrose and Stonehaven is in excellent repair, by which the Mail Coach passes, the one half near thereof is turnpike, and the distance much shorter than any other road travellers can use.[4]

The first timetabled operation was the 'Edinburgh and Aberdeen Fly' coach, which started on 5th March 1781 via Forfar and on 25th June 1781 was joined by another of the same name on the coast road via Montrose and Bervie. Both took two days and cost 40s (£2) single, an enormous amount of money by the standards of the day (£300 in today's money), though when the 'Royal Mail' coach started seventeen years later, the proprietors of the 'Fly' were quick to point out that the 'Royal Mail' was even more expensive.[5] Drivers were also noted for carrying intermediate passengers at 'unofficial' fares which were not mentioned on their waybills. In March 1785 the management placed an advertisement entreating passengers:

> not to allow the drivers to take up foot travellers between stages, and to inform of those who do. Such as will be carried, and not entered in the way-bill ... will be prosecuted with rigour for the imposition; and any driver carrying a hangy [sic] any part of the stage he drives, shall be liable in one guinea to the company for each so carried; masters to be answerable for their drivers.[6]

The advertisement was probably aimed at drivers and contractors as much as the passengers. For a time in 1783, with the impending new tax on coaches, it looked as if the 'Fly' coaches would be withdrawn due to the increased costs. A correspondent to the *Aberdeen Journal* in October that year reported that both the Brechin and coast-road 'Fly' coaches might be withdrawn and that:

> It is agreed on all hands that each Diligence going twice a week on separate days, might find sufficient employment. This, however, has been opposed equally by the proprietors of both machines, who have determined to set out on the same days, or give up altogether.[7]

The same correspondent reported a month later that one light post coach, drawn by two horses, would do for the traffic on offer, implying that larger, heavier vehicles were used. He added that the fares could go up to cover the extra taxes.[8] By March 1785 his wish was partly fulfilled. Although both coaches continued to run on Mondays, Wednesdays and Fridays from Aberdeen, returning on Tuesdays, Thursdays and Saturdays, the fare had risen to 42s 6d to pay for the new tax.[9] Once the roads were improved more services appeared, including the 'Union' coach from Aberdeen to Perth (1810) (renamed the 'Strathmore Union' coach from March 1811, when it was extended to Edinburgh) and the 'Telegraph' via Strathmore. In the advertisement for the 'Strathmore Union', the reason given for using the inland route was the *'known superiority of this road,* through the beautiful valley of Strathmore, to the circuitous and almost impassable road by the coast.'[10]

By 1817 the 'Prince Saxe Cobourg' was operating between Perth and Aberdeen in fourteen hours for the ninety-mile trip via Montrose. The stagecoaches probably reached their zenith with the 'Defiance' coaches, which operated to Edinburgh via Stonehaven, Laurencekirk, Brechin, Forfar and Perth, on the promise of speed, efficiency and good service. These had been introduced on 1st July 1825 by a partnership consisting of Captain Barclay of Ury, Ramsay of Barnton, Edinburgh, Lord Glenlyon and others. A particularly gushing account of them was printed in Barron's *Northern Highlands in the Nineteenth Century*, published in 1904, reprinting cuttings from the *Inverness Courier*.

Their coaches were luxurious and handsome, the horses beautifully matched and of the first character, harness in good taste and of the best quality. The drivers and guards in their uniforms of red coats and yellow collars were steady and respectable men, great favourites on the road, obliging, full of conversation and local knowledge and several of these played with no mean talent on the bugle and cornet. Time was kept to a minute and so complete and perfect were the whole establishment that a highly paid veterinary surgeon was employed to tend the horses and see that they were perfectly looked to.[11]

Captain Robert Barclay-Allardice at the age of 64.
R.M. Hodgetts after J.W. Giles; National Portrait Gallery, London

A description of Barclay as a young man was published in a lengthy article in the *New Sporting Magazine* in 1837 by an unidentified friend writing under the *nom de plume* of Nimrod. At a celebratory dinner held in Forfar in June 1835, Lord Arbuthnot:

contrasted the Defiance to the old 'Fly' which took three days in going between Edinburgh and Aberdeen – and with the more recent conveyance, the 'Telegraph', between Perth and Aberdeen through Strathmore, and the spavined cattle by which these coaches were drawn.[12]

Captain Barclay owned an estate of about 1,000 acres at Stonehaven, on which were 1,200 sheep and 100 head of cattle. He seems to have been regarded as a 'sporting' gentleman by others of his social class, and took great pleasure in taking bets on his own performance. On one occasion he made a bet that he could drive the mail coach from London to Aberdeen without a break, and having achieved that, offered to drive it back again for another bet (nobody took this on).

'Nimrod' finished his account by describing a run of the 'Defiance' from Aberdeen to Edinburgh, when he took alternate stages driving with Barclay.

We enjoyed our drive very much indeed; every thing went well, and I was pleased at the respect paid, by all descriptions of persons, to the Captain on the road. I noticed the time occupied in some of the changes. That at Cowden Beath was done in a minute, and I should think the average did not exceed a minute and a half, which is quite quick enough to be safe.[13]

In 1829 Barclay formed a new partnership with a Mr Watson of Keillor to run to Edinburgh in one day. Barclay wrote to Watson:

You will no doubt recollect that, about a year ago, I communicated a proposal to you for having a really good day coach, leaving Aberdeen at six in the morning via Strathmore, and arriving in Edinburgh at nine o'clock at night, and vice versa. This fell to the ground owing to – [possibly Ramsay] – backing out, after undertaking to cover the ground from Perth to Edinburgh.[14]

In fact the day coach did run via Strathmore in 1827, changing to the coast road in the winter of 1827-28, though in the light of Barclay's letter, it presumably ceased soon afterwards. Barclay was clearly seeking to organise the coaches on the Edinburgh service, because in another letter to Watson he says he had discussed a reorganisation of departures from Aberdeen with Machray, the Aberdeen innkeeper who controlled the 'Union' and the 'Times', proposing that the 'Defiance' and the 'Union' should be the only Edinburgh coaches, supplemented by a two-horse day coach between Montrose and Aberdeen. He proposed that all the stage innkeepers should become partners in the business.[15] It is not entirely clear how much of Barclay's plan came into effect; certainly on 20th April 1829 the 'New Times' coach started running a day service to Edinburgh leaving at 5am and arriving at 8pm via the coast road, while on 1st July 1829 the 'Defiance' started a new route via Laurencekirk, Forfar and Queensferry, departing Aberdeen at 6am and reaching Edinburgh at 9pm.[16]

It having been become a subject of general regret and reproach, that, for several years past, no public conveyance has been kept on this line of road, passing through one of the richest and most beautiful districts of Scotland; and that there is no choice for travellers but going thro' Fife, submitting to very inconvenient hours, two ferries, not at all times safe to pass, and coaches conducted more with a view to venting private animosities than to the safety and respectable conveyance of passengers ... a number of gentlemen along the line of road, aided by the most respectable innkeepers, have resolved on starting a Coach, to be called The Defiance, licensed to carry Four Inside and Ten Outside Passengers, which will commence running on Wednesday the first day of July next. [Fares £2 inside (125 miles) and £1 5s outside] ... every obstacle which could be devised has been thrown in the way of this coach being established, by a party too contemptible to be brought into public notice.[17]

The 'contemptible party' was presumably the proprietor of the 'Telegraph' coach.

Barclay and Watson were the sole proprietors of the 'Defiance'. They did not operate the coaches on the service, which were tendered for on three-year supply contracts, and they certainly did not own the vast numbers of horses required for the journeys, though they undertook the organisation of the horse allocation (thirty pairs of horses were required between Aberdeen and Montrose alone). The *New Sporting Magazine* reported that the operators in 1837 were three innkeepers at Aberdeen, Edinburgh and Queensferry. By this means they were able to spread the risk of operation, and ultimately to exit the business when the railways rendered long-distance coaching uneconomic.[18] Earnings were described as 'respectable', at an average of 2s 9d per mile.[19]

The 'Swift' was running northbound from Montrose in the morning and returning in the evening by September 1829.[20]

By May 1830 James Scott & Co. of the Star Hotel in Edinburgh, and (oddly) one of the 'Defiance' contractors, was bemoaning in the *Aberdeen Journal* the '*monopolizing system of the principal Coach Proprietors in Scotland.*'[21] The success of the 'Defiance' was also diverting traffic from Dundee to Strathmore and Perth. In May 1838, '*in consequence of the inconvenience which has been experienced from the discontinuance of a NIGHT Coach*',[22] a new light night coach called the 'Piper o' Dundee' started running from Machray's hotel at 9pm, arriving in Dundee via Laurencekirk at 5am; the 'Highlander' started on 22nd October 1838, running via Bervie to Dundee with connections to Glasgow and Edinburgh, and the 'Victoria' started about the same time, also via the coast. How successful these competitor coaches were is questionable, but in any case the 'Defiance' Edinburgh, Glasgow and Aberdeen network was recast with Dundee as the hub from 24th March 1845.[23]

Progress had been remarkable, and there is little doubt that Barclay was a prime mover in improving the speed and quality of coach services on the Aberdeen–Edinburgh routes. A journey to Edinburgh which would have taken four days in the mid-eighteenth century could be accomplished in 14½ hours, at the dizzying speed of 11mph.

Accidents were not uncommon, however. A particularly serious one occurred to the 'Saxe Cobourg' coach at East Mains of Rossie, just south of Montrose, as it headed to Aberdeen via Brechin in 1825, when:

it was met by a cart, the driver of which not being at his horse's head, the coachman, in order to clear his way, gave the horse of the cart a lash with his whip, in doing which he lost his balance and was precipitated from his seat and the coach passed over him. The horses finding themselves unrestrained, set off at full speed, and drove furiously along, until the coach came into contact with the side of Rossie toll bar, where it was overturned and almost shattered to pieces. Almost all the passengers are more or less hurt; one gentleman, a Mr Ferguson, from Aberdeen, is very seriously so. Mr Collier, junior, of East Mains of Rossie, promptly dispatched an express to Montrose for medical assistance, and to appraise the coach proprietors of the accident, who immediately sent out a post chaise to convey the passengers to Montrose, several of whom, with the guard, who is also hurt, were able to proceed on their journey in a post chaise. The gentleman who is most hurt lies at the Star Inn, where he is attended by an experienced medical practitioner. It is hoped he will recover. We understand no blame is attached to either guard or coachman, who are both sober careful men. It is remarkable that although the wheels passed over the coachman, he is not much hurt, and was able to bring the horses into Montrose.[24]

Coaches were a great improvement over the Post Office runners, and brought better passenger transport for the well-to-do few. The rest of the population had little need (or time) to travel, and such travel as they did need to do was done on foot, and within a few miles of home. Exceptions were fisher women, who regularly walked for miles with creels of fish for sale to inland districts, bringing dairy produce in return.

Local coaches – usually light omnibuses – also operated in the days before the railways, and as connecting services afterwards. A reminiscence in the *Dundee Evening Telegraph* recounts how 'Medicine Wally' used to amuse himself:

Scampering after the Bervie coach, a three-horse yellow and black painted vehicle, which passed on its outward journey about four in the afternoon.[25]

From contemporary advertisements after the opening of the railways it is also clear that coaches and omnibuses continued to run, but they became connecting services from railway stations, or were used for special services connecting the nearest station to the location of a farm sale or 'roup'. Hotel omnibuses were also common, such as the one connecting Stonehaven station to the principal hotels in the town. Occasionally, a former coach operator could be tempted to take on the railways, usually in response to an outcry about fares increases. In March 1850:

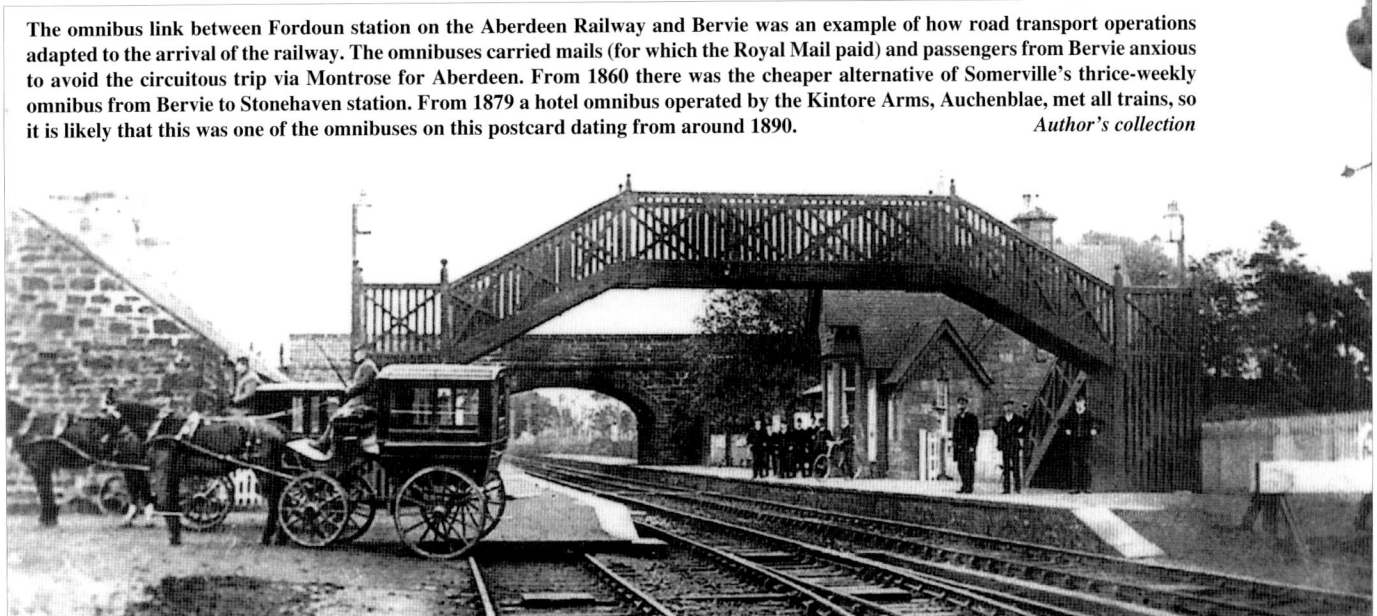

The omnibus link between Fordoun station on the Aberdeen Railway and Bervie was an example of how road transport operations adapted to the arrival of the railway. The omnibuses carried mails (for which the Royal Mail paid) and passengers from Bervie anxious to avoid the circuitous trip via Montrose for Aberdeen. From 1860 there was the cheaper alternative of Somerville's thrice-weekly omnibus from Bervie to Stonehaven station. From 1879 a hotel omnibus operated by the Kintore Arms, Auchenblae, met all trains, so it is likely that this was one of the omnibuses on this postcard dating from around 1890. *Author's collection*

Owing to the heightening of the fares and the circuitous route by Guthrie now adopted by the Aberdeen Railway Company, a stage coach has commenced running between ... Montrose and Bervie by Mr Moir, Innkeeper, Montrose, which is highly patronised.[26]

This seems to have been the forerunner of the later Somerville service which was in turn replaced by the Montrose & Bervie Railway. An example of a complementary rail service was Somerville's 1861 coach service between Bervie and Stonehaven station, supplementing a service already in operation to Fordoun station.

The old direct turnpike to the great north, which has been, as it were, dormant for many years, is about to be occupied with a conveyance running, as proposed, three days a week. Cheap rates of new coach will bring it below rates of Fordoun coach.[27]

The long-distance 'Royal Mail' coaches, though, were generally unsuitable for this kind of operation and were sold or scrapped after the railways were opened. An interesting later use for one of these was its export to New Zealand, probably facilitated by the strong ties between Aberdeen and Dunedin. The *Otago Witness* reported the story:

As an instance in the march of improvement, the good folks in Dunedin were rather surprised on Monday to see a 'royal mail coach' after the home fashion, standing at the Post-office to receive the mail for conveyance to the Clutha district, but at what number of knots an hour they are to be carried we are not prepared to state. The coach, which is a smart-looking vehicle, was built by Messrs Laing and Melvin, coachbuilders to Her Majesty, Aberdeen, from whence it has been imported, per Chile, by Mr A. Mollison. It is ornamented with VR, the arms of the granite city, and the names of the districts on the line of route. The inside of the coach is for the mail bags, and the top is seated for six passengers. It is fitted with a double set of patent springs, wheels, axles, drags etc., and is capable of being driven with two or three horses abreast. The total cost of it here was £160.[28]

The last remnant of the mail service from Edinburgh to Aberdeen was not withdrawn until 1890, when the Sunday mail gig (needed because of the lack of Sunday trains) ceased.[29]

Goods Carriers

Stagecoaches were passenger vehicles, though the *raison d'etre* of the 'Royal Mail' was the carriage of letters and packets. Goods transport by road was limited by the condition of the roads, and the capability of the horses, but still performed a useful function for local (and even some long-distance) trips. An 1830 guide listed two long-distance trips a week from Arbroath and Montrose to Aberdeen, a daily trip from Bervie to both Montrose and Aberdeen, and a twice-weekly run from St. Cyrus to Montrose, while Johnshaven enjoyed three trips per week to Montrose and a weekly trip to Aberdeen.[30]

By 1835/36 a fairly dense and frequent network of carrier services was operating, centred on Aberdeen,[31] and the contemporary guides, or 'remembrancers' list a number of wagons operating along the coast road between Montrose and Stonehaven.

Notes

1. *CM*, 4th Mar. 1775, p. 1. Driver had been butler to a local landowner (John Mill of Old Montrose) and on Mill's death in 1772 took the tenancy of the Ship Inn in Montrose (*CM*, 27th May 1772, p. 3).
2. The Bervie hotelier James Wynnas was recorded as offering a carriage for hire in the Wheel Carriage Tax Returns for April 1797 (NRS ref E326/8), but not in subsequent years although he remained in Bervie for some years until at least 1806. Of course it may just not have been declared for tax.
3. *CM*, 14th Jun. 1775, p. 1.
4. *AJ*, 6th Jul. 1803, p. 1.
5. *CM*, 2nd Jul. 1781, p. 4. Luggage allowance was 14 lbs, with any excess being charged at 2½d per pound. Intermediate passengers were charged 3½d per mile. The 'Royal Mail' fare for inside passengers was £2 12s 6d, but for outside passengers £1 11s, less than the 'Fly'. Intermediate fares were 3d per mile.
6. *CM*, 5th Mar. 1785, p. 1. By this date the fare to Aberdeen was 42s 6d.
7. *AJ*, 27th Oct. 1783, p. 3.
8. *AJ*, 24th Nov. 1783, p. 4.
9. *CM*, 5th Mar. 1785, p. 1.
10. *AJ*, 20th Mar. 1811, p. 1. This was, of course, before completion of the Bervie–North Water Bridge turnpike.
11. J. Barron, *The Northern Highlands in the Nineteenth Century*, Vol. 2 (Inverness, 1907), pp. xxxix et seq. The quotation was from an undated copy of the *Inverness Courier*. A news item on the death of Alexander Crichton, one of the *Defiance*'s guards, in *AJ*, 14th Mar. 1902, p. 5, stated that he used to carry two pistols to guard against highwaymen. *AJ*, 17th Jun. 1829, p. 2, noted the first run to be on 1st July 1829. There were ten outside passengers and four inside, with a staff of a guard and two coachmen who wore grey hats.
12. *New Sporting Magazine* [*NSM*] LXIX (1837) pp. 25-36, at p. 29.
13. Ibid., p. 34.
14. Correspondence published in *Fife Herald* [*FH*], 18th Jun. 1835, p. 4.
15. *FH*, 30th Jul. 1835, p. 4.
16. *AJ*, 29th Apr. 1829, p. 1, and 17th Jun. 1829, p. 2. W. Norrie, writing in *The Scots Magazine* in October 1892 states that the 'Union' coach was a day coach via Strathmore started in April 1826 by Alexander McNab of Edinburgh. After a short period of fierce competition between it and a rival 'Original Union' coach introduced by James Scott, of the Star Hotel, Edinburgh in June 1827, the 'Union' started running in conjunction with the 'Defiance'.
17. *AJ*, 24th Jun. 1829, p. 1. In September 1829 the 'Swift' coach started from Montrose to Aberdeen, so perhaps most of Barclay's plan came into effect.
18. The 'Defiance' coaches were supplied on tender to the partnership, as an advertisement asking for offers for three years' supply in *AJ*, 18th Sep. 1844, p. 3, demonstrates. The route was altered and curtailed as the railways extended towards Aberdeen; it was rerouted via Dundee and Granton instead of Perth when the railway opened (*AJ*, 2nd Apr. 1845, p. 1) and was eventually curtailed to operate between Montrose and Aberdeen by 1848 (*AJ*, 23rd Feb. 1848, p. 5). Barclay drove the last 'Defiance' coach trip in October 1849.
19. *NSM*, p. 31.
20. The 'Swift' settled down to be the daily coach from Stonehaven to Aberdeen and back from 1834, though in some seasons it was extended to Auchenblae.
21. *AJ*, 19th May 1830, p. 1.
22. *AJ*, 30th May 1838, p. 3.
23. *AJ*, 31st Oct. 1838, p. 2. The 'Piper' and the 'Victoria' were operated by Scott & Co, presumably in partnership with Machray and others. See also Norrie, op. cit.
24. *CM*, 10th Feb. 1825, p. 2; the fare from Aberdeen to Edinburgh single outside in 1814 was 42s 6d. This was far more than an average week's wage. A single fare outside from Aberdeen to Stonehaven in 1817 was 5s (£14.29 in today's money) for a 15-mile trip. *Bon-Accord & Northern Pictorial*, 8th Apr. 1949, p. 6, published a photograph of the ticket.
25. [*Dundee*] *Evening Times* [*ET*], 15th Oct. 1923, p. 2. This was probably operated by Somerville, whom the Montrose and Forfar Road Trustees agreed to charge a commuted rate of 6d per horse per day to in 1863 (*DA*, 11th Apr. 1863, p. 4).
26. *DPCA*, 19th Mar. 1850, p. 3.
27. *DPCA*, 15th Jun. 1861, p. 3.
28. *Otago Witness*, 12th Jan. 1861, p. 5.
29. *AJ*, 5th Nov. 1890, p. 4.
30. J. Mitchell, *Angus and Mearns Remembrancer* (Montrose, 1830).
31. K.L. Moore, 'Carrier Routes in the North-East of Scotland 1803-1914: Development and Change in a Service' in *Scottish Geographical Journal*, Vol. 119, part 4 (2003), pp. 325-40.

Chapter 5

Coastal Shipping and Canals

The carriers and coaches did little for bulk goods transport. Mail and stagecoaches had limited capacity for parcels on the roof, and these had to share space with 'outside' passengers and the driver and guard. Heavy freight had to travel by pack-horse or carrier to the nearest port in small consignments, and then by sea to its destination. Shipping services had been established between Aberdeen, Edinburgh and London in the late eighteenth century, and steam boat services to Leith – calling at Stonehaven, Montrose and even Johnshaven – were advertised in the 1820s.[1] Among the attractions of the trip on the paddle steamer *Velocity* was:

the most elegant accommodation for passengers, to whom every attention will be paid: and good entertainment, and the very best Wines and Liquors will be served on board.

Sadly, the *Velocity* was wrecked at the entrance to Aberdeen Harbour in October 1848, though fortunately without casualties.[2]

Shipping journey times were competitive with land, suffering only from the greater risk of loss in storms and the inconvenience of the rowing boat transfers from some of the ports of call along the way. A typical steamship trip to Edinburgh from Aberdeen cost 18s (cabin) and 10s (steerage) and the journey took twelve hours. By stagecoach the same trip cost 12s 6d (outside) and took fifteen hours.

Where the steamships dominated was in goods transport. Even though small by today's standards, the new ships were 290-ton vessels and could take far more than the small parcels carried by the stagecoaches, or indeed the loads on contemporary carriers' wagons.

Canals could provide efficient and safe bulk freight transport, but required locks to overcome any gradients, involving long delays. The Aberdeenshire Canal (the only canal actually constructed in north-east Scotland), between Aberdeen and Inverurie, was opened in 1807 and provided a smooth, if still slow, transit between mid-Aberdeenshire and Aberdeen Harbour until 1854.[3] A number of canal schemes were hatched for south Kincardineshire and Forfar; this is perhaps not surprising in an era before the development of railways, or later when steam railways still consisted of short lines between collieries and canals, and their cargoes were hauled by horses or under-powered locomotives with limited range.

In his 1876 *History of Arbroath*, George Hay recounts the various schemes round Arbroath:

The Town Councils of Arbroath and Forfar contemplated a very considerable work in the formation of a canal between the two towns, to be called the Strathmore Canal. The first survey, which extended from Arbroath to the ruins of Restenneth Priory, was made in 1783 by Mr Whitworth, CE. The matter was more thoroughly gone into in 1817, when, at the request of Provost Duncan, Mr Robert Stevenson, the engineer of the Bell Rock Lighthouse, made a survey. The immediate cause of the scheme being taken up there was the want of fuel in Strathmore from the failure of the peat mosses, and the great expense of land carriage. The expense of cartage from Arbroath to Forfar was from 14s to 15s per ton, and by the canal it was to be reduced to 7s. Power was to be taken to extend the canal westwards

Left: One of the earliest shipwrecks of Aberdeen coastal steamers was the loss of the *Brilliant* on 12th December 1839 when it hit Aberdeen North Pier in a storm. Fortunately most of the passengers and crew were able to scramble to safety.

Right: The PS *Duke of Sutherland* in a less exciting view. However it too was wrecked at the entrance to Aberdeen Harbour, on 1st April 1853. Of the fifty-two crew and passengers, sixteen were lost.
Illustrated London News, *9th April 1853*

This postcard is captioned 'Arrival of Aberdeen Steamer' at Newcastle, but unfortunately the name of the vessel is not visible. Perhaps it is the SS *Aberdonian* of 1906. The huge crowd awaiting it are presumably not all passengers! *Author's collection*

to Coupar-Angus, and eastwards to Brechin. At Arbroath it was to communicate with the harbour by means of a lock. It was anticipated that the trade of the town would be much developed by the canal, and that the Magistrates would be enabled to extend and improve the harbour. In 1824 the Town Council subscribed £200 for another survey. In the following year they had a report from Mr Stevenson with regard to a proposal to form a railway from Arbroath through Strathmore, and the canal scheme then finally fell out of sight.[4]

Hay does not pass any comment on whether such a proposal would have been economically viable, but it seems fairly obvious that transport by road to the canal, then transfer at the other end into a ship would have been as unprofitable as the Aberdeenshire Canal was. A proposal for a canal from the Howe of the Mearns to Perth was mentioned in Robertson's 1810 survey,[5] but nothing more was heard of this until July 1820 when Robert Stevenson published '*a memorial regarding the propriety and importance of opening the great valleys of Strathmore and Strathearn, by means of a railway or canal*'. This would have been a freight-only line, designed to carry coal, lime and weaving materials inland, and export agricultural and industrial produce, horse operated and using stationary steam engines to haul loads up rope-worked inclines. No dividends were promised, but Stevenson hoped the benefits of opening up the area for trade would be enough to induce weavers and landowners to invest. It was not, and they did not.[6] In 1826 Stevenson tried again, with a slightly less ambitious route from Perth to Brechin and Montrose, with a branch to Arbroath, but this time it was a railway scheme.[7]

Notes

1. The *Tourist*, operated by the Leith & Aberdeen Steam Yacht Company, was advertised to operate three times a week between Aberdeen and Leith, calling at Stonehaven, Montrose, Arbroath, Crail, Anstruther, Pittenweem, Ely and Dysart, while the Aberdeen, Leith & Clyde Shipping Company was operating the *Velocity* (256 tons burthen and two 110hp engines) between Aberdeen and Newhaven on the days when the L&ASYC did not operate, calling at most of the same stops (*AJ*, 1821: 30th May, p. 3, 6th Jun., p. 3, 25th Jul., p. 3). By 1824 the *Velocity* was calling at Johnshaven (*AJ*, 12th May 1824, p. 1).
2. *AJ*, 1st Nov. 1848, p. 4; more detail of the wreck (and the ship) are given in I.G. Whittaker, *Off Scotland: A Comprehensive Record of Maritime and Aviation Losses in Scottish Waters* (Edinburgh, 1998).
3. The inland terminal of the canal was at Port Elphinstone, a mile or so east of Inverurie.
4. G. Hay, *A History of Arbroath to the Present Time, with Notices of the Civil and Ecclesiastical Affairs of the Neighbouring District* (Arbroath, 1876), p. 375.
5. The standard history of the canal is 'The Aberdeenshire Canal' in J. Lindsay, *The Canals of Scotland* (Newton Abbott, 1968). The canal was purchased by the Great North of Scotland Railway in 1845, mostly to be used as trackbed for the line to Huntly. The canal cost £44,000 to build and revenues built up from £311 in its first year of operation to £3,062 in its last.
6. R. Stevenson, *A Memorial Relative to Opening the Great Valleys of Strathmore and Strathearn by means of a Railway or Canal, with Branches to the Sea from Perth, Arbroath, Montrose, Stonehaven and Aberdeen; Together with Observations on Interior Communications in General* (Edinburgh, 1821).
7. R. Stevenson, *Report Relative to Lines of the Railway, Surveyed from the Ports of Perth, Abroath, and Montrose into the Valley of Strathmore ... in the Year 1826* (Edinburgh, 1827).

Chapter 6
The Railways

The Railway Route to Aberdeen

Even during the heyday of the turnpikes, it was clear that trade was limited by the speed of horse haulage. The fastest mail coach took 14½ hours to reach Aberdeen from Edinburgh, and the trip from Bervie to Montrose was a leisurely 1½ hours.[1] While coach speeds had increased, the total number of passengers on a coach would be somewhere around ten or twelve, so that even three coaches a day to Montrose or Stonehaven would carry fewer than forty passengers, and many of these would be through passengers from Aberdeen or Dundee whose impact on the local economy would be limited to buying meals at the coaching inns.[2] Fares were very expensive (unless a 'side deal' could be done with the coachman – apparently a fairly common practice) for often unsociable departure times. Loads carried were light, and costs were high, limiting both the availability and quantity of imported items and exported goods. Only ships could carry larger loads, and once landed, goods usually faced steep gradients from the harbours of the coastal villages.

By the early 1830s, railways were beginning to emerge from the experimental and novel stage so that they could be seen first as local and regional carriers of both passengers and goods, and then as part of what was soon envisaged as a national network.

The first railway in the north-east of Scotland was the Dundee & Newtyle; this was a line which connected Dundee with Strathmore by means of several steam-driven, rope-worked inclines, connecting the relatively level sections of line on which the feeble locomotives of the time were able to run. It opened in 1831. The first scheme for a railway further north was the subject of a survey carried out in 1826 by Robert Stevenson for a line from Perth via Coupar Angus and Forfar to Brechin and Montrose, with a branch from Forfar to Arbroath, again with rope-worked inclines, but using horse haulage at 3mph on a line with passing loops every one third of a mile. It did not proceed beyond the planning stage.[3]

At first there was no concept of individual railways being anything more than local carriers, built to deal with a particular, local, need. The first railways in Angus were based on the Newtyle line, which had a gauge of 4 feet 6½ inches, and the Dundee & Arbroath Railway, opened in 1836, which was built to a gauge of 5 feet 6 inches. The contemporary lines in Central Scotland were mainly built to what became the 'standard' gauge of 4 feet 8½ inches, but even here there were exceptions.

The initiative was also in the hands of local landowners, who were seeking to develop their estates; Lord Wharncliffe owned the lands in the Meigle area, while Lord Panmure was the Chairman of the Dundee & Arbroath line.[4]

By the mid-1840s, however, the situation was changing rapidly. Speculation in railway shares, or more often share allocations, was a tempting way of rapidly getting rich; when railway shares were allocated, often at minimal deposits, it was easy to purchase these with borrowed money, watch the value of the allocation rise, then sell and repay the loan while walking away with the profit. For some speculators this was not racy enough; they applied for allocations and hoped to sell them on without even paying the deposit.[5] As with most investment bubbles there seemed only to be an upside, only winners in the escalating price of railway securities. A significant railway investment bubble developed in the mid-1830s, but it was in the 1840s that the largest nineteenth-century railway share bubble was seen. Schemes for railways appeared almost daily in the newspapers, always accompanied by glowing descriptions of how little the line would cost to build, and how much traffic it would carry. The deadline for submission of railway schemes for the 1846 session of Parliament brought about 800 applications.

During 1846 Parliament approved 4,538 miles of railways, so that, combined with the 3,500 miles approved in 1844-45, the country was supposedly on track to getting 10,000 miles of railway in total by 1850/52, compared to the 2,000 miles it had in 1843. On top of that, a further 1,354 miles were approved in 1847, and 371 in 1848. (Of the total of almost 12,000 miles all these approvals represent, only 60% were actually built.)[6]

Aberdeen was the fourth largest Scottish city and the largest place in the northern half of Scotland by a considerable margin, with a population in 1831 of 35,370.[7] The next largest place was Inverness, with a population of 14,304, so it too was a natural destination for railway schemes from central Scotland and beyond. Although railways were built northwards as separate, local, concerns, it was widely regarded as only a matter of time before these separate companies would be joined as one through service, or at least operated by one company. Between Perth and Aberdeen three separate companies were established in the 1840s – the Scottish Central Railway (SCR) from Greenhill (on the Edinburgh–Glasgow main line near Falkirk) to Perth, the Scottish Midland Junction Railway (SMJR) from Perth to Forfar, and the Aberdeen Railway (AR) from Forfar via Brechin to Aberdeen, with a branch to Montrose.

On 12th March 1844 the SCR promoters were told by letter of the SMJR plan to reach Forfar, and by January 1846 the SMJR had obtained powers to buy the Newtyle group of railways. In 1845 the AR received parliamentary sanction to build a line from Guthrie (between Forfar and Arbroath) to Aberdeen via Laurencekirk and Stonehaven with branches to Brechin and Montrose. It seems certain that the SMJR always envisaged that they would lease their line to a larger company and there was an attempt by the rapidly emerging Caledonian Railway to lease both it and the SCR in 1848.[8]

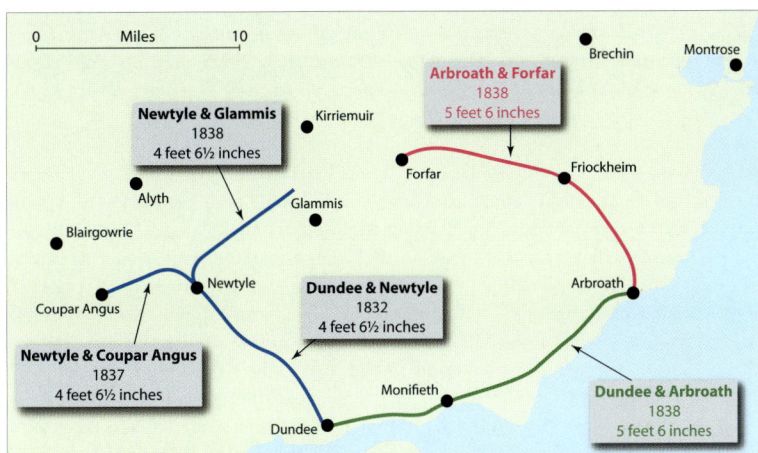

Map 3 Early railways in Forfarshire may have radiated from Dundee, but were built to three different track gauges (the Dundee & Perth was 4 feet 8½ inches) in an age when railways had a purely local focus. Note the use of the old spelling of Glamis in the railway's name.
After Map 11 in C.J.A. Robertson, **The Origins of the Scottish Railway System, 1722-1844** *(Edinburgh, 1983)*

However, these attempts were thwarted by the collapse in railway share values in the late 1840s as the investment bubble burst, leaving the AR and the SMJR to amalgamate in July 1856 as the Scottish North Eastern Railway.

In his pioneering study of early Scottish railways, Robertson[9] says that the SCR, SMJR and the AR were all local lines, asking nothing from the Caledonian but general support, but all were crucial to the Caledonian's plans to dominate the trade to Aberdeen.

THE ABERDEEN RAILWAY AND THE EAST COAST OF SCOTLAND JUNCTION RAILWAY

The line which was most important to the development of Kincardineshire was the Aberdeen Railway, and it was to emerge as the favoured scheme of the several alignments which were proposed in the 1840s.

In early 1844 *Inland Railways* published a review of lines then being promoted in Scotland:

> It has even been in view to project a line northwards to Aberdeen or Inverness, but the want of trade and intercourse sufficient to remunerate such an outlay has led to the abandonment of this embryo design.[10]

In the *Aberdeen Journal* for 20th March that year an advertisement appeared for the Aberdeen, Dundee & Perth Railway, which was hoping to build from Aberdeen to Perth via Stonehaven and Strathmore. The editorial welcomed the news:

> We have at length the satisfaction to announce that our good city, never far behind in the march of improvement, is about to participate in all those advantages – social, commercial and agricultural – which have invariably followed in the train of Railway communication.[11]

Two days later the *Dundee, Perth and Cupar Advertiser* thought that:

> It is now a matter of certainty that within a very short period a complete line of Railway will be established between London, Edinburgh and Glasgow; and proposals are also being actively carried forward for connecting Dundee and Perth with these Cities. Communication by Railway will thus be completed as far northward as Arbroath.
>
> The time has therefore arrived when steps should be taken for securing the same advantages to Aberdeen and the intervening districts, as it is obvious that, unless this be accomplished, they must lose their relative importance.
>
> It has already been ascertained, by a survey made some years ago, that no engineering difficulties present themselves to a line from the Harbour of Aberdeen to the Arbroath and Forfar Railway at the Friockheim Station; and, from the large traffic already existing, and the great increase that must follow from a continuous line connecting Aberdeen and the intermediate towns with London, and the East and West Coasts, the returns cannot fail to be ample and remunerative.
>
> It is hoped, however, that a new survey should be immediately made, with a view to adopting all the improvements which experience has suggested, the result of which, with accurate estimates of the expense and traffic, will speedily be laid before the Public.[12]

Immediately below this editorial, the Dundee legal agents, Sheill and Small had placed an advertisement for a Dundee and Perth Railway, which went on to say:

> the Dundee and Arbroath, and Arbroath and Forfar lines, will be joined by the Aberdeen Railway at the Friockheim Station of the latter line and thereby a continuous Railway will extend from Aberdeen, by Brechin, Montrose, Forfar, Arbroath, Dundee, Perth, Stirling, Falkirk, etc, to Glasgow and Edinburgh, and connect with lines leading to the Metropolis of the Kingdom.

Letters to the press followed, including one from 'Friend to Improvement' extolling the virtues of the Strathmore Railway which would go *'from Glamiss to cross the Dee a little below the romantic village of Banchory-Devenich [sic]'*. He felt that the only problem was leaving Montrose out,

> but the expense of forming a line from Montrose northward along the coast to Aberdeen, would be totally disproportionate to any revenue which could ever be expected to arise from its traffic.[13]

On the next page of the same newspaper appeared the prospectuses for the Aberdeen, Dundee & Perth Railway via Strathmore, and the Aberdeen & East Coast Railway via Montrose and Bervie. The AD&PR prospectus mentioned the possibility of adopting the atmospheric system, as on the Dublin & Kingstown railway, thereby saving 40% of the cost, it was claimed.[14] A footnote said:

> an experienced Engineer has surveyed a considerable portion of the Northern Division of the projected line; and it is asserted that the only practicable egress (except at an enormous expense) by means of Railway communication from Aberdeen Southwards is by adopting the Line along the North side of the River Dee, and crossing that River opposite the Estate of Durris, proceeding through that Property and the Parish of Glenbervie, near to the Village of Auchinblae, and thence by Laurencekirk and Brechin.[15]

An *Aberdeen Journal* editorial on 27th March pondered the merits of the two schemes. The writer wondered about the cost of running a line round the coast, given the *'rugged and rocky'* nature of the terrain. He concluded that the Strathmore proposal was more practicable, going via the north bank of the Dee, crossing it at Durris, and then via Glenbervie and Auchenblae, Laurencekirk etc.:

> On the whole, then, as regards the rival Lines of Railway from Aberdeen, the question seems to be this – will the superiority of traffic with the town of Stonehaven, and villages of Bervie and Johnshaven, over the villages of Auchinblae, Laurencekirk, and the town of Brechin, not including Banchory on Deeside, compensate for the more expensive Line of Railway along the rocky coast of Kincardineshire?[16]

On 29th March, the *Dundee, Perth and Cupar Advertiser* carried an advertisement from the Aberdeen & East Coast Railway which said that a report had been commissioned from the engineers Grainger and Miller of Edinburgh in 1837 on the rival routes to the south. Grainger and Miller favoured the coastal route because it was shorter, cheaper, and passed through more towns and villages. Nothing more was done because of the state of the markets at the time. Now four lines were being promoted in the Tay Valley: the North British, the Edinburgh & Northern, the Perth & Stirling and the Dundee & Perth. As a result, the East Coast Line from Aberdeen to Arbroath was being promoted to connect with these new lines. Gibb & Son, engineers, were to resurvey the line, but the preferred route would be Aberdeen–Stonehaven–Bervie–Johnshaven–Montrose–Arbroath, or to meet the Arbroath & Forfar line at Friockheim. The promoters had not intended to move yet, but their hand was forced when they noted the rival (Strathmore) scheme being announced.[17]

However, within a few days the promoters of the two schemes had

CHAPTER 6: THE RAILWAYS

agreed on a joint survey to chart the way forward. The *Aberdeen Journal* noted with some satisfaction that:

> *It is hardly necessary farther to add, that, from the junction of parties which has now taken place, all risk of Parliamentary opposition will be avoided; and that, when the Promoters of this line shall have obtained their Engineer's final Report, they will be able to come before the public with such support as cannot fail to command undivided confidence.*[18]

A week later the Prospectus of the Aberdeen Railway was published. There was an impressive list of subscribers, with Chairman Lord Provost Blaikie, and a massive provisional committee made up of many of the dignitaries of the North East. These included James Farquhar of Hallgreen. Capital was to be one million pounds in shares of £20. The 1837 survey was mentioned, but the route chosen was Aberdeen–Stonehaven–Mearns–Brechin, with a branch to Montrose. The promoters predicted the usual handsome return of 8%, and the *Dundee Courier*, quoting a report in the *Aberdeen Constitutional*, plainly encouraged subscribers to speculate on the share allocations. With only a 10% payment required to secure the share options, it was a very attractive proposition to purchase them, sell once they had increased in value, and pocket the difference after repaying a loan for the 10%. And this was not in an era where subscribers would be warned that share values could go down as well as up.

Within a few days a further scheme was being floated, this time by the Great North of Scotland Railway, for a direct line from Aberdeen to Perth, though nothing more was heard of the scheme.[19]

> *The stock of the Scottish Central Line, of which the Aberdeen Railway forms a continuation, bears already a premium; more than 9000 shares, over and above the number allotted, having been applied for. This circumstance, therefore, warrants us in stating that in the course of a month at farthest, the Aberdeen Railway scrip will bear a similar premium, especially when we take into account the large amount of stock already subscribed.*[20]

When the Aberdeen Railway was examined by the Parliamentary Commission on 2nd June the following year, the promoters said they had originally wanted the coastal route via Bervie, but had found that costs would be £15,000 per mile higher than for the route eventually selected.[21] However, the coastal route did not seem to be dead yet, for on 14th October 1845 a preliminary announcement appeared in the *Dundee Courier* for the East Coast of Scotland Junction Railway from Arbroath to Stonehaven via Montrose and Bervie. This was, said the editorial, promoted by the '*most respectable and highly influential*' persons, and the engineer was the famous Joseph Locke, who had designed the Lancaster & Carlisle Railway among several other major lines.[22] The capital was to be £750,000. Three of the

A contemporary and very stylised print, probably by W. Bartlett, and published by William Mitchell, Aberdeen, of the Aberdeen Railway approach to Aberdeen from the Kincardineshire bank. Apart from the slightly odd locomotive, and the massively over-scale North Church tower, the Dee Viaduct was actually built as a steel girder structure. The suspension bridge is the Wellington Bridge, over which one of the Kincardineshire toll roads left Aberdeen.

Hygra.com

LEFT: A very early and faded photograph taken at Drumlithie probably around 1854. Note the two children posing on the opposite tracks! *Gordon Will collection*

FACING PAGE: Another photograph at Drumlithie, probably on the same occasion.
Gordon Will collection

supporters were Captain Barclay of Ury, David Scott of Brotherton, and James Farquhar of Hallgreen, Bervie, names we shall come across again.

Unlike some lines promoted in the second investment bubble in the 1840s, it does appear that this line was being actively developed; after a slight hitch when Joseph Locke wrote a letter to the legal agents, Kinnear & Monro of Stonehaven, saying he had no connection with the line,[23] surveying began in earnest. Even here, however, there were minor problems. One of the landowners affected, Hay of Letham, obtained an injunction stopping the surveyors from entering his land, only withdrawing it when he received an assurance that trains would slow down '*for hounds in cry after hares or foxes*'.[24] The new engineer, John Miller, reported that he could see no major problems in construction, though he did envisage the need for a 400 yard long tunnel.[25] On 8th December 1845 the Management Committee announced that Parliamentary Standing Orders had been complied with.[26] The plans had been lodged on 30th November.

The ECSJR was soon in trouble, however. At a shareholders' meeting on 17th January 1846 it had been agreed:

in consequence of the state of the money market, and the general prospects of railway business, to defer making application to parliament for a bill in the present session.[27]

Worse was to come. At a meeting of shareholders in Gibb's Royal Hotel in Edinburgh on 19th April, it was revealed that although 26,000 shares had been allocated, with a paper value of £650,000, in fact only a small proportion of the 10% deposits had been paid – a sum of £10,709, representing 4,010 shares of which only £5,009 was left after deduction of fees and expenses. Divided among 4,010 shares, that would repay 25s per share (a loss of £1 7s 6d per share). Moreover, it was reported that there had been repurchasing of letters of allotment in order to encourage allottees to pay their deposits and that the Edinburgh brokers had purchased 500 more shares than they had authority for. It was said that this had been done '*in the purest and best bona fides*', but many were less convinced. One shareholder said that they should go after the defaulters so that the expenses could be more evenly shared out. However, it emerged at the meeting that some of the defaulters were people who had been named as members of the Provisional Committee, and who were not in fact on it. As a result it was agreed to let matters rest. Nevertheless a committee was appointed to go after defaulters, and 1s of the 25s was allocated for that purpose.

The committee reported at the beginning of May 1846. However, their report was criticised as being '*not a very intelligible document*'.

The committee stated that they found that there had been a practice of buying in on behalf of the company the letters of allotment at a premium, with a view to induce allottees to take up their shares; and it appeared that a considerable portion of the funds of the company had been misapplied in this manner; but the trick had been unsuccessful, as not a sixth part of the shares allotted had been taken up.[28]

By way of consolation the brokers' accounts had been reduced by £57 as they had exceeded their authority.

The *Railway Herald* was scathing:

The shareholders were fools enough to pass the resolutions which the committee, under these circumstances, brought forward, for an interim payment of 25s per share, and appointing a committee to prosecute the defaulting allottees. We believe this affair is about the grossest job which the breaking-up mania has brought out; and it altogether exceeds our comprehension how any respectable body of shareholders could give it their sanction. Even supposing the liability of allottees had been settled, the wholesale rigging, so unblushingly laid bare, is quite sufficient to deprive the parties, on the ground of fraud, of any legal rights which they might otherwise have maintained.[29]

In the *Glasgow Herald* on 26th June 1846 the allottees took out a notice saying that they would contest the action by the ECSJR to recover their deposits.[30] The Management Committee were determined, though. In the final report in the *Dundee, Perth and Cupar Advertiser* in November 1849, the Chairman reported that after paying out the 25s per share, there was no money left, and in fact John Miller was owed £105. The only source of further funds was by getting the claim of 5s per share against the many allottees (20,135 out of 26,000) who had not paid their deposits, two of whom were on the Provisional Committee. Legal action had recovered £1,025 since April 1846, but no payment had been received on 12,000 shares. Of the £1,025, only £445 remained after expenses. The Committee

recommended paying a further 2s. The Chairman said he thought:

they might congratulate themselves sincerely that they had got out of the scrape so easily; for if they had gone into the scheme sooner, when the railway mania was at its height, the probability was that the deposits would all have been paid, they would have gone to Parliament for a bill, and entered into contracts, when after the thing would assuredly have stuck fast, and he himself would have been the loser to the extent of eight or ten thousand pounds.[31]

The ECSJR was not the only north-east scheme in trouble at the unravelling of the second railway investment bubble. The *Scottish Railway Gazette* reported in October 1846 that only twenty miles of the Aberdeen Railway had been completed to Dubton from the south. A large embankment was being constructed towards the River South Esk,

But the [work]force is altogether even miserably inadequate to the extent of the works.

The line beyond Stonehaven had nobody working on it:

Deserted, and apparently in the course of serious deterioration, the splendid viaducts and bridges seem veritable ruins in the eyes of the passing stranger, and altogether they present a spectacle of the most painful kind.[32]

At a shareholders' meeting in early December 1846 it was reported that twelve miles of main line and the six-mile branch to Brechin had been open for seven months, worked in conjunction with the Arbroath & Forfar. It was hope to complete twenty-five miles of line in 1847, thanks to the support of the Edinburgh & Northern, NBR and York, Newcastle & Berwick, who were subscribing £276,000. The shareholders were less than impressed:

Various shareholders, sensitive to the present prostrate condition of their interest in the line, gave free expression to their views in regard to the conduct of the Directors.[33]

By January 1849 the Aberdeen Railway shareholders were meeting to decide how to extract their company from its difficulties. While Blaikies of Aberdeen had been building locomotives,[34] and parts of the civil engineering work were complete, large sections of the line had ground to a halt. The Edinburgh & Northern had pulled out its investment and there was a need to raise £270,000 in new preference stock. The Directors, seeking to put a brave face on matters, said that Locke, their engineer, had declared that *'once the works recommenced'*, they could reach a point 11½ miles south of Aberdeen in only four months, and to the south end of the Dee Viaduct at Craiginches in another four.[35]

By September 1849 things had progressed sufficiently for the Directors to take a trip from Erskine Street, Montrose, to Stonehaven – *'where the snorting of a locomotive had never been heard before'* – with the expectation that the line would have reached Limpet Mill, just north of Stonehaven, in another two weeks.[36] They had only slightly longer to wait. On 27th October a trial train was run from Dubton to Limpet Mill. However, they could not get beyond Marykirk, as the contractor, Mr Mitchell, had lifted part of the line in protest at not being paid. A stand-off developed with a railway official instructing the workers to relay the track and Mitchell countermanding the order. In the end the police were called and the train returned to Dubton.

A further trip was organized on 1st November, with *'local militia and armed men from Craigo'* on board. Another stand-off resulted, and once again the train had to return to Dubton.[37] At least the stagecoach operators could see that it was only a matter of time before the Aberdeen Railway could use its line, for a few days later it was announced that mail coach fares were being reduced to railway levels. Aberdeen–Montrose would be 7s 6d inside (5s outside) with intermediate fares adjusted in proportion.[38] The connection was even closer; Lord James Hay, Chairman of the Aberdeen Railway, was credited with having been one of those involved in starting the 'Defiance' coach to Edinburgh.[39]

The 'Royal Mail' coach was reported as running between Aberdeen and Montrose for the last time on Saturday 12th January 1850,[40] though oddly, the Kincardineshire Turnpike Minute Books report the last run much later, on 25th April 1851. This latter date may indicate the expiry of the contract rate with the Turnpike Trust, as it seems hardly credible that the coach would have run so long after the opening of the railway, and when the local press report is quite specific. The same minute books report the last 'Defiance' as running on 31st October 1849, the 'Union' and the 'Swift' on 22nd September the same year.[41]

On 3rd April 1850 the Aberdeen Railway was opened to Ferryhill, just south of Aberdeen city centre, without ceremony. Omnibuses and cabs provided the connection.[42]

However, even though there was now a rail connection to the south, there was considerable dissatisfaction in Montrose that it was effectively at the end of a branch line, with no connection either to Arbroath or Stonehaven.[43]

Notes

1. Pigot, 1837.
2. Apart from the 'Royal Mail' coach from Edinburgh, in 1837 there were the 'Swift' and 'New Times' coaches from Montrose and Perth respectively. The 'Royal Mail' called at Bervie at 3.30am, the 'Swift' at 7am and the 'New Times' at 2pm; southbound times were 5.30pm, 7.30pm and 10am respectively (Pigot, 1837 guide).
3. R. Stevenson, *Report*.
4. P. Marshall, *The Railways of Dundee* (Witney, 1996) and *Scottish Central Railway* (Witney, 1998).
5. This was clearly what was being done by some investors in the East Coast of Scotland Junction Railway. The railway spent years in a fruitless quest to recover all the allocation fees.
6. A. Odlyzko, *Collective Hallucinations and Inefficient Markets: The British Railway Mania of the 1840s* (Minnesota, 2010) p. 78 (preliminary version published on line at www.dtc.umn.edu/~odlyzko/doc/hallucinations.pdf).
7. Dundee had a population of 45,355 in 1831; Aberdeen surpassed it for the first time in 1921.
8. D. Ross, *The Caledonian: Scotland's Imperial Railway – A History*. (Catrine, 2013), p. 47. The Caledonian withdrew its attempt to lease these two lines and the Dundee & Perth Railway in 1849.
9. C.J.A. Robertson, *The Origins of the Scottish Railway System 1722-1844* (Edinburgh, 1983) p. 295; a planned sequel, to be called 'The Railway Mania and its Aftermath in Scotland 1844-54' was planned, but the author died before he could complete it. The papers and unfinished chapters are in the University of St Andrews Special Collections.
10. Quoted in *AJ*, 14th Feb. 1844, p. 4.
11. *AJ*, 20th Mar. 1844, p. 3.

12. *DPCA*, 22nd Mar. 1844, p. 3.
13. *Dundee Courier* [*DC*], 26th Mar. 1844, p. 2. Note yet another unusual spelling of Glamis.
14. The 'atmospheric' system was a means of propulsion which involved using a vacuum tube to propel vehicles. The vehicles were fitted with pistons and a partial vacuum was created in the tube ahead of them to cause them to move. The system was used for a time on lines at Dalkey in Ireland, on the London & Croydon Railway and on the South Devon Railway. All these installations suffered technical problems and the system was abandoned in each case after a short time. On 29th March a letter from 'An Observer' appeared in *DPCA*, referring to a report of 1833 on the extension of the Dundee & Newtyle Railway which had said that the Dundee, Strathmore & Aberdeen Railway could be connected to the Newtyle line and worked on the atmospheric principle.
15. *DC*, 26th Mar. 1844, p. 3.
16. *AJ*, 27th Mar. 1844, p. 3.
17. *DPCA*, 29th Mar. 1844, p. 3.
18. *AJ*, 10th Apr. 1844, p. 2.
19. *AJ*, 1st May 1844, p. 2.
20. *DC*, 23rd Apr. 1844, p. 2.
21. *AJ*, 4th Jun. 1845, p. 2.
22. *DC*, 14th Oct. 1845, pp. 3-4. The list of backers on the Provisional Committee included Lord Cranstoun, Captain Barclay-Allardice of Ury, David Scott of Brotherton, James Farquhar of Hallgreen, James Raitt of Annistoun, James Fitzmaurice Scott of Commieston, Dr William Young of Fawside, Wm Stewart, baker, Stonehaven, William Jameson, Provost of Montrose, Baillie Watson, Acting Chief Magistrate of Bervie, and many others, including Eagle Henderson, Deputy Chairman of the North British Railway.
23. *DPCA*, 7th Nov. 1845, p. 4.
24. *DC*, 18th Nov. 1845, p. 2.
25. *DPCA*, 21st Nov. 1845, p. 4.
26. *CM*, 8th Dec. 1845, p. 1.
27. *London Daily News*, 20th Apr. 1846, p. 4.
28. *Yorkshire Gazette* [*YG*], 2nd May 1846, p. 3.
29. *Railway Herald*, quoted in *YG*, 2nd May 1846, p. 3.
30. *Glasgow Herald* [*GH*], 26th Jun. 1846, p. 3.
31. *DPCA*, 13th Nov. 1849, p. 2. The meeting approved the payment of the 2s and to continue hounding the defaulters. It is not reported whether they had any further success.
32. Quoted in *DC*, 4th Oct. 1846, p. 2.
33. *DC*, 6th Dec. 1846, p. 2.
34. The first one was examined in late December 1847. *AJ*, 29th Dec. 1847.
35. *DC*, 24th Jan. 1849, p. 1.
36. *AJ*, 19th Sep. 1849, p. 5.
37. *DPCA*, 2nd Nov. 1849, p. 1.
38. *AJ*, 7th Nov. 1849, p. 1. Two trips a day were run: 2.28am and 10.30am from Aberdeen, returning from 'Montrose Victoria Station' at 8am and 6.18pm. There is no further reference to Montrose 'Victoria'.
39. *AJ*, 10th Oct. 1849, p. 5.
40. *Montrose Herald*, reported in *AJ*, 16th Jan. 1850, p. 6.
41. Minute Books of Kincardineshire Turnpike Trusts (Second District and Consolidated District Minute Book 1849-50 Annual accounts, *Aberdeenshire Archives*, ref. KC2/3/3).
42. *AJ*, 3rd Apr. 1850, p. 5.
43. A detailed account of the promotion and construction of the Aberdeen Railway can be found in J.J. Waterman, *The Coming of the Railway to Aberdeen in the 1840s* (Aberdeen, nd).

Johnshaven station staff around 1890. *Norris Forrest collection*

Chapter 7
The Bervie Railway

First Steps

It nevertheless took several years for this dissatisfaction to turn itself into a scheme for a railway along the coast. A meeting of promoters of the Montrose & Bervie Railway was held in Montrose on 7th October 1859 when a prospectus drawn up by the civil engineer Edward H. Blyth was discussed. He estimated the cost of the thirteen-mile line at £60,000, so recommended a capital requirement of £70,000. A railway contractor '*intimately acquainted with the district*', but unnamed, suggested a '*low line*' which would only entail a slight deviation and would cut costs to around £44,000. This was agreed to and the capital requirement was set at £65,000. Of this, £22,000 had been subscribed, mainly by the principal landowners in the area – Farquhar of Hallgreen, Bervie, Scott of Brotherton, Porteous of Lauriston and Forsyth-Grant of Ecclesgreig, St. Cyrus – but with some participation by farmers in the district. Kinnear & Monro of Stonehaven and Ross of Montrose were appointed as legal agents and the engineers were Benjamin and Edward Blyth.[1]

An entry in the official *Edinburgh Gazette* on 15th November 1859 announced the incorporation of the Montrose & Bervie Railway Company and its intention of applying for an Act to build the line, and to enter into a working arrangement with the SNER. Plans and sections were to be available for public inspection on 30th November at the Sheriff Clerk's offices in Stonehaven and Forfar.[2]

Montrose Town Council had earlier decided to help by making land within its control available at £1 per acre, rather than the market value of £5.[3] The challenge, however, was to increase the capital raised from £22,000 to the target of £65,000, when all the major local sources of capital (those whose land values were likely to increase) had already been tapped.

The first port of call was the obvious and stated one of approaching the SNER for a contribution. An agreement was reached with the SNER for it to contribute £15,000, though Porteous (who had become a Director of the SNER principally to pursue the interests of the M&B, according to his testimony to the Parliamentary Committee examining the later extension scheme) was never able to pin down the SNER Chairman, Stirling, on this. Stirling claimed later that his board would not agree to such an arrangement, and that had they done so, it would have been in return for a commitment from the M&B not to extend north of Bervie. In May 1860 it was reported that the SNER Directors looked upon the Bervie line '*with considerable suspicion*' but on further consideration had concluded that it might be advantageous '*or at least not so disadvantageous as to make them oppose it*'. At the same meeting they decided to subscribe the £15,000.[4] The money never arrived.

The Montrose and Bervie Railway Act received the Royal Assent on 3rd July 1860.[5]

Fortunately the new line was able to benefit from a strategic dispute between larger railway players in the area.

The 'Kittywake Line' – the Aberdeen, Montrose & Dundee Railway

The Scottish North Eastern Railway, successor to the original Aberdeen and Scottish Midland Junction railways in 1856, had become embroiled in a major dispute with the Great North of Scotland Railway over the need for a line through Aberdeen. The Highland Railway, based in Inverness, was in the process of building a new direct line to the south to join the Aberdeen–Perth line just north of Perth, at Stanley, and it was clear that once this was completed, a large part of the traffic from north and west of Aberdeen would migrate to the new line. In Aberdeen the Great North of Scotland Railway had a terminal station in the eastern docks at Waterloo, and the only through connection with the SNER station at Market Street was via the dockside

Map 4 Gordon's map of Bervie in 1832 was surveyed well before the arrival of the railway, but it had not changed much. The station was built on the shore, down at the bottom of Kirkburn, far less convenient for the town than the station proposed for the Stonehaven Extension scheme, which would have been located in the Broadyards at the east end of the High Street, the main north west to south east street on this map.

By permission of the National Library of Scotland

railways; through passengers were even more inconvenienced, and it was not uncommon for them to arrive from an SNER train by cab to find the gates at Waterloo closed and their northbound connection being prepared for departure. The fact that the GNSR closed the gates five minutes before departure could even mean that passengers were able to witness their connection being prepared for departure and then leave without them.[6]

Since a significant proportion of the GNSR traffic to the south was consigned by ship from Aberdeen, often by the Aberdeen Steam Navigation Company, in which the Deputy Chairman, John Stewart, had a direct financial interest of approximately 50% of the equity, the GNSR was less concerned than the SNER to counter the Highland threat. Negotiations had dragged on between the two companies over the construction of a through line via the Denburn Valley in Aberdeen, but matters came to a head when the GNSR, alarmed at the estimated cost of the Denburn line at around £200,000, decided to withdraw from the discussions. The SNER concluded that only a solution independent of the GNSR would secure their through traffic from north of Aberdeen, and on 20th November 1861 an advertisement appeared in the *Aberdeen Journal* promoting an Aberdeen avoiding line leaving the SNER main line just north of Stonehaven, at Limpet Mill, crossing the Deeside Railway at Culter and joining the GNSR main line at Kintore. An incidental benefit would have been access to the Echt and Skene area. The cost of this scheme was estimated at around £150,000, slightly more than the SNER's share of the Denburn scheme.[7]

This development thoroughly alarmed the GNSR. Their first action was to take a perpetual lease on the Deeside Railway to close off that approach to Aberdeen. According to Stewart, their concern was that the SNER would just build the northern leg (from Culter to Kintore), establishing a bridgehead into '*Great North territory*', and take a lease on the Deeside Railway.[8] At the nineteenth half-yearly meeting of the GNSR in April 1862, Stewart protested that the GNSR had always wanted to bring through traffic by way of Aberdeen, but it is clear from his remarks that the GNSR wanted to hedge their bets on the new Highland line to Perth:

> *if we spent £60,000, £70,000 or £80,000 in making the Denburn Junction, we are bound, by this additional outlay, for ever to bring the through traffic this way; and if you allow us to keep the money in our pockets, and have no such material guarantee, it will be £4000 per annum saved to us, and we can send it the nearer way up the Highland road.*

Meanwhile the SNER had leased the Dundee & Arbroath Railway in what seemed to be a retaliatory move, and the GNSR had decided to invest in the Montrose & Bervie as each company vied for strategic advantage.[9]

A few days later the Parliamentary hearings for the Stonehaven–Kintore ('Limpet Mill') line began. Reith, manager of the SNER, pointed out that the GNSR Chairman owned about half of the Aberdeen Steam Navigation Company, implying that the GNSR were ambivalent about sending freight south by rail. He also referred to an earlier scheme for a line from Culter to Echt and Alford in 1855, suggesting that there was a precedent for a railway through the area. More dirty laundry was aired when it was revealed that the GNSR had, in addition to taking a large share of the stock in the Montrose & Bervie, also been negotiating with the Dundee & Arbroath to take a lease. At the end of the proceedings the Limpet Mill scheme was approved, subject to a twelve-month standstill to allow the Denburn scheme to proceed to an Act. If that happened, the Limpet Mill powers would lapse.[10]

The GNSR response was to promote '*a ditch extending from Hutcheon Street to the Clay Hills 10-23 feet deep*' as the *Aberdeen Journal* described the 'Circumbendibus', an Aberdeen avoiding line skirting the outskirts of the city.[11] The *Aberdeen Journal* was scathing about both the Circumbendibus and the '*Kittywake Line*' (as it described the coast line via Bervie). The nickname had apparently been coined by the *Aberdeen Herald* to describe the East Coast of Scotland Junction Railway as serving only the Kittywakes of Fowlsheugh and little else, but was used with some relish by the *Aberdeen Journal* in its campaign to see the proposal defeated.

Given the difficulties in raising capital for their line, all this was excellent news for the Montrose & Bervie. At the fourth half-yearly meeting held in the Star Hotel, Montrose, at the end of April 1862, the Directors were able to announce that the share capital was now fully subscribed, '*due to the subscription of parties interested in a through route*'. However they recommended a pause in starting work until October 1862 to allow for redesign of the route, as it would now probably form part of a through line to the north.[12] Fully subscribed the share list might have been, but in October, following a deputation from the Company to Montrose Town Council, the Council agreed to subscribe £1,000 on condition the deposit was returned if the line was not built; this decision was not universally popular within the Council as some members felt it was over hasty and possibly illegal.[13] The *Caledonian Mercury* also carried a report of the meeting. Their report stated that possibly two-thirds of the capital required for the through route had now been subscribed, suggesting that the earlier declaration by the Directors that the capital was fully subscribed referred to the branch line scheme only. Engineers B. & E. Blyth predicted that the through route would cost about £10,000 per mile and the return on capital would be between 5% and 6½%.[14]

At the following half-yearly meeting in November 1862, the M&B announced that the through route was now being developed, and that a meeting of shareholders would be called once the plans were finalized. However, the through line had caused some changes in alignment: gradients had been eased between the North Esk Viaduct and St. Cyrus, and a high level approach to Bervie had placed the new station there just east of the Square, rather than on the beach at the foot of Kirkburn. At a subsequent public meeting in Montrose Guildhall, Provost Savage urged support for the new scheme and described it as follows:

> *It will commence by a junction with the Arbroath and Forfar Railway near the church of St. Vigeans, and traversing the rich agricultural district embraced in the parishes of St. Vigeans, Inverkeillor, Lunan, Maryton and Craig, it will cross the Southesk by a viaduct nearly on a level with, and close by, the west side of the present Suspension Bridge. From thence it will pass through the Basin on the west side of the town, cross the Northesk Road at the south end of Victoria Bridge, and the Montrose Branch Railway a little on the east side of the turnpike road in a direct line to the Northesk, which it will cross by a bridge immediately below the present bridge. From thence it will proceed through the farms of Comieston, Warburton, and Kirkside – Kirkside House being on the west side – sweep past the east end of the Free Church of St. Cyrus, and northwards very close to the east side of the turnpike road till it reaches the burgh of Bervie. It will then cross Bervie water by a bridge, keep the east side of Craig David, pass very near the farmhouse of Fernieflatt, and proceed from thence very near the top of the Cliffs until it reaches the high table-land on the south side of Stonehaven. The valley there will be crossed by a viaduct passing over the top of the woollen manufactory on the left bank of the Carron, and it will join the Scottish North-Eastern Railway very near the manse of Fetteresso.*

It was intended to apply for running powers over the SNER to Aberdeen, and over the Dundee & Arbroath, Dundee & Perth and Arbroath & Forfar lines to reach Dundee and Perth. The Provost pointed out that the new station at Montrose would move the shore line into the flow of the South Esk River, avoiding '*the whole noxious* and pestilential deposits which are now thrown upon the Bank Sands' at the east bank of the Montrose Basin. Meston, one of the M&B auditors, followed the Provost, saying that railways were now cheap to make due to 'late discoveries in engineering' (which he did not specify) and that the only heavy work required would be the South Esk Viaduct and the Bank Sands embankment. Although he agreed with Blyths on the cost of construction, he estimated working expenses at only 45% of revenues, and a return of over 6%. Presumably as evidence of the 'advances in engineering', he said the South Esk Viaduct would be a five-arch structure, with piers 'made out of double tubing, filled with concrete or stone and lime'.[15] All this optimism had an effect; canvassers reported sales of 298 shares of £10 after the meeting.

The roadshow then moved to Arbroath. Meston gave further details of the proposed line. Talking of the estimated revenue per week, he said that the M&B estimates of three years before had been £10 per mile, and the Arbroath & Montrose estimates in 1856 were £14. The Scottish branch line average was £7 to £8, so their estimates had been revised downwards to £6 on the Bervie–Stonehaven section, giving an average of £10 over the whole line from Arbroath. This compared with £37 on the Dundee & Perth, over £40 on the Dundee & Arbroath and about £40 on the SNER. The estimated value of through traffic was put at £30 a week. With one third of the capital borrowed at 4½%, and 45% working expenses, that left 6% for a dividend. Despite some hostile questioning from two SNER employees in the hall, Messrs Dewsbury and Kerr, the meeting was deemed a success. The *Dundee Advertiser* reported on the questions, and it is worth reproducing them in full, given the endemic over-estimation of revenue and under estimation of costs common in railway schemes.

Dewsbury, of the SNER, said he was in favour of line to Montrose, but it was not often that railways were constructed for the estimated cost.

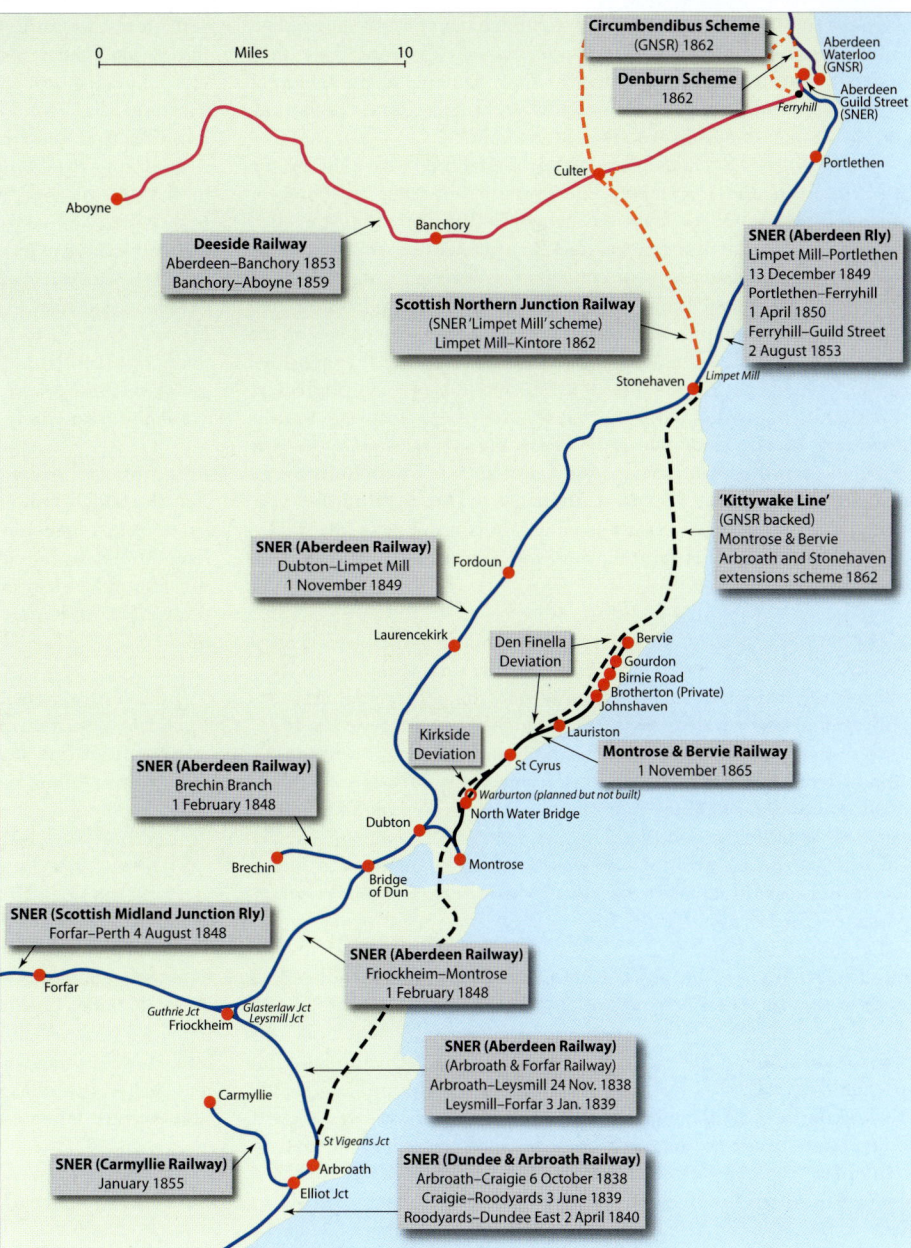

MAP 5 The railways south of Aberdeen in the early 1860s, showing the extent of the ambitions of both the SNER and the GNSR.

1. On costs:-
   What was cost of Montrose viaduct?
   How was the valley midway between Arbroath and Montrose to be crossed, whether by bridge, viaduct or embankment?
   If cost of these two items were deducted from the £120,000, what was then cost per mile?

2. On revenues:-
   On what data were traffic returns based?
   With reference to a 'southern company' coming to help with line. 'He would like to know what company it was and whether it was a responsible one, before he invested his money in the proposed undertaking, and he was sure that the Arbroath people, who were much longer headed than he was, would be of the same opinion (laughter).'

Kerr, of the SNER, asked:

1. What material would be used in Southesk viaduct.
2. What was the cost of the Northesk viaduct?
3. What were the gradients?

Monro refused to answer most of the questions, just saying that Blyth's reputation was enough.

Mr. Dewsbury having made some farther observations, to which Mr. Monro replied, the audience meanwhile getting rather impatient.

Kerr proposed that the landowners pay for the line themselves. The Arbroath Provost ruled that out of order. Dewsbury then proposed an amendment that while the line was a good idea, they needed further information. Clearly that was not what the audience wanted to hear, and the motion of support was passed decisively.[16]

By the time the show had moved to Stonehaven, in late November, with the predictable enthusiastic support being registered, the Public Notice had been published, listing the four elements of the scheme – the Kirkside (St. Cyrus) deviation, the Den Finella–Bervie deviation, and the Arbroath and Stonehaven extensions.[17]

The promised Extraordinary General Meeting was held in the Star Hotel on 2nd December. There was a reference to the *'very general feeling'* soon after the passage of the M&B Act that it needed to be extended to Stonehaven and Arbroath. The support from Montrose and Arbroath town councils was strong, and canvassing for shareholders had been very successful. Many applications had been for small amounts, but with one of £20,000 from *'one of the southern lines'*, £137,000 had been subscribed for the through line, and £70,000 for the Bervie line alone. Porteous, the M&B Chairman, said that all the rail for the Bervie line had been secured, to take advantage of low iron prices, but then mused on what name the new line should adopt. Perhaps the Scottish East Coast Railway, he thought, or better, the Aberdeen, Montrose & Dundee Railway.

Some of the gloss started to come off during the next few weeks, as attacks intensified from the press. This editorial in the *Aberdeen Journal* was typical:

> *The Scottish North-Eastern may not be conducted so well as it might be in some respects. It may not pay due attention to its local traffic. We think it not unlikely; but if so, it is greatly owing to the burdens with which it was so fearfully encumbered at the outset. It is because too much money has already been sunk in forming our connection with the south. Let this new line be made, it will be so much more money sunk to no adequate end, for all of which the public will pay some day, when they will find that the purpose of additional through communication, they have about as much use for the 'Kittywake' line as a cart has for a third wheel.*[18]

Kinnear & Monro, the M&B's Stonehaven agents, felt obliged to write to the *Aberdeen Journal* on 18th February 1863, complaining about the *'ignorant and senseless'* articles in it. Much of this revolved around an alleged agreement that the M&B had made not to extend beyond Bervie in return for a subscription of £15,000 stock from the SNER, and that the extensions were really a GNSR ploy to put pressure on the SNER. Kinnear & Monro wished to refute the first allegation, saying that while the SNER had asked the M&B not to build north of Bervie, that *'had been refused at once'* and that in fact the £15,000 had never been received. As to the second allegation, they could say that the GNSR did not hold any stock in the M&B. As will become clear, this was misleading in the extreme.[19]

Even in Arbroath Town Council, dissenting voices were heard. At a meeting a couple of days later, one councillor said that the M&B had not proceeded because of lack of capital, and was only now being resurrected because the GNSR wanted to use it as a bargaining chip with the SNER.[20] However, more organisations gave their support to the scheme, including Aberdeen Town Council (following an open letter from 104 merchants and manufacturers urging such action), Dundee Town Council (largely because they feared an emerging Caledonian Railway monopoly) and Stonehaven Town Council.[21] Those who continued to speak out against it were even in some personal danger; a witness to the Parliamentary Enquiry opposed to the scheme was burnt in effigy outside his Montrose house.[22]

The House of Commons Committee was reported in detail in the local press.[23] The value of fish landings at every village was examined in minute detail (often to the irritation of the Committee Chairman), and the allegations of breach of faith over the extension with the SNER were examined. While the Chairman of the SNER (John Stirling) was adamant that it was *'quite understood that there was to be no extension of the line'* and that while he had considered investing in the line, it was a proposition he could not put to his Board. Under cross-examination he had to admit there was no restriction in his agreement with the M&B, and there was a strong suspicion that the SNER were merely playing for time, knowing that the line was under-subscribed, and that its powers were due to expire in a short time. Porteous did not come out well in the proceedings, it being apparent that he was either outwitted by Stirling, or careless of what had been agreed. In his evidence, he claimed always to have opposed the *'low route'* (the one subsequently built), because it would not be possible to extend it. Porteous gave evidence that he:

> *did not recollect of any pledge being given by us that we should not extend beyond Bervie, but we would have been glad at that time to have made any terms, in order to obtain assistance.*[24]

At a further meeting with Stirling, he said that he had been told that the SNER Directors would not agree to any assistance and that he therefore considered the matter closed. Unfortunately a letter from Monro to the SNER was quoted, saying they would not extend the line in return for the SNER subscribing £15,000. Pressed on the role of Anderson and Stewart of the GNSR, Porteous answered that:

> *Our law agents are Messrs. Adam and Anderson, who happen to be also the solicitors of the Great North. Mr. Stewart is Deputy Chairman of that Company. If we do not get this Bill, Messrs. Adam and Anderson will pay the expenses (laughter).*
> MR. MUNDELL (FOR THE SNER). *And exonerate the directors and shareholders of the Montrose and Bervie Company?*
> WITNESS. *Yes (laughter).*
> MR. MUNDELL. *That's very candid, at any rate.*

The SNER made a good job of demonstrating that it would face damaging competition from a new line which would be uneconomic in itself. James Campbell, a farmer from Bellfield, about three miles from Bervie, was called as a witness to prove there was need for the line. He said there was a two-horse coach running three times a week in summer only and a carrier running twice a week from Bervie to Stonehaven. When asked about the local markets, he said:

> *I believe there is a cattle market at Bervie.*
> MUNDELL. *How often?*
> JAMES CAMPBELL. *Every year (laughter). I believe there is a sort of weekly market for grain at Bervie – some two or three dealers go (laughter renewed) …*
> MUNDELL. *Of course coming from so far north you would send them [sheep] by the cheapest route (laughter).*
> JAMES CAMPBELL. *Of course; six miles is no great distance to drive cattle, or to cart grain. I use manure – some of it brought from a distance; I also use 'sharn' and other manures (great laughter).*

A lot is probably lost in the translation from broad Doric to Hansard English.

Probably the decisive factor was the revelation that in March 1862 Anderson (Lord Provost of Aberdeen and law agent for GNSR) and Stewart (GNSR Vice-Chairman) had offered assistance on the basis of subscribing £35,000 if £10,000 could be found in the district, the line extended from Arbroath to Stonehaven, and £40,000 additional funds contributed locally. The GNSR paid the deposit and agreed to pay Parliamentary expenses, but the M&B's law agents were still able to claim that these were 'private investments' and not by the GNSR.[25]

The Parliamentary Committee understood the game that was being played by the GNSR and the SNER. The Bill was thrown out and the post-mortems started at the sixth half-yearly meeting of the M&B,

CHAPTER 7: THE BERVIE RAILWAY

where Porteous said the company now needed to get on with building the Bervie line. He was still clinging to the belief that the scheme could be resurrected; mysteriously, he said:

> At present I will only say further, that we shall give our best attention to the subject, and still hope to get satisfactory arrangements made with those that take an interest in our progress.

Hercules Scott, obviously still smarting from the accusations of bad faith by the SNER, said that while some things were discussed, nothing was agreed, and when negotiations restarted with the SNER they would be '*from scratch*'. Perceptively, he added that the failure of the scheme was due in his opinion to the '*pleas of poverty*' by the SNER and the '*involvement of GNSR proxies*', which had damaged their credibility.[26] A suggestion that the deviations should still be made to keep the extension alive was rejected when it was revealed that these would cost an additional £30,000 and cause more delay.

The commentary in the *Aberdeen Journal* was justifiably harsh:

THE 'STATUS QUO ANTE BELLUM'.

> *A good fight must be a great luxury, if we may judge by the cost. How many wars end where they began, plus the expenditure of lives, limbs, blood, sorrow, and hard cash! We have a specimen of this sort of thing in our recent Railway campaigns. How much money have the Scottish North-Eastern and the Great North spent during the past two years? We should be glad to hear that they are under two-thirds of a 'plum.' Yet we find them both congratulating themselves on a victory which leaves them standing on the ground which they occupied in 1861. They have fought two campaigns; and now they furl their banners over a treaty which restores them to their two-year-old status quo without any great store of laurels to compensate for the lack of material advantages. We shall not moralise over such matters. That may be left to the shareholders. It is their privilege. If they have no other, they may be left in undisturbed possession of that, at least. No doubt they will exercise it when they contemplate the grand scale in which one or two gentlemen can indulge their personal animosities and promote their party schemes, till they spend more money than would stand, ounce for ounce, and pound for pound, in good gold in the balance against both Railway Boards, duly weighed and stamped by the Dean of Guild's officer.*
>
> *In 1861, the Scottish North-Eastern and the Great North seemed about to join hands and make the Denburn Junction on Messrs. Gibb and Willett's plan, with a station near Union Bridge. There was some hope of it for a week or two. But after negotiations had been hung up till the latest moment by the Great North, objections were started, and it was given up. Then, all of a sudden, out came the Scottish North-Eastern with the Limpet Mill line, which was passed, subject to suspension for twelve months, to allow the Great North to try their hand at a more popular measure. Next came the 'Circumbendibus,' and with it the lease of the Deeside, and the new East Coast project; while the Scottish North-Eastern cut in ahead again with a lease of the Arbroath and Dundee. And the result is, that the 'Circumbendibus' has supplanted the Limpet Mill, but is suspended, in its turn, to allow the Scottish North-Eastern to try what they can do next where the Great North has failed. As for the other schemes, the Deeside lease stands unsanctioned; the Dundee and Arbroath is as yet undecided on; the 'Kitty wake' [Montrose & Bervie extension] is confined, in prospect, to its original habitat in the vicinity of Fowlsheugh and Whistleberry Point; and we are all back to the position of 1861, with certain weighty obligations in behalf of good faith, and, let us hope, some wisdom gleaned in the costly field of Parliamentary experience.*[27]

The *Inverness Courier* added:

> *After the decision of the Parliamentary Committee on the bills before them, the companies have conferred together, and have come to a mutual agreement, on the following terms:— The citizens are to get the Denburn route; the Scottish North-Eastern is to make it, receiving a subscription of £125,000 from the Great Northern [sic]—the estimated expense of the circumbendibus. The Great Northern [sic] gets three-fourths of the fare on the junction: and the Scottish North-Eastern one-fourth; and the maintenance of the joint-station, which is to be in the immediate vicinity of the Glass Works, will be paid for by each company according to the use they make of it. The question has been the subject of constant discussion, and some rather stiff quarrelling in Aberdeen for the last six months, but it may be hoped to be now finally settled.*[28]

The repercussions for the Great North management were far reaching. Sir James Elphinstone, GNSR Chairman, sought to place the responsibility for the dispute with the SNER. However the Denburn scheme eventually cost the GNSR far more than it would have done with promised contributions from the SNER and the Inverness & Aberdeen Junction Railway in the early days before the Highland line to Perth was mooted. Stewart had been removed by the end of 1864 and the financial position of the GNSR deteriorated rapidly, so that from paying 7% dividends in 1863, it was paying none at all in 1865, a position it remained in until 1874.[29]

BUILDING THE MONTROSE & BERVIE LINE

For the M&B it was, as the north-east saying goes, '*back to auld claes and porridge*'.[30] After the excitements and dreams of being part of a through route, albeit a slow single-track one, the company now had to get on quickly with construction if it was not to face the expiry of its Parliamentary powers in 1865. The invitation to tender (ITT) for the 'St. Cyrus Contract', the 5½ miles from Montrose to Bush (Lauriston) was issued by Kinnear & Monro on 26th October 1863,[31] and the *Aberdeen Journal* reported that at the half-yearly meeting it was expected that the contract would be let in mid-November for an immediate start.[32] The Chairman added that because the northern portion was relatively light, it was not expected to take long. Presumably he was not thinking about the North Water Bridge contract.

Events did not move quite as quickly as that. The *Montrose Standard* reported on 9th January 1864 that Mitchell & Ireland had won the St. Cyrus contract for £35,000 (£6,363 per mile),[33] and on 23rd March a tender was issued for sleepers for the section.[34] The ITT for the Bush–Bervie section (the 'Brotherton Contract') was not issued until 6th April.[35]

At the half-yearly meeting in the Star Hotel, Montrose, on 29th April, it was reported that the St. Cyrus contract was proceeding well, and that tenders had been received, but not decided on, for the Brotherton contract. Porteous was able to say that:

> *The contractors for the first half of the line are pushing on the works vigorously, and in the course of a few weeks the second half of the line will, we hope, be begun.*

However Hercules Scott took a less optimistic tone, when he added that the company was running into some difficulty in its land acquisition negotiations, and was still short of capital:

The North Esk Viaduct was the largest structure on the Montrose & Bervie line, and survives as a walkway. This photograph, probably taken in the 1950s, shows a Class 'J37' locomotive returning to Montrose with the daily goods. *Author's collection*

I do ... trust that we may yet find that the right hand of fellowship will be held out to us by friends and neighbours through whose properties we are going, and whose interests along with our own must ... be benefitted. It is not too late in the day for such gentlemen to see their true interests, and ... in the course of a short time, the list of shareholders will be swelled by names which as yet do not appear on our register[36]

By 4th June the *Dundee Courier* was able to report that:

The works on this line are proceeding favourably. The land-piers on the north side of the North Esk are now rapidly approaching completion; and the workmen have commenced with the piers in the bed of the river. Though it might appear that this would be a far more difficult piece of work than the other, on account of the mass of water, yet it seems that the pumps can accomplish the work with actually less labour. At other points the works are being carried on actively.[37]

A couple of months later, the same newspaper published a lengthy and detailed description of the line:

The construction of this railway was commenced in February, at several points of the proposed line, and the contractors have made so much progress that already nearly a fourth of the whole work is completed.[38]

Also, that the North Esk Viaduct was 200 yards long and 50 feet high. There were skew arches each of 50-foot span in the main structure, and two small arches at south end. The only other important work was a viaduct at Den Finella 130 feet above the water, carried on three 40-foot spans and one of 20 feet. Both these stone-built viaducts used stone from local quarries. Finally, a stone sea wall was being constructed just south of Gourdon. Contractors for the two contracts were Ireland & Co. of Montrose, who were due to be finished by the end of June 1865 when the statutory period for completion expired. At the half-yearly meeting of the Company on 28th October, Scott reported that fourteen bridges had been built, or nearly completed, and that the North Esk Viaduct piers had been raised and work was '*in a very forward state*'. He invited shareholders to walk the line and see for themselves. At the same meeting it was announced that John Duncan, Chairman of the Deeside Railway, had joined as a Director. Duncan had been appointed Deputy Chairman of the Great North of Scotland Railway in succession to John Stewart in September 1864 and is credited with rescuing the company from its dire financial situation over the following years.[39] Even though at this stage the GNSR would have been entitled to nominate a Director because of their shareholding, it was useful to have a close relationship with the new GNSR Directors while the M&B was seeking to recover its costs for the extension scheme.[40]

Sadly, the first accident on the line occurred on 29th June 1864. One of the construction gang, a young lad named White of Lochside, Montrose, was killed when a wagon ran over him.[41]

The contract for station construction was let to John Gordon, of Montrose, in March 1865, and the station names were decided on.[42] Progress was not fast enough, however, and this was beginning to be apparent to the Board. At the half-yearly meeting on 28th April 1865 it was notable that Porteous was talking about a '*reasonable prospect*' that the line would be open by July, though he felt it necessary to talk about delays caused by the lock-out in the iron trade in England, which had delayed the delivery of rails. It was also notable that when Porteous seemed to be favourably inclined to provide a station at North Water Bridge to placate a local farmer, Scott quickly intervened to say that they should concentrate on finishing the line before thinking about enhancements.[43]

By the middle of June, the *Montrose Standard* was reporting that while the contractors were pushing on as fast as possible, the rail shortage now meant that completion was more likely in the second week of August. Eight miles of permanent way had been completed, but two of the arches of the North Esk Viaduct were incomplete, and would take another three weeks.[44]

On 18th July 1865, another workman was killed. Kenneth McKenzie was run over by a wagon at Johnshaven and his legs crushed. He died two days later in hospital, '*leaving a widow in such circumstances as to deserve the consideration of the benevolent.*'[45]

Finally, on 16th August, the *Aberdeen Journal* was able to report that:

A locomotive engine, to which was attached a number of trucks, has passed over the Montrose and Bervie Railway. There were a good number of passengers on the train.[46]

The report somewhat lost its impact when it turned out that the train was only running between Johnshaven and Montrose. It was, however, proof that the North Esk Viaduct was complete.

On 1st September the first official train ran over the whole length of the line, though nearly involving another serious injury:

CHAPTER 7: THE BERVIE RAILWAY

The Den Finella Viaduct was short but very high.
Graeme Davidson

The directors … passed over the line yesterday, prior to its being opened for traffic … in about a fortnight. The workmen engaged on the line are hard at work; so that we will soon have the benefit of Railway communication with Bervie and the district which lies between. On Friday last, a portion of the embankment fell upon one of the navvies, and nearly suffocated him. In a short time, however, the debris was cleared away; and the poor fellow was extricated, comparatively little injured. We understand he is now recovering.[47]

Meanwhile, work on finalizing the working agreement with the SNER was proceeding. A public notice was published by the SNER that a motion to approve the agreement would be proposed at the next half-yearly meeting on 21st September, as well as contributing £15,000 to the cost.[48] The GNSR-owned stock was clearly at risk of coming on the market just at the time the SNER would require it to make their contribution to the M&B, thereby apparently depriving the M&B of much of the additional capital. The GNSR had in fact agreed a sale at par to the SNER, and then offered to sell the stock to the M&B if it wished to buy them on the same basis.[49] A proposal that the M&B principal shareholders should take the stock was also floated. A few days later, on 25th September, the GNSR half-yearly meeting approved the sale of £12,000 of stock to the M&B, payable in M&B debentures with a maturity of three, five and eight years hence at 3% per annum.[50] Farquhar, Porteous and Scott took the stock.[51] This was a good deal for the M&B, as they were effectively able to convert the GNSR shares into debt at a relatively low interest rate (the local bank lending rate was 4½% at the time) and as events were to prove, it would take some time for the GNSR to recover their money.[52]

On 27th September the *Aberdeen Journal* reported that:

The new line is almost ready for general traffic. On Wednesday the usual notice was issued by the Board of Directors to the Government Inspector; and as he is bound to make his official examination of the line within ten days after receipt of notice, the probability is, that the line will be opened by the end of the week.[53]

That was not to be, however. The inspection was carried out by Captain Rich, RE, accompanied by Porteous, Scott, the manager of the SNER (William Esplin), and T.R. Yarrow of the SNER locomotive department. There were also a *'few friends'*.

The train consisted of a large engine and tender, the whole weighing 40 tons, and three carriages conveying the company. The train left Montrose at 9.30, and after carefully inspecting the whole line, and particularly the stations, bridges etc, arrived at Bervie at 2.40pm. There was considerable enthusiasm displayed at various points in their progress, flags being displayed and numbers of people turned out. On reaching Bervie, the party were met by the whole inhabitants, who turned out to give them a welcome. The inspection was very satisfactory, and the Inspector expressed himself satisfied with the work of the contractors – Messrs. Ireland & Co. The result of the inspection has been that the railway is to be opened for goods traffic on Monday first [2nd October] while the passenger traffic will not be opened for three weeks at least, as several alterations have to be made. These are trivial in their nature, but the rule of inspection is so strict that Government will not allow passengers to be carried until the utmost letter of the law has been complied with. The day was very fine, the heat of the sun being tempered by a fresh cool breeze off the sea, and the whole company were in the highest spirits.[54]

However, the inspector's report was not as favourable as this made out. Many minor defects were found, but the most serious shortcoming related to the absence of an operating system, the need for a turntable, and gradient easing at St. Cyrus and Johnshaven.

To the Secretary, Board of Trade, Rlys Dept.
Edinburgh, 29th September 1865
Sir,
I have the honour to report, for the information of the Lords of the Committee of Privy Council for Trade, that in compliance with minute of the 26th Inst., I inspected the Montrose and Bervie Railway yesterday.

The New Line forms a single Junction with the Scottish North Eastern, about a mile from Montrose, at Broomfield, where the Montrose & Bervie Ry. Co. has erected a small station.

The New Line is 12 miles 6 ch long. It is single throughout, with sidings. No land has been taken for doubling the line. The gauge is 4ft 8½ins. The Stations are Broomfield, St. Cyrus, Lauriston, Johnshaven, Gourdon and Bervie. The Permanent Way consists of a Single headed rail, in lengths of 18, 21 & 24 ft., which weigh 65 lbs. per lin^r yard. It is fished & fixed with wooden keys, in chairs which weigh 24 lbs. ea. The Chairs are spiked to sleepers, laid transversely, at an average distance of 3 ft. These next to rail joints are only 2 ft. 6 ins. apart.

The Sleepers are [writing unclear] 9 ft. long 10x5/9x4½. [dimensions in inches].

The line is ballasted with gravel.

There are 10 over and 12 under bridges, principally built of stone – eight having cast iron girders and timber cross bearers. The North Esk Viaduct which is about 50 ft high consists of eleven square segmental arches, of 50 ft span and five of 55 ft span on the skew.

The Den Finella Viaduct consists of three semi-circular arches of 40 ft span and one of 20 ft span.

The viaducts are 15 ft wide and are built of stone.

The masonry in several under bridges shows slight cracks and the lines of the viaducts are not true. The North Esk Viaduct shows cracks and settlements in several places.

I recommend that all cracks are at once pointed, with cement or a mixture of cement and mortar, so as to afford the means of judging whether they move any more. The North Esk Viaduct requires more ballast and it would be desirable to place a guard rail on the curve at the north end.

St. Cyrus Station is on a gradient of 1 in 70 and Johnshaven on 1 in 100. These gradients should be altered to 1 in 230. The South Distant signal at Lauriston requires raising.

The Signals generally require painting and the lamps attaching. Indicators are required at all facing points and clocks at the stations.

Spring stop buffers are required at Bervie and the siding leading to the turntable should be taken off the loop, instead of the main line.

The fencing is incomplete opposite Mr. Scott's residence, at Johnshaven and at Gourdon. The rubbish requires clearing away in many places where it forms ramps to the fencing and the fencing adjacent to the under and over bridges generally requires making good. Some fangs or through bolts are required on the cast iron under bridges.

A turntable has been provided at Bervie. It will be necessary to obtain an undertaking to provide one at Broomfield if the Co are to have working arrangements with the Scottish NE into Montrose.

I have received no undertaking the proposed mode of working this single line, which I submit, cannot be opened for passenger traffic without danger to the public using the service by reason of the incompleteness of the works.

Your Obedient Servant
J.H. Rich (Inspector)[55]

CHAPTER 7: THE BERVIE RAILWAY

On receipt of Rich's report, the Board of Trade directed that the opening should be delayed one month to no earlier than 30th October 1865.

The second inspection, held on 24st October, found these alterations had been made satisfactorily, but Captain Rich also conducted *'various severe tests'* on the North Esk Viaduct, no doubt to establish whether the settlement he had noted at his first inspection had stabilized.[56]

Rich's report, dated 25th October 1865, noted that:

> *The works reported incomplete in my letter of the 29th Ult have been attended to and I enclose an undertaking as to the proposed mode of working which appears satisfactory as far as the New Line is concerned.*
>
> *It will be desirable, however, to obtain one from the Scottish North Eastern Co for the working between Broomfield Junction and Montrose. They have promised to submit one and it is further desirable to obtain an undertaking from the Bervie & Montrose Co to erect a turntable at Broomfield Junction in case any alterations should take place in their working arrangements with the Scottish North Eastern Railway, by which they would not have the use of that company's turntable at Montrose.*
>
> *The guard rail on the Esk Viaduct should be made 150ft long instead of 75ft which it is at present and should be plated with angle iron.*
>
> *At least three fang bolts should be inserted in each length of rail all round the curve leading on to the Esk Viaduct from the North and over the Viaduct.*
>
> *Gradient boards are required and proper clocks at the stations.*
>
> *The Chairman and Engineer have promised that these matters shall be attended to at once.*
>
> *Should the Co. hereafter desire to change the working arrangements to the Train Staff System, a double junction will be required at Broomfield and the siding arrangements at Lauriston St[ation] will require slight alterations so as to have no facing points, except those at the end of the loop. The new line should be worked with great care and not at high speed. The incline north of the Esk Viaduct is 1 in 50 for 2 miles and there is a sharp curve coming on to the viaduct.*
>
> *I submit that the Bervie & Montrose Railway may be opened for passenger traffic so soon as the undertakings referred to in this report are received.*

The undertakings requested were speedily submitted and authority was given to open the line to passenger traffic. The M&B published their initial timetable on 31st October (Table 3).[57]

The M&B had not managed to complete its line within the statutory period for completion, but this seems to have been quietly forgotten. It opened without ceremony on 1st November 1865, with a lengthy description of proceedings being published in the *Dundee Courier* the following day:

> *This railway was opened for general traffic on Wednesday, and the first day was a very successful one in a financial point of view. A very large number availed themselves of the first opportunity of visiting what had, in many cases, been to them an unknown territory. The day was by no means a fine one. The sky was overcast, and frequent showers fell, yet this circumstance did not damp the ardour of many who had previously resolved to have a trip on the opening day. The first train departed for Montrose at 7.15 a.m., and very few passengers went with it, perhaps not over one dozen. That early hour is not at all suitable for excursions in the month of November, so most of those who intended going waited for the second train, which was announced to leave at 11.45 a.m. This was on the arrival of the down mail train from the south. Some delay took place, however, and it was close upon 12 noon ere the train started. It was a pretty large one, there being nine carriages in all, and the most of them were filled. On reaching the first station, at Broomfield, there were a number more waiting to be taken on, after which the train proceeded to St. Cyrus, where many of them left, but their places were taken by an equal number. The same process was repeated at all the stations till the train reached the Terminus at the ancient Royal Burgh of Bervie, where, for the present, the line terminates. The time of arrival was 12.45, being fifteen minutes after the advertised time. The return train left Bervie at 1.30, and again consisted of nine carriages all very well filled. This time, however, most of them were Bervie folks, as the shops there were all shut, and a sort of half-holiday instituted to commemorate the auspicious event. On the train reaching Gourdon, a large proportion left. Another clearance was effected at Johnshaven, and when the train reached Montrose at 2.15 there were not many passengers in it. The first up train which left Bervie at 9.45 brought a large number of sight seers right on to Montrose where they spent the day till 4 p.m., when they had to depart. Several of the directors of the line went along the train, among whom were Mr. Porteous, of Laurieston, the Chairman; Mr. David Mitchell, Kirksidehouse; Mr. Munro of Messrs. Kinnear & Munro, writers, Stonehaven, secretaries to the Company. Mr. Alexander, of the S N E was also engaged all day on the line superintending arrangements, which all wrought well, there being no hitch whatever. In regard to the goods traffic, this being the opening day not much could be done, but sufficient indications were shown that a good deal may and will be done in the goods department. There were at various points waggons being loaded, and several were brought in with this train. At Johnshaven the train had to be stopped and a waggon of herring in barrels put on; and again, at Lauriston, two waggons of grain were taken on. At Bervie also a covered waggon was being filled with yarn. These were all signs of traffic, and none more so than that of the baker's boy, who got a box of bread put into the van to assist him to the next station. The working arrangements seem to [be] very complete. The train is worked by a very powerful engine (No. 47), and*

TABLE 3: MONTROSE & BERVIE, OPENING TIMETABLE							
	DOWN TRAINS				**UP TRAINS**		
STATIONS	1	2	3	**STATIONS**	1	2	3
Montrose	7.15	11.45	4. 0	Bervie	9.45	1.30	6.45
Broomfield Road Jn	7.19	11.49	4. 4	Gourdon	9.49	1.34	6.49
St. Cyrus	7.33	12. 3	4.18	Johnshaven	9.59	1.44	6.59
Lauriston	7.37	12. 7	4.22	Lauriston	10. 7	1.52	7. 7
Johnshaven	7.45	12.15	4.30	St. Cyrus	10.11	1.56	7.11
Gourdon	7.55	12.25	4.40	Broomfield Road Jn	10.25	2.10	7.25
Bervie	8. 0	12.30	4.45	Montrose	10.30	2.15	7.30

the carriages are all first and third class, there being no second class on the line.

For the information of those who may not have seen the above line, we may give a faint outline of its course. Passengers for Bervie take out their tickets at the usual ticket office, Montrose. The train then moves on up the Montrose line till the first station is reached, being Broomfield junction, where the Bervie line breaks off and turns eastward and proceeds through the low lying grounds at the bottom of the Bay of Montrose till it approaches the North Esk, when it begins to rise, and that river is crossed by a viaduct perhaps 50 feet high, and consisting of five arches. Shortly after passing the river the line begins to ascend a very steep incline, the gradient being 1 in 50, till it reaches the house of Kirkside (D. Mitchell, Esq). At this place there is a small gap on the south side of the line, which enables the passenger to look down upon the famed 'auld kirkyard' of St. Cyrus, so well known as the spot where the unfortunate author of 'John o' Arnha'' put a period to his existence, and where his mortal remains lie interred. A more dreary looking place on a November day could hardly be looked for. The next station reached is St. Cyrus, a thriving-like village, consisting mostly of new houses. The next station is Lauriston, near which is seen, among the trees by which it is surrounded, the mansion house of Alexander Porteous, Esq., the chairman, and one of the chief promoters of the line. Passing onwards, the line begins to sink a little, and the engine seems to have less to do. The celebrated Den of Finella is passed, on an arch, or arches, at a height of 135 feet above the water. This den is a favourite jaunting-place for the young folk of Montrose and other places. Proceeding now down the incline of 1 in 66, the fishing village of Johnshaven is reached, the line passing it on the north. It is still so high, that the passenger has only a sort of bird's-eye view of the town below, or, rather of the roofs of the houses. Leaving Johnshaven, and proceeding eastwards, the fine new mansion of Brotherton (Hercules Scott, Esq.) is passed on the left hand, the line at this spot running along the sea-beach. The house of Brotherton is a fine-looking mansion. The old house has been so, and the new one, not yet finished, is built on to it, the two forming one house. It stands at an elevation of perhaps 50 feet above the level of the sea, and at a distance of 150 yards inland. The line, which was so high at St. Cyrus, has now been sunk down to the level of the sea-beach, and continues so till it passes the town of Gourdon. This is a pretty considerable place, and has a regularly built harbour, small no doubt, yet large enough for its present requirements. There was only one vessel, a schooner, in it, which did honour to the event, by displaying a profusion of bunting. After leaving Gourdon, the line is carried along the beach almost on the level of the sands till it reaches the terminus between the burgh of Bervie and the sea. The station is about 250 yards on the south side of the High Street, or turnpike road which passes through the town, and a more convenient site could not have been selected.

From the above outline it will be seen that one of the leading features of the new line is steep gradients. This will require the line to be wrought by heavy engines. On Wednesday, No. 47 went up the ascent at Kirkside of one in sixty without much effort; and in returning, at Johnshaven, where the gradient is one in sixty-six, its existence was ignored. Of course it will not be so easy after the coal and lime traffic is begun; but the whole distance being so short, 13½ miles, a few extra minutes can be devoted to it. The line as a whole does not seem to have presented any great engineering difficulties. For the first two miles or so, and the last three or four, all that has been required has been to fence in the ground and lay down the rails. The cuttings have been by no means heavy. The best feature in the plan seems to have been that of making the line a succession of gentle curves, and thus avoiding the enormous expense which would have been entailed had the old idea of 'straight lines' been followed out.

This railway has opened out a large and well-peopled tract of country, which has to most travellers been a sort of terra incognita, but has now been thrown open to the influences of commercial intercourse.[58]

At the M&B half-yearly a few days later, Porteous, still full of bonhomie after the opening of the line, declared that the SNER were *'our natural allies'*. He obviously had a short memory.

The local coach operator was also quick to adjust. Somerville, who had operated the Montrose–Bervie coach since 1849, immediately withdrew his service to Montrose and altered his thrice-weekly service from Bervie to Stonehaven to run daily to connect with the first arrival in Bervie, reaching Stonehaven in time for the fast train to Aberdeen, meeting the evening mail at Stonehaven and connecting with the last train to Montrose. An admirable example not only of business agility, but of transport integration.[59] A less agile response was seen on the Bervie Turnpike. In April 1866 it was reported that the Trust had had difficulty letting the tolls for the North Water Bridge. It had been offered at £110, the average of the past five years, No offers were received, and none when the price was reduced to £100. Finally, the present tenant was asked for his views and said it was now worth £35. The Trustees were not having that, so they offered it a third time without a price when the tenant offered £36. Somebody else offered £73 and it was let.[60]

EARLY FINANCIAL PERFORMANCE

Now that the line was built and open, it is interesting to compare what was promised by the promoters and what actually occurred. Andrew Odlyzko, in his study of the 1840s railway mania,[61] recounts the difference between estimates and delivery; engineers' cost estimates were *'reliably unreliable'*, traffic estimates were usually too high, and operating cost estimates were always too low. To what extent was this true of the M&B?

The original cost estimate for the Montrose & Bervie by Blyths was £60,000. Based on that, the capital requirement had eventually been set at £70,000. The cost given by Scott was £86,000, 43% more than Blyths' estimate. The actual engineering cost (which is presumably what Blyths were referring to) was £74,000, but even on pure construction costs the overspend was £14,000 or 23%. In addition, the land cost of £8,000 and Parliamentary and legal fees of £4,000 exceeded the allowance of £10,000 in the promoters' presentations by 20%.

It will be recalled that the original subscriptions only amounted to £22,000, so it is worth examining where the balance came from. The largest 'external' contribution came from the GNSR, which it will be recalled was using the M&B as part of its strategic battle with the SNER and had invested £12,000 through its proxies. As part of the working agreement, the SNER undertook to replace this sum by £15,000, half in cash and half in SNER 4½% preference stock.[62] The value to the M&B was ultimately less because of the part payment in stock.[63] This arrangement brought the nominal share capital on a fully-paid basis to the £70,000 required. The shareholders were as shown in Table 4.[64]

Apart from the SNER, the major shareholders were James Farquhar of Hallgreen Castle, Bervie, Alexander Porteous of Lauriston, and Hercules Scott of Brotherton, Johnshaven. Between them they owned 66% of the company.

In terms of debt, the Company had borrowing powers, and for most of its existence these were used to the extent of between £18,000 and £19,500, supplemented initially with temporary overdraft facilities. Farquhar, Porteous and Scott held much of this debt, and by the end of the Company's independent existence, their family

CHAPTER 7: THE BERVIE RAILWAY

holdings were £2,500 each, with about half the remainder overdue GNSR holdings.

The M&B was built for £86,000, which was the equivalent of £7,200 per mile, including two major viaducts. Compared with other Scottish branch lines the line was cheaply built; the stations were modest wooden structures and there was no evidence of extravagance in the facilities provided. Even staff uniforms were a luxury avoided by the M&B.[65]

Trying to Make Ends Meet – An Overview

It rapidly became clear that the revenue of the line was lower, and the costs of operation higher, than the M&B had predicted; the Chairman, Porteous, sought to explain the poor results at two successive half-yearly meetings by blaming the weather (always a good excuse in the north-east of Scotland) and on the time taken to divert traffic from '*their accustomed routes*'. During the exciting times of the Kittywake Line campaign, £10 per mile per week had been promised for the M&B in its prospectus, while a more conservative estimate would be £7 for that section of the line. That would have implied revenue of between £4,368 and £6,240 per annum. As Table 5 indicates, the promoters were right to be conservative, as the average revenue for the fifteen complete years of the line's existence was £4,315, and the best year was £5,168, or £8 5s 6d a mile. The traffic took much longer than expected to build up, and it was 1874 before revenue regularly exceeded £4,900 per annum.

However, traffic expenses had been estimated at 45% (operating ratio, or expenses as a percentage of receipts) in the Kittywake prospectus. Table 6 shows how this compared with reality.

Despite the company's best efforts, the percentage of receipts absorbed by operating expenses averaged around 65%, and never went below 58%, leaving around £1,000-£1,200 per annum to cover interest payments on mortgages and debentures (usually around £880) before any dividend could be considered. The initial years were especially difficult, where the weak or '*developing*' traffic was compounded by high initial working expenses, partly due to the heavy charges for use of Montrose (CR) station. By January 1869 the accumulated losses, after all charges, amounted to £867, and it was a major achievement for the M&B under Scott's leadership to reverse

Table 5: M&B Revenue, 1866-80

Year	Passengers + Parcels (£)	Goods (£)	Total incl Misc (£)
1866	2,002	1,280	3,281
1867	1,995	1,434	3,429
1868	1,915	1,479	3,421
1869	1,935	1,666	3,627
1870	1,927	1,689	3,647
1871	2,005	1,891	3,917
1872	2,119	1,830	3,975
1873	2,350	2,168	4,537
1874	2,573	2,322	4,932
1875	2,596	2,368	4,988
1876	2,638	2,260	4,920
1877	2,633	2,510	5,168
1878	2,629	2,379	5,030
1879	2,409	2,522	4,956
1880	2,407	2,473	4,899

Note: Figures are from published M&B accounts (NRS BR/RAC/S/1/116). Copies missing in this sequence can be found bound in the M&B Minute Books.

Table 4: Montrose & Bervie – Principal Shareholdings

Holder	Shares (£10)	Total Shares
Local Holders		
James Farquhar of Hallgreen, Bervie	1,434	
Alexander Porteous of Lauriston	1,173	
Hercules Scott of Brotherton, Johnshaven	983	
Captain Frederick Grant Forsyth-Grant of Ecclesgreig, St. Cyrus	100	
David Mitchell, Montrose	99	
FB Paton, Montrose	20	
William Mitchell, shop owner, Montrose	20	
Bervie Town Council	20	
David Dickson, baker, Laurencekirk	10	
Local owners (5 shares or less)	53	
Total, local owners		3,912
Other Holders		
Edward Moor, merchant, Liverpool	100	
TN Farquhar, solicitor, London	20	
Thomas Tyler, solicitor, London	980	
Total, other owners		1,100
Railways		
SNER	1,500	
Total Corporate		1,500
Total		6,512

Notes:
1. It will be noted that the total does not match the £70,000 nominal value which was fully taken up. Some shareholders have not been identified, and the share register has not survived.
2. There was a further consolidation when 51 of the 53 shares owned by local proprietors with five or less shares, and all the allocation to Thomas Tyler of 980 shares were declared forfeit and purchased by Farquhar, Porteous and Scott, making their holdings 1,844, 1,512 and 1,264 respectively.

Table 6: M&B Receipts, Operating Expenses and Operating Ratios, 1866-80

Year	Revenue (£)	Working Expenses (£)	Op. Ratio (%)
1866	3,281	2,794	85.1
1867	3,429	2,573	75.0
1868	3,421	2,296	67.1
1869	3,627	2,256	62.2
1870	3,647	2,302	63.1
1871	3,917	2,383	60.8
1872	3,975	2,467	62.1
1873	4,537	2,896	63.8
1874	4,932	3,433	69.6
1875	4,988	3,078	61.7
1876	4,920	3,228	65.6
1877	5,168	3,255	63.0
1878	5,030	2,917	58.0
1879	4,956	2,995	60.4
1880	4,899	3,344	68.3

Note: Source of figures as for table 5. Some reports in newspapers and elsewhere used variants including or excluding small items, so may differ. These figures have been used to calculate the operating ratio.

these so that by 1873 the accumulated loss had been eliminated and a modest dividend of 1% was declared. This dividend was repeated in 1874, and for most of the remaining years of the company's existence a dividend of between 0.5% and 3% was achieved.[66] The next chapter deals in more detail with the cost and revenue challenges the company faced.

Notes

1. *DC*, 12th Oct. 1859, p. 3. Kinnear & Monro was misprinted as Kinnear & Home in the *DC*; it was also misspelt Munro occasionally.
2. *Edinburgh Gazette*, 15th Nov. 1859, pp. 1500-2.
3. *DC*, 11th Oct. 1859, p. 3.
4. *DPCA*, 4th May 1860, p. 4.
5. *DPCA*, 6th Jul. 1860, p. 3. *23 and 24 Vic, c. 142*. The Act passed without any challenge, both the Board of Trade and the Admiralty having been satisfied at preliminary enquiry stage.
6. An example is given in F. Fletcher, *Directors, Dilemmas and Debt* (Aberdeen, 2010), pp. 39-40, of the correspondence this gave rise to in August 1858. One man's wife and children were allowed to board, but he was not, as he was delayed paying the cab!
7. *AJ*, 15th Jun. 1861, pp. 1 and 8. The Skene and Echt district never did get a railway service, and repeated efforts to promote light railways in the late nineteenth century and early twentieth came to nothing. Eventually a pioneering road motor service was established by the GNSR.
8. *AJ*, 2nd Apr. 1862, p. 10. The SNER did in fact bid for the Deeside lease, causing the GNS to pay rather more than they had intended.
9. *AJ*, 2nd Apr. 1862, pp. 8 and 10.
10. *AJ*, 16th Apr. 1862, pp. 6, 9-10.
11. *AJ*, 10th Dec. 1862, p. 8.
12. *Dundee Advertiser* [*DA*], 30th Apr. 1862, p. 4; *DC*, 1st May, p. 3.
13. *DA*, 15th Oct. 1862, p. 4.
14. *CM*, 16th Oct. 1862, p. 2.
15. *DC*, 1st Nov. 1862, pp. 3-4.
16. *DC*, 12th Nov. 1862, p. 3.
17. *DA*, 14th Nov. 1862, pp. 1, 3.
18. *AJ*, 28th Jan. 1863, p. 8.
19. *AJ*, 16th Feb. 1863, p. 8.
20. *DC*, 20th Feb. 1863, p. 4.
21. *DC*, 7th Apr. 1863, p. 2; *AJ*, 8th Apr. 1863, p. 5; *AJ*, 22nd Apr. 1863, p. 9.
22. *DA*, 17th Apr. 1863, p. 3.
23. First day (21st April): *DA*, 23rd Apr. 1863, p. 3; *DC*, 24th Apr. 1863, p. 3. Second day (22nd April): *DA*, 24th Apr. 1863, p. 4; *DPCA*, 24th Apr. 1863, p. 6. Third day (23rd April): *DA*, 25th Apr. 1863, p. 3; *DC*, 25th Apr. 1863, p. 3; *DPCA*, 28th Apr. 1863, p. 6. Fourth day (24th April): *DC*, 27th Apr. 1863, p. 2. Fifth and final day (27th April) *AJ*, 29th Apr. 1863, p. 5.
24. *Evidence before Parliamentary Commission*, quoted in *DA*, 25th Apr. 1863, p. 3.
25. *AJ*, 29th Apr. 1863, p. 5.
26. *DC*, 16th May 1863, p. 4.
27. *AJ*, 20th May 1863, p. 8.
28. *Inverness Courier*, 21st May 1863, p. 6.
29. Fletcher, op. cit., pp. 65 et seq. A shareholders' Committee of Enquiry appointed in 1865 found that *'for the amount expended, and yet to be paid for the Montrose and Bervie Railway, your Committee cannot find the slightest excuse, and must characterize it as a wasteful expenditure of your funds'* (Fletcher p. 76). Elphinstone lasted as Chairman until 1867.
30. An English translation would be *'back to ordinary life'*. *'Claes'* in Doric = *'clothes'* in English.
31. *AJ*, 28th Oct. 1863, p. 5.
32. *AJ*, 11th Nov. 1863, p. 8.
33. Quoted in *DC*, 9th Jan. 1864, p. 4.
34. *AJ*, 23rd Mar. 1864, p. 1.
35. *AJ*, 6th Apr. 1864, p. 1.
36. *DC*, 30th Apr. 1864, p. 4.
37. *DC*, 4th Jun. 1864, p. 4.
38. *DC*, 29th Aug. 1864, p. 4.
39. Fletcher, op. cit., p. 71, has a photograph of Duncan. He became Chairman of the GNSR in 1867.
40. *DC*, 31st Mar. 1864, p. 3, reported that at the GNSR half-yearly meeting a motion had been put by shareholder Stephen Louden of Stonehaven that the expenses and stock contribution of £35,000 be disallowed. He did not receive a seconder.
41. *DC*, 2nd Jan. 1865, p. 4.
42. *Montrose Review*, 3rd Mar. 1865, p. 4. Subcontracts as follows: Ford & Balfour (masonry), Brown & Webster (slaters), Chas Middleton & Son (Plumbers), Hogg (plasterers), C&A Gray (painters). Wood on stone foundations. Stations were to be called 'Broomfield Junction', 'St. Cyrus', 'The Bush', 'Johnshaven', 'Gourdon' and 'Bervie'. The Bush was actually named 'Lauriston' on opening, after the nearby residence of Porteous; Bush is the roadside hamlet nearest the station. Warburton had evidently been deleted from the plans by this time (see Appendix 2).
43. *DC*, 29th Apr. 1865, p. 4.
44. Quoted in *DC*, 17th Jun. 1865, p. 4.
45. *AJ*, 26th Jul. 1865, p. 8.
46. *AJ*, 16th Aug. 1865, p. 5.
47. *DC*, 2nd Sep. 1865, p. 3. A fuller account of this trip was published in the *Stonehaven Journal & Kincardineshire Advertiser*, 7th Sep. 1865. The train consisted of a tender locomotive, two carriages (one First and one Third) and a brake van.
48. *AJ*, 13th Sep. 1865, p. 1.
49. M&B Minute Book No. 1 [MMB1], p. 109 (Directors' Meeting, 10th Jul. 1865), NRS, Ref. BR/MBR/1.
50. *DC*, 25th Sep. 1865, p. 2.
51. MMB1, p. 117 (Directors' Meeting, 28th Sep. 1865). The entry states that the Directors *'agree ... to take the ... shares to themselves at par in proportion to the shares ... at present held by them respectively – the price of the shares to be paid to the Montrose and Bervie Company in exchange for a similar amount of Debenture Bonds, payable in equal proportions at three, five and eight years, and bearing three per cent interest, to be given to the Great North of Scotland Railway Company in lieu of the said shares but without security.'*
52. The GNSR debentures were split into £500 portions – twenty-four of them – which should have given a clue to the GNSR. £4,000 was due in October 1868, £4,000 in October 1870 and the remainder in October 1873. No repayments were made until January 1871, and by the date of the NBR takeover in 1881, only £5,500 had been repaid. The GNSR's lawyers threatened foreclosure, but the M&B pointed out that such a course would ensure they never got their money. See M&B Register of Debentures and Mortgages, NRS Ref BR/MBR/2.
53. *AJ*, 27th Sep. 1865, p. 3.
54. *DC*, 29th Sep. 1865, p. 4. The line did not open for Goods on 2nd October, as the *DC* had hoped.
55. MSS report of inspection, The National Archives, file MT 6 36/1. In one or two places the handwriting is quite difficult to decipher.
56. *AJ*, 1st Nov. 1865, p. 3.
57. *DC*, 31st Oct. 1865, p. 1.
58. *DC*, 3rd Nov. 1864, p. 4.
59. *DA*, 30th Sep. 1865, p. 4.
60. *DC*, 16th Apr. 1866, p. 2. The rental remained at £73 for another year, then increased to £80 in 1868, and decreased to £70 in 1869, before falling dramatically to £25 in 1870. It then averaged £36 from then until the end of tolls in 1878, so it appears the tenant was right. The tollgate had been the most profitable one on the Aberdeen–Montrose road until the opening of the railway.
61. Odlyzko, op. cit.
62. MMB1, p. 115 (Directors' Meeting, 11th Sep. 1865). The cash/shares split of 50/50 was in the meeting of 24th Mar. 1866.
63. The SNER shares were 50% paid in SNER 4½% debentures, which the M&B sold to Farquhar, Porteous and Scott at 95% of their value, £7,200, in September 1868 (noted at M&B Board meeting, 22nd Sep. 1868, see MMB1, p. 241). The cash value of the SNER investment was therefore £14,700.
64. MMB1, p. 88 (Directors' Meeting, 14th Feb. 1865).
65. It was agreed on 7th February 1866 that staff could be issued with caps (MMB1, p. 132, Directors' Meeting, 7th Feb. 1866). In October 1871, in response to a request from the staff, the M&B agreed that Station Agents would get a cap and tunic, provided the agents paid half the cost of the tunic, and that ticket clerks would get a cap. The agents declined to pay and as a result they were only issued with a cap (MMB1, Directors' Meeting, 11th Sep. and 27th Oct. 1871).
66. 1878 was the best year, when a total of 3% dividend was declared (2% in July 1878 and 1% in January 1879).

CHAPTER 8
OPERATING THE BERVIE RAILWAY

THE COLD LIGHT OF DAY: CONTROLLING COSTS AND REVENUE DEVELOPMENT

The costs of operating the M&B were much higher than predicted, and it was clear almost from the start of operations that the company could not afford the charges levied by the SNER as part of the working agreement. At the Board meeting on 28th February 1867 the Directors considered the accounts from the SNER for the first nine months of operation and the Caledonian Railway invoices for the following three months, and a very strongly worded minute was recorded:

> *The Directors notice with much regret the very large Charge entailed on this Company under the operation of the Agreement scheduled to their Act for the joint use of the Montrose Station.*

These charges amounted to £366.

> *They further find that during the month of November the proportion payable under the said Agreement amounts to £44 13s 5d. It is observed that the said charges amount to upwards of eleven per cent on the gross revenue of the line for the first twelve months, which if the above monthly charge incurred in November be maintained throughout the current twelve months, a sum of upwards of £500 will be payable to the Caledonian Coy. for the use of the said station. The Directors cannot but feel that the operation of the said Agreement, if continued, must prove disastrous in the last degree to the prospects of their line, the payment being out of all proportion to the value derived by the line from the use of the Montrose Station as also to the whole revenue of the line.*[1]

As a result, they decided to seek a meeting with the CR to see if a reduction could be negotiated, and to ask the auditors to check whether the charges were correct. Scott was deputed to deal with the CR, but to refer any agreement back to the Board.

At the fourteenth half-yearly meeting in April 1867, the company announced a fifteen-month loss of £501 16s 5d. The losses were blamed partly on the CR charges, but:

> *The Traffic on the line would probably have improved more rapidly but for the general stagnation in the trade of the country, which has seriously affected all Railways. The revenue has also suffered from the severe and protracted snow storms in winter, by which the traffic was stopped, and which occasioned expense in clearing the line of the snow.*

Two new halts were opened, at North Water Bridge on 1st June 1866, and at Birnie Road on 10th August 1866. The traffic from these would have made almost no difference to the passenger receipts, especially since the latter would be served by one train each way on Fridays only. In contrast, North Water Bridge (which was a late addition to replace the intended Warburton station) was served by all trains, but there were only a few farms and houses within reach of it.[2]

The pressures may have been too much for Alexander Porteous as he announced that:

> *in consequence of the state of his health he was unable longer to give that attention to the affairs of the Company which they required.*[3]

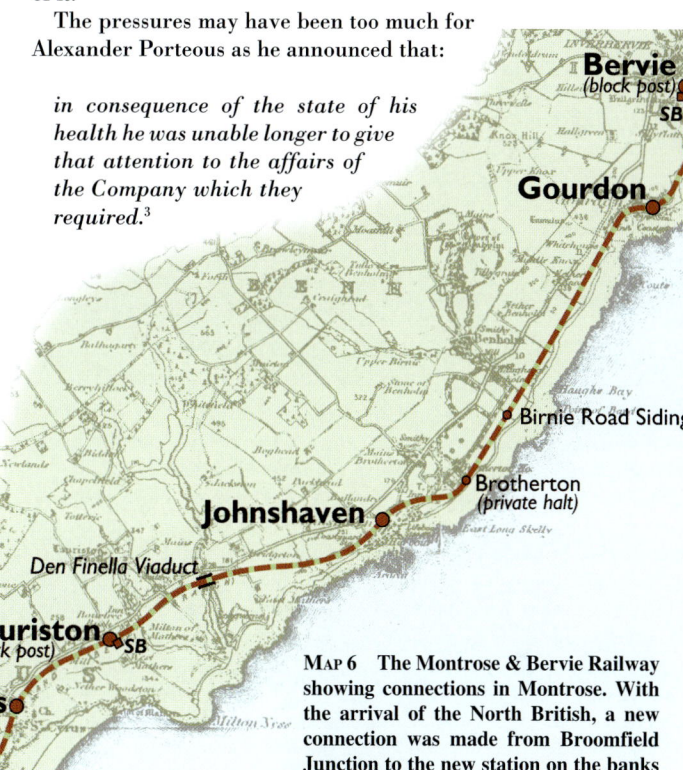

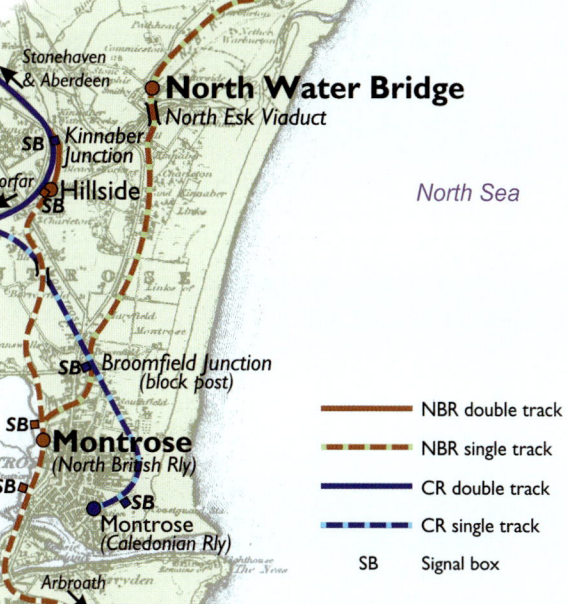

MAP 6 The Montrose & Bervie Railway showing connections in Montrose. With the arrival of the North British, a new connection was made from Broomfield Junction to the new station on the banks of the Basin.
Allan Rodgers

Hercules Scott circa 1895.
Walter Blakeman collection

Caledonian No. 510 with a mixed train at Bervie circa 1875. No. 510 was built by Vulcan Foundry in 1862 for the SNER as their No. 43. It was renumbered 702 by the CR in 1877 and 538 in 1881. It was withdrawn in 1886. Note the station building before the addition of the Caledonian Railway extension of 1897. *Allan Rodgers collection*

Scott was elected Chairman and to him fell the task of trying to bring costs under control and to improve the revenue position.

The most pressing issue was clearly the CR charges. The agreement operated in a very mechanistic way; according to the agreement, the station was valued in respect of the building and plant, the monthly cost of clerks, porters and horse haulage was then added, and the total was apportioned 50/50 between passenger and goods traffic. Then the costs were apportioned according to the passengers and goods transmitted by the CR and the M&B. During the fifteen months, the M&B had to pay £481 on £4,100 traffic. The 80,777 M&B passengers, of whom 37,367 came from Montrose, each cost 2d for the use of the station and 1d for the use of the CR line as far as Broomfield. The fare to Broomfield was 1d, so the M&B made a loss of 2d on every passenger. The fare to North Water Bridge was 3d, and that was absorbed by the charges.

Scott's reaction was to propose terminating all Third Class passengers and freight at Broomfield and using road transport to transfer them to Montrose.

A request for a renegotiation had been put to the CR, but their Northern Committee were not to discuss it until June, and that was too slow.[4] Perhaps to apply some pressure on the CR, as well as to save some cost immediately, the M&B Board decided to terminate all goods at Broomfield, and contracted with Alexander Neilson, a local carrier, to transfer all freight between Montrose and Broomfield. Neilson would receive all goods for the Bervie line at his shed in Ferry St, Montrose, while John Bates of Murray St, Montrose would also be an M&B agent, for which he was to receive the sum of £1 for his services during July. Neilson was to make one return trip to meet the first train from Bervie, and be paid a guarantee of 1s 3d, or 1s 0d if the cart was full. He was also to meet the last trains, but at his own revenue risk.

Passenger services were altered to reduce the Montrose station charges: from 1st July 1867 the last train from Montrose would leave at 7.25pm and arrive at Bervie at 8pm as previously, and the only through journeys to be booked by Third Class passengers would be on the 6.30am from Bervie and the 9.20am from Montrose. Return tickets would be issued between all stations and Broomfield at a 50% supplement on the single fare, but this facility would be available for Third Class passengers on Wednesdays and Saturdays only, the returns for Saturday being valid on the following Monday. No new season tickets would be issued to Montrose.[5] The M&B were probably bluffing, of course, because the terms of the Inspecting Officer's report (which the M&B had accepted) were that in these circumstances a new turntable would have to be provided at Broomfield. This would undoubtedly have cost more than whatever savings were being made by stopping short of Montrose.

At the following meeting two weeks later, Scott reported that he had found a number of errors in the CR accounts and had written a letter pointing these out.[6]

The meeting with the CR Directors finally took place on 8th August 1867. Scott and David Mitchell, a recently appointed Director and Provost of Montrose, represented the M&B. The entire CR Board of the Chairman and eleven others arrived by special train and the *Aberdeen Journal* reported that:

the conference was of the most amicable kind, and that an arrangement was agreed to, on terms mutually satisfactory, which will enable passengers, as formerly, to start from, and arrive at, the Montrose Station, instead of being compelled to proceed to Broomfield Station. We learn also that in various other points the Caledonian Directors met the views of the Bervie Board in a liberal spirit; and that the new arrangements resolved upon, while intended in the first instance to benefit the public, will also prove advantageous to both Companies.[7]

Scott had proposed an annual fixed charge of £150, and this was accepted by the CR, who even offered to backdate it to 1st February 1867. This was a triumph for Scott, as new Chairman, and he sought to follow it up by proposing that the station at Broomfield be closed saving most of the staff there.[8] However, at the following meeting the secretary could not say whether such a move was legal (even though he had been present when the matter was discussed), so it was deferred. Scott's irritation is clear from the minute: '*The Secretary was instructed to prepare himself to advise the Board as to their legal powers.*'[9]

The Minutes from here on contain a blizzard of cost-saving proposals; questions were raised about the costs of the telegraph service provided by the CR, as well as a demand for more detailed accounts of the shunting power provided.[10] Surplus property (including an area over an acre in extent near Brotherton House) was identified and sold, while attempts were made to dispose of surplus rails and materials.[11] A number of staff reductions were made, including dispensing with the ticket clerk at Gourdon,[12] and the staff wage bill, which had been running at £466 per annum in 1867 had been reduced to £396 three years later.[13] Even the Directors were squeezed; it was decided that all future meetings of the Board would be held at Montrose station (presumably to avoid refreshment costs at the Star Inn.) The fees for the secretary were fixed at £50 per annum, including all extra work,[14] and more control was exercised on the station agents, for example in keeping detailed records of arrival and departure of wagons,[15] while one, who had been supplementing his income from the receipts, was sacked.[16]

The shunting power supplied by the CR was yet again under scrutiny when the locomotive supplied was said to be '*slow in reverse*'. The CR claimed that it was '*fully adequate to draw 40 waggons.*' Scott disputed this, saying:

Six loaded wagons in addition to the ordinary Passenger Carriages was the utmost the said engine was practically able to work.[17]

At the fifteenth half-yearly meeting in November 1867 it was noticeable that there was no more talk of '*trade depressions*' and other excuses; Scott merely confirmed that the Board were now working on reducing expenses.[18] By the sixteenth half-yearly in April the following year, Scott was able to report that working expenses had decreased by £123 and revenues were up by £91. The focus of the Board would be on developing revenue and cutting expenses, which were still too high because of the high cost of track maintenance and charges by the CR.[19] However, he also noted that the line had cost precisely £85,999 0s 9½d and that the capital raised was £82,000. A number of damage claims arising from the construction also remained, though progress was being made in settling most of them.

The *Dundee Courier* observed that at the seventeenth half-yearly meeting in November 1868 the revenue was almost stationary for the previous eighteen months, with revenues varying only by a few pounds, but good progress had been made on operating costs, which had declined as a percentage of revenue from 78% to 72% and 67%. However, the first of the GNSR debentures was due at £4,000, and the company did not have the funds available to repay it or the means of refinancing it. A threatening letter from the GNSR's legal agents was brushed aside, the Board instructing the secretary to reply that:

The Directors regret exceedingly the inability of the Company at present to pay ...; that the Directors have failed in their attempt to borrow money to enable them to do so; that negotiations are about to be opened by the Directors with the Caledonian Railway Company for a readjustment of the Working Agreement with that Company, which, if successful, the Directors anticipate will improve the position of the Company; that the whole plant on the Railway which is worked by the Caledonian Railway belongs to that Company; and that proceedings under the Bond, while they cannot wait for the recovery thereof, will have the almost certain effect of defeating the intentions and exertions of the Directors to obtain money for the payment of the Bonds. In these circumstances the Directors hope that the threatened proceedings will not be taken.[20]

In other words, if the GNSR wished to take legal action, they would not only have no assets to seize, but would prevent the M&B paying at all. The ploy worked, and the GNSR did not again threaten legal proceedings, even though eventually all their bonds became overdue. Although the GNSR effectively found itself in the position of a forced lender, the M&B did keep up the interest payments on them, and by 1881 had paid about half of them back.[21]

The M&B did, however, have one avenue of unused finance. In the initial promotion of the line, a number of small businesses in the area had taken a couple of shares each, but had failed to meet the calls on them, while a London lawyer had taken 980 and failed to meet any calls apart from the deposit, no doubt hoping to sell the allocation on at a profit as had been the common practice during the 'mania' years of the 1840s. The M&B now moved to forfeit all these shares (keeping the £51 actually paid on them) and sold them to the three principal shareholders in proportion to their existing holdings. David Mitchell bought one share, which rounded up his holding to 100. The effect was to increase the cash available to the company by over £10,300 without increasing the nominal capitalization.[22]

1869 was a bad year for the M&B, but a terrible year for the Chairman. In the course of seven days from 29th January to 4th February, Hercules Scott and his wife, Anna, lost four of their five children to diphtheria, leaving one daughter.[23] The company reached the highest point of its accumulated losses, at £867. Scott remarked that the results were '*far from satisfactory*' but that several recent changes should shortly start to make an effect. Working expenses had been reduced and £7,500 of additional loans had been raised, raising the capital to £89,500, covering the cost of construction, while still leaving unused borrowing power of £3,500. The SNER 4½% preference stock had been sold at a loss of £465, but had been turned into cash (£7,200) instead of an investment. Scott and the other two major shareholders purchased the stock.[24]

By the nineteenth half-yearly meeting in November 1869 the position was improving and the Company was able to declare a tiny surplus. Scott was ever diligent in following up every aspect of the M&B's business. In the March Directors' Meeting he reported that he had noticed that the rate for carrying stone traffic from Lauriston to Montrose and then to Dubton was higher than from Lauriston to Dubton, and would follow this up with the CR. At the same meeting the secretary was directed to find out if the CR would run a Composite Second/Third Class carriage in place of the Third Class one, and once again whether the present locomotive could be replaced as it was '*too slow in reverse*'.[25]

The following half-yearly meeting was noted as having a '*meagre attendance*' – perhaps not surprising as most of the shares were now in the hands of three Directors and most of the smaller shareholders had been dispossessed for non-payment, but Scott was quite up-beat. The Company had '*reached a turning point in the success of the railway*', he declared and by October 1870 revenue was again up and expenses down, while the telegraph wires (another CR property subject to what the M&B considered extortionate charges) had been bought from the Caledonian.[26]

Better Times on the M&B

During the 1870s the Bervie line performed adequately well; costs were kept under firm control (though the staff were awarded a pay increase in 1873) and traffic increased. The *Dundee Courier*'s St. Cyrus correspondent thought the increase was well-deserved:

The increase, the Directors may rest assured, will not be thrown away on the Montrose and Bervie officials, for their civility in the past has been noticeable, and will not be less so now.[27]

There was some competition from Gourdon Harbour, through which a sufficient quantity of fish and merchandise were exported to merit comment at the half-yearly meeting.²⁸ A newsworthy success was the departure of a double-headed livestock train from Johnshaven with 455 sheep for Kirkcaldy and Edinburgh in thirteen wagons,²⁹ while by 1875 Scott was amazed by the number of passengers the line carried:

*When they bore in mind the fact that at the opening of the line less than ten years ago, a single omnibus three days a week served the whole of the public requirements between Montrose and Bervie, it seemed incredible that they should have drawn nearly £2400 from passengers alone during the past twelve months.*³⁰

In October 1874 it was reported that at last freight was starting to pick up, with goods up by 1,163 tons on the corresponding half-year twelve months before, and minerals up by 1,745 tons. It was also noted that traffic receipts on the line had increased considerably since 1867.³¹

The deficit, meantime, had continued to decline, and from the high point of £867 in January 1869 had been eliminated by January 1874. Dividends were now a possibility for the long-suffering shareholders.³²

At the twenty-ninth half-yearly in April 1876, Scott apparently announced that:

*receipts for the last six months were the largest that had yet been drawn during any corresponding period, and admitted of a dividend of £3-4 per cent.*³³

Although a hurried correction by the newspaper two days later that '*the dividend for the past year is ¾% and not as stated on Saturday*' indicated either that the reporter had allowed himself to be somewhat carried away, or a printer's error.³⁴

Even though Hercules Scott was actively involved in the management of his own estate as well as the M&B Chairmanship and the Kincardineshire Turnpike Trustees, while also finding time to give evidence for the Montrose & Arbroath Railway and act as a Director of the Dundee & Arbroath line, there were signs that he would have to consider reducing his commitments. In November 1872 he had had to withdraw from a contest for the local Parliamentary constituency, citing the recurrence of the health problems which he suffered whilst a civil servant in India. Porteous had died in 1872 and Farquhar in 1875, so that Scott's control of the line had considerably increased, though nominally he was not the largest shareholder. As he himself remarked during the sale to the North British in 1881, both the other original major shareholders were his brothers-in-law.³⁵

1878 was probably the high point of the financial performance of the line, with a dividend of 2% being declared in July; however at a meeting chaired by Scott's nephew, D.S. Porteous, there were the stirrings of discontent among the other shareholders. In April Captain Alex Watt complained about the rates for lime, which he said were about double the CR rate, and criticism was made of the apparent inability of the Board to borrow money at less than 5%. David Mitchell complained that the dividend policy was too cautious, as the GNSR were paying 1½%, and consequently their shares were trading at £66 to £67 per £100 whereas the M&B shares were worth only £25. The GNSR, he claimed, were able to borrow at 4-4½%. The meeting, at which there was a '*fair attendance*', was no longer prepared to be impressed by Porteous' tale that Scott had noticed they were being charged by the CR for a night-shift signalman at Broomfield when the M&B ran no night trains.³⁶

At the thirty-seventh half-yearly meeting in October, Mitchell returned to the attack. He objected to the Directors' report as:

there was nothing before them to verify the statements which they were requested to adopt. The Secretary had spent the income of the Company without consulting the Directors, and when a sight of the books had been sought it was refused.

He complained that meetings should be in Montrose (near where he lived) rather than in Stonehaven (where the secretary's office was located, and where Scott attended Turnpike meetings). Scott defended himself and the secretary robustly in a lengthy speech, it was reported, and said that:

when meetings had been called the Directors did not attend, and that an inspection of the books had not been refused.

The Company had never been in better shape, Scott added. As if to emphasise the point, he declared the first (and also the last) 2% dividend in the Company's history.

The following year was far less promising; receipts were down, as were expenses. For the first time, Scott seemed on the defensive. Unseasonable weather was felt to be a factor and while a like-for-like dividend (that is, 1%) would be possible, it would leave a very slender amount to carry forward to the next half year. Once again fish exports from Gourdon had dented the freight business, while the experimental reduction in rates for lime (presumably to satisfy Captain Watt, who had campaigned for it) had resulted in no increase in business. David Mitchell once again went on to the attack. He moved the non-adoption of the Directors' Report (even though he was a Director):

on the grounds that the accounts had never been submitted to the directors, that the chairman ignored his co-directors and treated them as nonentities, and because the line at present was grossly mismanaged.

Nobody seconded his motion. Mitchell then objected to the reappointment of the auditors on the grounds that they should be based in Montrose and not Aberdeen. Scott dismissed the charges as '*utterly baseless*', adding that he had seen Mitchell before the meeting and after a disagreement had told him he might as well '*just hammer away*'. One of the other shareholders was reported as saying that it was a shame such charges '*should go forth in public*'.³⁷

At the fortieth meeting in April 1880 Scott reported that a dividend of ¾% should be possible, as trading was improving, but this did not satisfy David Mitchell, who once again attacked the management of the Company. The *Dundee Courier* reported that:

Baillie Mitchell took strong exception to the manner in which the affairs of the Company were conducted. Accounts were paid without any of the Directors having seen them, and it was altogether absurd that they should have a Secretary in Stonehaven residing twenty miles away from Montrose. He maintained that the Company's affairs throughout were not properly managed, and pointed out various items in which a better state of things could be brought about.

Scott responded that as the line was managed operationally by the CR the Directors had little power, and '*after some discussion*' the Directors' Report was adopted. Mitchell then proposed that a Mr Baxter be appointed as auditor, as he lived in Montrose, but once again this was not seconded, Mr Meston of Aberdeen being elected.³⁸

The harvest of 1879 was described as '*disastrous*', with M&B revenue being £187 down and expenses about £50 up, according to the *Glasgow Herald*.³⁹ Shares in the M&B were trading at £3 5s per £10 share and a ¾% dividend was declared at the forty-first meeting in October 1880, but at least there was no reported infighting between the Directors.⁴⁰ It was clear, however, that little improvement in the overall position of the M&B could be expected, with expenditure already being tightly controlled, and revenue (particularly freight)

CHAPTER 8: OPERATING THE BERVIE RAILWAY

subject to trade fluctuations. Crucially, also, the working agreement with the CR was due to end in late 1881, and there was a clear risk that some of the terms which had been so '*harmoniously*' agreed with the 1867 CR Board might not be so easy to replicate. It was also fortuitous that the NBR seemed keen to extend its influence as far north as possible, and that it appeared to regard the Bervie line as a potentially strategic possession.

THE KITTYWAKE FLIES AGAIN

For a time in 1871 it looked as if the two great rivals, the CR and the NBR, would combine, and a proposal to do so was passed almost unanimously by the CR shareholders. However, the NBR Extraordinary General Meeting was extremely stormy, and the motion was only passed by the use of proxies. It was clear that the companies' hearts were not in the merger proposals, and the scheme collapsed.[41]

By that time, the NBR was promoting a line from Arbroath to Montrose as part of its renewed drive to Aberdeen, awakening dreams of an independent through line there. The *Aberdeen Journal* had even hoped that:

> These proposals point to direct communication between Arbroath and Montrose, and with Aberdeen, through the extension of the Montrose and Bervie line.[42]

And this at a time when the Bervie line was only just emerging from its burden of accumulated losses.[43]

The Caledonian and Scottish North Eastern Railway Amalgamation Act had given the NBR the right to promote, unopposed for five years, an extension of its line northwards via Montrose to Aberdeen, and in June 1871 the Montrose and Arbroath Railway Bill was published. Significantly, the M&B Chairman, Hercules Scott, was appointed Chairman of the line, indicating the close relationship he was forming with the North British. The new line ran from Arbroath along the coast to Montrose, where a station was built on the west side of the town, on the banks of the Basin. From there, the line swung west to join the Caledonian main line at Kinnaber, while a new connection in cutting, and with a short tunnel under the Stonehaven road, linked the new station to the M&B at Broomfield. Despite the hopes entertained by the *Aberdeen Journal*, the city was to be reached by running powers over the Caledonian from Kinnaber, rather than by extending the Bervie line to the north.

THE NORTH BRITISH TAKES OVER

At a Special General Meeting in January 1881 the NBR agreed to move forward with a Bill to '*amalgamate with*' (that is, take over) the Bervie line. The meeting believed that at £5 a share (plus the debt) it would still yield an ample profit. The *Glasgow Herald* revealed that Walker, General Manager of the North British, and Scott had agreed a provisional sale at a meeting on 29th October 1880. The same report said that the North British were in fact offering £6 a share (not £5) plus the debt. The favourable terms were said to be due to the construction of the Arbroath & Montrose Railway, and Scott was quoted as saying he hoped the '*Bervie extension*' (presumably to Stonehaven) would soon follow.[44]

Apart from some concerns from the Montrose Harbour Board that freight rates might be increased by the NBR,[45] and predictable opposition from the CR, including a claim that the shares it owned should be bought at full par value instead of at a 40% discount (rapidly dismissed by the Parliamentary Commissioners),[46] there was little opposition to the Amalgamation Bill, and it swiftly passed its Parliamentary stages in May and June 1881. The takeover was scheduled for 1st October 1881. Since there was to be a change from Caledonian Railway operation to the North British, considerable preparation was involved. The *Dundee Advertiser* on 1st October 1881 reported that:

> The officials of the North British Railway Company were busily engaged yesterday in making the arrangements necessary for the taking over of the Montrose & Bervie line. A careful examination of the points and signalling apparatus between the North British Station and Broomfield Junction was made by Mr. Hogg of the North British, and in the afternoon a train of three or four carriages left the station for Bervie. Mr. Bell, engineer, Mr. Drummond, superintendent of locomotives and Mr. McDougall went on with the train to examine the stations and make arrangements for the traffic being opened this morning. The engine and carriages were to remain at Bervie all night and bring in the passengers in the morning. Several men were engaged in fitting up the commodious booking office at the Montrose Station.[47]

The *Dundee Courier* took up the story on the same day:

> On Thursday a large number of carriages for goods and passengers arrived at the North British station, which proceeded yesterday afternoon to Bervie, preparatory to the line being handed over to the North British Company today. Until

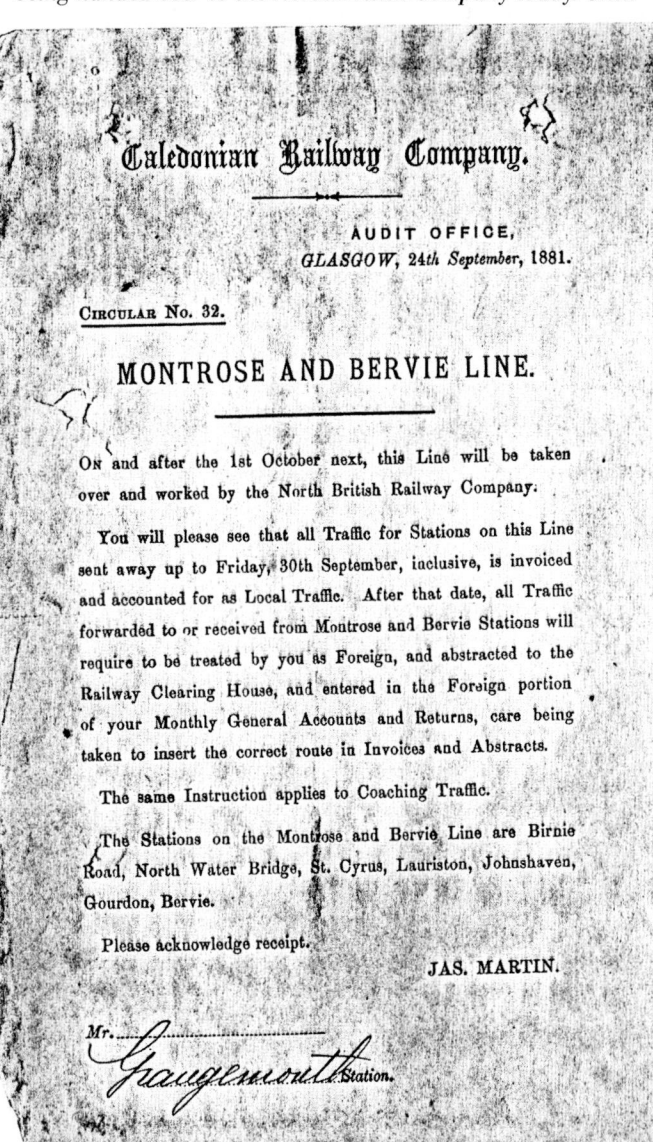

Keith Jones collection

the new bridge is completed a 'bus will convey the passengers to the Caledonian Station. Vigorous operations are ... to be commenced next week on the new viaduct over the Southesk, and when it is completed it is to be hoped that Montrose will at least be partially freed from the line of delightful junctions, from which it has never derived any substantial benefit.[48]

The final actions of the M&B was to wind up the company, and this was done in a sequence of meetings culminating in the last formal session of the Montrose & Bervie Railway Company on 18th November 1881. Among the affairs to be settled was the allocation of the final balance, which amounted to £569. The proposal was to award the secretary 120 guineas (£126), and a '*substantial testimonial*' to Scott. This was approved.[49] A letter to the *Dundee Advertiser* a few days later from '*a shareholder*', but quite probably David Mitchell, complained that:

The Bervie line has been a losing concern from the beginning, and in such circumstances it is very inappropriate to wind up the Company in such an extravagant manner.[50]

The '*shareholder*' would probably have been further incensed to read that the '*memorial*' to Scott was a portrait of himself by the noted Scottish artist John Henry Lorimer. This hung in Brotherton Castle for many years.[51]

ACCIDENTS AND EXCITEMENTS

We are accustomed in the early twenty-first century to regard the railways as an extremely safe place on which to travel and to work; several years have passed with no major passenger accident, and serious injuries, let alone fatalities, are thankfully very rare. In the mid-nineteenth century the situation was very different, and a number of serious accidents and injuries occurred on the M&B in its independent existence. In that respect it was far from unusual; railway safety was far less well developed, and mishaps to passengers and (particularly) staff were regarded as inevitable and relatively routine. In the Board of Trade annual report of accidents for 1874, it was reported that 201 passengers were killed and 1,981 injured, while 788 railwaymen and contractors were killed and 2,815 injured.[52] In contrast, between 2008 and 2013 two passengers were killed and fourteen injured.

Accidents on the Bervie line were no more common than on other similar lines, and were usually caused by locomotive malfunctions or shunting accidents. There were also unrelated (and sometimes unexplained) injuries to trespassers as well; for example the Lauriston blacksmith was found lying on the track between Johnshaven and Lauriston with severe cuts to his head and several other injuries in October 1866, possibly received as a result of walking along the track.[53] In December 1875 an elderly labourer named William Jack was run over about a mile from Montrose. The *Dundee Courier* reported that '*his body was shockingly mangled*', so we can assume he did not survive.[54] A more puzzling accident took place the following year when a weaver, John Milne, was run over near Montrose station.

He had been waiting for Bervie train to proceed [to Montrose station], and by some means or other had gone on the Bervie portion of line, and it is supposed he got dazed. The Bervie train was being shunted, when it passed over his legs and arms, terribly mutilating them, from the effects of which he died fifteen minutes afterwards.[55]

Sometimes it was livestock which were run over. In 1880 the *Northern Warder & Bi-weekly Courier & Argus* published a story under the headline '*Quick Dispatch of Wandering Ducks*'. Apparently four ducks wandered onto the line at St. Cyrus and were killed by the midday train from Bervie. A week later the same thing happened, with seven killed and one suffering a broken leg. The unfortunate ducks belonged to Mr Moncur, the baker and confectioner in the village.[56] On one occasion trespassers interfered with the line deliberately. The *Dundee Courier* reported an '*ATTEMPT TO UPSET THE MONTROSE AND BERVIE TRAIN*' in September 1873. The driver of the 7.15pm from Montrose, Robert Petrie, felt a bump about one mile south of Johnshaven and reported it at Bervie. The wayman reported that he had found two pieces of wood placed on the track at Den Finella. The *Courier* added: '*There are just now plenty of railway accidents, without attempting to manufacture them.*'[57] The perpetrators were never caught.

Railway operating mistakes and mechanical failures caused most accidents on the line. Throughout the existence of the M&B Company, all trains were run as mixed goods and passenger services, which among other things meant that delays at intermediate stations were common while wagons were shunted on and off trains. On 14th May 1867 the 3pm train from Montrose to Bervie left the station without its passenger coaches because the couplings had not been done up between the wagons at the front of the train and the coaches. The train reached Broomfield Junction before the mistake was noticed. Fortunately nobody was hurt and the train left fifteen minutes late after setting back into the station to collect the coaches.[58]

A more serious failure occurred on 21st October 1872 when Driver Robert Petrie noticed one of his tender axles had snapped as the 3pm from Montrose was nearing St. Cyrus. He sent his '*stoker*' on a hired horse to Montrose with the train staff (the token giving the train authority to enter the line) to allow an assisting engine onto the branch, and the train proceeded to Bervie after an hour and a half, by which time most of the passengers had got off and walked. However the *Dundee Courier*'s St. Cyrus correspondent reported that Petrie had '*augmented the popularity which travellers by the Montrose and Bervie Railway had formerly accorded to him.*'[59]

Thankfully the other recorded locomotive accidents did not result in injuries either; on 27th November 1876 the 11am from Montrose burst a boiler tube near Johnshaven and put the fire out. Another locomotive was sent for from Montrose and the train reached Bervie three hours late.[60] On 13th November 1880 the 7.45pm from Montrose suffered a burst boiler tube on the bank approaching St. Cyrus, the driver and fireman having what the *Dundee Courier* described as a '*narrow escape*'. Most of the passengers got off and walked, but the train was drawn back to Broomfield and eventually reached Bervie three hours late.[61]

The most serious accident during the independent period of existence of the M&B was undoubtedly on 12th April 1876 when the driver of the 5.10pm from Bervie had his arm severely crushed while helping to shunt some loose cattle wagons there.[62] The driver was John F. McIntosh, who went on to achieve distinction as the Chief Mechanical Engineer of the Caledonian Railway from 1895 to 1914, being responsible for the 'Dunalastair' and 'Cardean' class locomotives which achieved fame for the company.[63]

Damage to the track was very rare. Only one instance of a landslip (near Johnshaven) was recorded – in 1872[64] – but snowstorms regularly closed the line, often for days at a time.[65]

Public transport accidents also happened on the roads at this time; in July 1879 the *Aberdeen Evening Express* reported that one of three buses, described as a '*heavy, three-horse machine*', returning attendees of the Aberdeen Wapinschaw from Stonehaven to Bervie was involved in an accident at '*Stonehaven Bridge*' (presumably Bridge of Carron). Happily, '*the party inside the machine fortunately escaped scathless* [sic].'[66]

Even M&B Directors were sometimes involved. On 3rd January 1878 the *Dundee Courier* reported that Mr D.S. Porteous (son of the late M&B Chairman) and his wife's carriage was thrown in the ditch when the horse shied as the first train to Bervie was starting from North Water Bridge. There was apparently little damage and no injuries, but they did miss their train from Dubton.

CHAPTER 8: OPERATING THE BERVIE RAILWAY

The beach at Bervie was a moderately popular holiday destination in the early twentieth century, despite the cold wind and the complete absence of any sand. Amazingly, the boat winch the children are playing with is still there! J. Valentine B2927 is a postcard from 1950. *Author's collection*

Notes

1. MMB1, p. 167 (Directors' Meeting, 28th Feb. 1867).
2. *DC*, 30th May, p. 1, and 9th Aug. 1866, p. 1. The 9.45am from Bervie and the 3.5pm from Montrose called on Fridays only. The Guard issued tickets at 2s 3d (First) or 1s 1½d (Third) to Broomfield or 2s 6d (First) and 1s 3d (Third) to Montrose, but did not give change.
3. MMB1, p. 174 (Directors' Meeting, 29th Apr. 1867). Porteous died in 1872.
4. *DC*, 30th Apr. 1867, p. 4.
5. MMB1, p. 177 (Directors' Meeting, 15th June 1867).
6. Ibid., p. 180 (Directors' Meeting, 28th June 1867).
7. *AJ*, 14th Aug. 1867, p. 3.
8. MMB1, pp. 183-4 (Directors' Meeting, 9th Aug. 1867).
9. Ibid., p. 185 (Directors' Meeting, 15th Aug. 1867). Broomfield was not closed until 1st February 1869 because some of the other Directors took more persuasion.
10. Ibid., p. 190 (Directors' Meeting, 13th Sep. 1867). The CR accepted that errors had been made in shunting charges.
11. Ibid., p. 188 (Directors' Meeting, 13th Sep. 1867).
12. Ibid., p. 192 (Directors' Meeting, 9th Oct. 1867).
13. M&B half-yearly accounts.
14. MMB1, p. 194 (Directors' Meeting, 26th Oct. 1867).
15. Ibid., p. 192 (Directors' Meeting, 9th Oct. 1867).
16. Ibid., p. 206 (Directors' Meeting, 2nd Dec. 1867). Pilfering was nothing new, of course. Wm Caird, employed as station master at Johnshaven from 5 August 1866 to 14 May 1867 was in front of the Aberdeen Circuit Court of Justiciary for theft of £24 4s 11d from charges to Findlay, Fishcurers there. He pleaded Guilty. Sentence was deferred (*DC*, 20th Sep. 1866). At the Directors' Meeting of 6th January 1868 it was decided to raise a civil action against Caird for the sum he had stolen (MMB1, p. 209).
17. Ibid., p. 206 (Directors' Meeting, 2nd Dec. 1867).
18. *DC*, 1st Nov. 1867, p. 4.
19. *DC*, 1st May 1868, p. 4.
20. MMB1, pp. 244-5 (Directors' Meeting, 6th Oct. 1868).
21. There were twenty-four GNSR mortgages of £500 each, falling due in three batches of eight in October 1868, October 1870 and October 1873. The first batch was redeemed between January 1871 and January 1881, and three of the second tranche were redeemed in January 1881. The other £6,500 was assumed by the North British Railway as debt in 1881.
22. MMB1, p. 247 et seq. records the series of meetings where the forfeiture was carried out. *DC*, 6th Jan. 1869, reported that 1,069 shares were forfeited, but the Minute Book records a total of 1,031, with these being sold to Porteous (410), Farquhar (339), Scott (281) and David Mitchell (1).
23. Mary Isabella (6 years 8 months) died on 29th January, Edward Uchtred (3 years 11 months) died 1st February, Hercules James (8 years 7 months, the eldest son) died 3rd February and Helen (5 years 5 months) died 4th February (*Sheffield Daily Telegraph*, 6th Feb. 1869, p. 3). The surviving daughter was Anna Katherine (born 10th June 1868). Hercules and Anna Scott had a further daughter on Christmas Day 1869, appropriately called Margaret Rose de Noel. Anna Katherine inherited the estate and lived at Brotherton Castle until her own death in July 1948.
24. *DC*, 30th Apr. 1869, p. 4. The figures quoted in this newspaper for working expenses are wrong.
25. MMB1, pp. 281-2 (Directors' Meeting, 6th Mar. 1869).
26. *DC*, 29th Oct. 1870, p. 3. The secretary was also instructed to complain to the CR about the '*disgraceful state of the carriages on the line*'.
27. *DC*, 14th Aug. 1873, p. 3.
28. *DC*, 1st May 1875, p. 2. Freight volumes could still be volatile, depending on market conditions and competition. It was reported that fish forwarding had decreased by 693 tons, mainly because of exports via Gourdon harbour; grain was down 252 tons, and there had also been decreases in flax, tow and yarns from Bervie and Gourdon. However meal, flour and timber had registered an increase of 400 tons. These fluctuations were sufficiently unnerving for the Board to postpone a dividend.

29. *DC*, 8th May 1872, p. 4.
30. *DC*, 1st May 1875, p. 2.
31. *Northern Warder & Bi-Monthly Courier & Argus* [*NW*], 27th Oct. 1874. The numbers published by the *NW* do not correspond with those in the published accounts, but their conclusions are correct. The figures quoted probably excluded some headings in one, and included others in the other.
32. M&B half-annual accounts.
33. *DC*, 29th Apr. 1876, p. 2.
34. *DC*, 1st May 1876, p. 4.
35. *AJ*, 29th Jun. 1881, p. 7.
36. *ET*, 22nd Apr. 1878, p. 4.
37. *AJ*, 30th Apr. 1879, p. 5, and *DC*, 1 May 1879, p. 2.
38. *AJ*, 30th Apr. 1879, p. 5.
39. *GH*, 30th Oct. 1880, p. 3.
40. *DC*, 11th Nov. 1880, p. 2.
41. *GH*, 2nd Dec. 1871, p. 3. See also D. Ross, *The Caledonian, Scotland's Imperial Railway – A History* (Catrine, 2013) p. 107 and also his *The North British Railway – A History* (Catrine 2014) pp. 90-1 for more detail on the CR/NBR amalgamation discussions.
42. *AJ*, 22nd Sep. 1869, p. 8.
43. *DC*, 16th Jun. 1871, p. 3, reported that in the 1866 CR/SNER amalgamation Act the CR was prohibited from objecting to an NBR line to Stonehaven via Bervie within five years of Act. Even though that period had now elapsed, the implication that a through line was still a practical possibility was clear.
44. *GH*, 29th Jan. 1881, p. 3. The *DC* got the offer wrong; £6 per share is what the NBR paid.
45. *GH*, 3rd May 1881, p. 4.
46. *DC*, 10th May 1881, p. 5.
47. *DA*, 1st Oct. 1881, p. 6.
48. *DC*, 1st Oct. 1881, p. 3.
49. *DC*, 22nd Nov. 1881, p. 3.
50. *DA*, 22nd Nov. 1881, p. 7.
51. *AJ*, 28th Aug. 1884, p. 2. Lorimer specialized in painting the rich and famous, including Sir Thomas Sutherland, Chairman of P&O shipping line, Bishop Chisholm and Sir Joseph Lister. Many of his paintings are exhibited in his former home at Kellie Castle in Fife. The location of the painting of Hercules Scott, or whether it survives, is unknown.
52. The figures for 1874 are quoted in *Edinburgh Evening News* [*EEN*], 13th Apr. 1876, p. 3.
53. *DC*, 27th Oct. 1866, p. 4. It was not reported whether the blacksmith, appropriately called Mr Black, recovered.
54. *DC*, 20th Dec. 1875, p. 2.
55. *AJ*, 9th Feb. 1876, p. 3.
56. *NW*, 30th Mar. 1880, p. 3.
57. *DC*, 2nd Sep. 1873, p. 3.
58. *Montrose Standard*, quoted in *Stirling Observer*, 16th May 1867, p. 3.
59. *DC*, 24th Oct. 1872, p. 4.
60. *EEN*, 28th Nov. 1876, p. 2.
61. *DC*, 15th Nov. 1880, p. 2.
62. *EEN*, 13th Apr. 1876, p. 2.
63. I am grateful to Jim MacIntosh of the Caledonian Railway Society for pointing out this connection. J.F. McIntosh (1846-1918) joined the SNER as an apprentice at the Arbroath workshops at the age of 14. In 1865 he passed out as a fireman and qualified as a driver in 1867, moving to Montrose. The Bervie accident cost him his right hand and his driving career, but after a series of supervisory and management posts he replaced John Lambie as Chief mechanical Engineer of the Caledonian Railway in 1895 when Lambie died suddenly (http://en.wikipedia.org/wiki/John_F._McIntosh). His locomotive designs are discussed a some detail in A.B. MacLeod, *The McIntosh Locomotives of the Caledonian Railway 1895-1914* (London, 1948).
64. *AJ*, 2nd Oct. 1872, p. 7. On Thursday morning, between 4am and 5am, there was a landslip one mile south of Johnshaven. Twelve feet of embankment slipped, leaving rails and sleepers hanging. The 7.15am from Montrose was delayed three hours. '*No other detention occurred through the day, Mr Jamieson, Inspector of Way, and a staff of men, having soon afterwards put all to rights.*'
65. That in 1874-75 was typical. The *DC*, 7th Jan. 1875, p. 4, reported that the 3.15pm from Montrose on Friday was stuck at Lauriston until Saturday evening. '*Such a storm as that of Friday last no one here has ever seen*'.
66. [Aberdeen] *Evening Express* [*EE*], 11th Jul. 1879, p. 2.

The Castle Hotel, Bervie, built in 1867 was '*within three minutes walk of the Bervie Terminus of the Montrose and Bervie Railway*'. This Tuck postcard, number IV 4, probably dates from about 1952. The building still exists, but not as a hotel. *Author's collection*

Chapter 9

The Montrose & Bervie Railway Company in Retrospect

Shareholders' Aspirations

We acted both for the improvements of our estates, and for the general good which we believe we have very greatly promoted by our line.[1]

It is clear from this and other answers which Scott gave in his examination by the Parliamentary Committee investigating the Amalgamation Bill that the M&B was promoted as a means of developing the estates along the east coast of Kincardineshire, rather than as a specifically commercial venture on a stand-alone basis. However, that was not to say that the shareholders did not try to make it commercially successful. Scott makes clear in his evidence that he was disappointed in the performance of the line, and that the returns were not what they had hoped for.[2]

The line was burdened from the start by the working agreement with the SNER, and then the Caledonian, and though the M&B was able to reverse the accumulated deficit of the early years and earn a modest profit, the returns were poor, and the prospects were grim. It is also clear that if the bondholders (principally the GNSR) had not been prepared to accept interest on overdue bonds, the line would have been unable to continue.

Walker's evidence indicates that the NBR purchased the M&B partly as a strategic acquisition in their attempts to get nearer Aberdeen, and possibly also with a mind to using it as part of a through route further north. In the immediate term it was thought that the NBR could operate the line profitably because it would not have the burden of the CR working agreement and could reduce costs by perhaps 15 to 20%, bringing the operating ratio down from about 70% to around 50%, as well as developing the traffic more than the M&B had been able to do. One of the first acts of the new owners was to abolish mixed trains and run separate passenger and goods trains;[3] in 1885 all the station platforms were lengthened, new upright palings and gates erected round them, and the station offices were repainted '*giving them a clean and tidy appearance*'.[4]

The M&B is not, of course, separately accounted for in the NBR accounts, but at the half-yearly meeting in March 1882 the Chairman reported that:

The traffic of the Montrose and Bervie Railway, of which the Company took possession on the 1st August last, has quite justified the expectation of the Directors that the acquisition of the line would prove advantageous.[5]

The local shareholders were also very pleased with the sale, even though they had taken a 40% loss on the value of the investment. Anyone (and there were apparently a very small number)[6] who bought the shares prior to the announcement of the sale to the NBR at the then trading price of £2-£3 a share would have made a very handsome profit, but Scott, Farquhar and Porteous had purchased all their shares at par (£10) value.[7] They had, by Scott's calculations, taken dividends of an average of 10s 3d per £100 share over perhaps ten years of dividends, so that returned about another 5.6% of the value, while the principal shareholders had received feu duties on the line, amounting to about 8.6%. However, at most, the local large shareholders would have been able to recover perhaps 75% of the initial value. So why were they pleased?

On 28th January 1881 at a special meeting of the shareholders, Scott gave part of the answer.

The calculation that was made was this. Supposing you have a traffic of £5,000 a year, and supposing working arrangements, such as the North British company have already made with the Penicuik and other lines were established in our case, then we should have had £2,750 over. Out of that, £1,000 would have to go to pay the interest at 4 per cent on £18,000 of debt, and between £250 and £300 for Feu duties, and we should have had £1,450 over, which would have given us a dividend of 2 per cent upon current capital. I took this basis in my arrangements and negotiations with Mr. Walker, and it appeared to be a fair and reasonable one. I think you will find that the price the North British are to pay us – namely £6 for every £10 share – is a full and ample equivalent for the dividend which, under a fair and reasonable working agreement with the company we were feeding with our traffic, we were likely to have realised. That has been the basis of the arrangement that has been made.[8]

Scott had pulled off a remarkable deal with the North British. Not only had he convinced Walker that the 'fair' profit per annum was about double what the M&B was actually making, but that the NBR should pay £42,000 (60% of £70,000) for it, about forty-seven times the actual profit or about twenty-nine times the 'fair' profit. In addition to that, the NBR were taking on the debt. He then convinced the shareholders that this was more important than recovery of their original investment, perhaps not too difficult when he only had two other major landowners like himself to convince.

The other large shareholder, the Caledonian Railway, was far from pleased. Not only had they lost control to their main rivals of what was still seen as a strategic asset, but they were faced with a £6,000 write-down on the value of their investment. An attempt at the Amalgamation Bill proceedings to have their shareholding given preferred treatment – in effect to return 100% of its value – was always doomed to failure.[9]

Perhaps the answer also lies in the fact that through Scott's sale to the NBR he had secured the future of the line and ensured that it would still be able to play a part in the development of the area. The uncertain future negotiations with the Caledonian had been avoided, and their investment had returned more than it would have done in a distress sale (potentially close to nothing). The debentures had also been assumed by the NBR, so that was a further burden removed from the investors. Given a choice between 60% and nearly nothing, this probably seemed a good place to be.

Then there was the increase in value of the estates through which the line passed. It has not been possible to establish specific changes in valuations for the estates owned by Farquhar, Scott and Porteous, but an indication can be gained from the valuation data for the parishes in which they were situated. Their estates were respectively Hallgreen in Bervie Parish, Brotherton in Benholm and Lauriston in St. Cyrus. Table 7 shows how the three coastal parishes south of Bervie fared against the county average in the period between roughly the opening of the turnpikes and the opening of the railways, and then just after the NBR takeover.

The valuation of the three parishes increased with the opening of the turnpikes, though not as rapidly as the county as a whole, partly due to spectacular increases in parishes adjacent to Aberdeen.[10] Valuations increased again over the eighteen years following the opening of the railway. For example, Bervie increased more than it had during the whole of the turnpike era. Even though by 1881 the railway itself was accounting for a small proportion of the parish

Table 7: Valuation of South-East Kincardineshire Parishes			
	1803-04 (£)	1864-65 (£)	1882-83 (£)
Bervie	1,243	3,015	7,038
Benholm	3,059	6,589	9,705
St. Cyrus	6,758	15,149	19,447
Kincardineshire	63,389	191,133	260,063

NOTE: The average change per decade in the period 1865-83 was 6.81 times that in the period 1804-65 for Bervie Parish, with corresponding rates of 2.65 times and 1.54 times for Benholm and St. Cyrus. The difference for the county was 1.62 times.
SOURCE: Annual valuations by parish.

valuation, it is a reasonable assumption that the valuation increase of the three estates after 1804 was because of the turnpike road improvements and that this increase was accelerated by the M&B.[11]

THE RAILWAY'S EFFECT ON THE EAST KINCARDINESHIRE ECONOMY

The effect on the wider economy was also likely to have been considerable, though this is more difficult to prove. In terms of population, Kincardineshire's population rose by 10% between 1831 and 1861, but then remained static until 1881. Johnshaven and St. Cyrus slowly declined throughout the century, while Gourdon increased rapidly along with Bervie as the mills increased their workforce, a development only made possible by the arrival of the railway.[12]

The fishing industry in this part of Scotland had mixed fortunes in the nineteenth century. Johnshaven took some time to recover from the depredations of the Royal Navy press gangs during the Napoleonic Wars but developed rapidly in the second half of the century,[13] while the rapid centralization of the fishing fleet at Aberdeen between 1870 and 1879 after the harbour improvement there had the effect of reducing the output of the smaller ports.[14] We have already seen that Gourdon Harbour handled at least some of the export fish market. At best, this was probably a trade sporadically influenced by the M&B, although Scott considered it a growing source of traffic.

Table 8: Population Trends in South-East Kincardineshire 1831-81			
	1831	1861	1881
Bervie (Parish)	1,137	1,561	2,106
Bervie (Burgh)	757	952	1,094
Gourdon	238	497	919
Johnshaven	1,027	1,089	1,041
St. Cyrus	1,598	1,552	1,487
Kincardineshire	31,431	34,468	34,464

SOURCE: Decennial census.

The railway undoubtedly developed one industry in a way which could not have been foreseen by the proprietors. The early shareholders' meetings contain references to how surprised the Directors were to note the volume of passengers, and although the number only slowly increased throughout the line's independent existence, over 40,000 passenger a year were using the line from the earliest days, with some years seeing over 47,000. Of the 1872 revenue, 53% was attributed to passengers and in the last year for which data has survived – 1880 – this proportion was still 49%.

In 1867 the Castle Hotel was opened a hundred yards from Bervie station. This had obviously been designed to handle excursion traffic as the advertisement made clear. The new hotel was:

within three minutes walk of the Bervie Terminus of the Montrose and Bervie Railway ... Since the opening of the ... Railway, a large Trade has sprung up with the surrounding district, and in the summer months there is, in addition, a great influx of visitors from Montrose, and other Towns, for whom hitherto the accommodation in Bervie has been quite inadequate.[15]

Advertisements for farms to let usually emphasized how near the railway they were, demonstrating how important that feature had become to their businesses.

Scott survived his railway by another sixteen years, becoming rather more infirm as a result of the attack of rheumatic fever he had suffered in 1874. However, he continued to play a very active part in the community and continued to invest in transport improvements, including a major improvement to Johnshaven Harbour which took two years and was completed in 1884.[16] A biography of Scott can be found at Appendix 10.

NOTES

1. House of Commons. Minutes of Proceedings before the Select Committee on Railway Bills on the North British and Montrose and Bervie Railway Companies' Bill (Group 11), response to Q105. See Appendix 10 for detail of the Parliamentary proceedings.
2. See Appendix 6 for details of the evidence. From Scott's reported surprise that there were so many passengers, it seems likely he expected the line to be principally a freight carrier.
3. *DA*, 22nd Nov. 1881, p. 11.
4. *DC*, 19th Dec. 1885, p. 4.
5. *DC*, 2nd Mar. 1882, p. 2.
6. House of Commons. Minutes of Proceedings, op. cit., Wednesday 4th May 1881, Q121-Q123 (NRS ref: BR/PYB/S/1/569).
7. Three share sales by auction at the Star Hotel in Montrose were reported in *ET*; two were sold for £2 12s each in May 1879 (*ET*, 12th May 1879, p. 4), twenty were sold for £2 15s each in August 1879 (*ET*, 23rd Aug. 1879, p. 4), and ten were sold for £3 2s 6d each in November 1879 (*ET*, 1st Nov. 1879, p. 4). The shares were quoted in November 1880 at £3 5s each (*DC*, 11th Nov. 1880, p. 2).
8. *Stonehaven Journal & Kincardineshire Advertiser*, 3rd Feb. 1881.
9. See Appendix 6.
10. Nigg parish valuation increased by 558% between 1803 and 1864.
11. In 1877-78 the railway accounted for 7.6% of the total Bervie Parish valuation, 4.6% of Benholm and 3% of St. Cyrus.
12. Theoretically, the small harbour at Gourdon (designed by Telford in 1819 and enlarged in 1842) could have handled at least some of this output, as it did from time to time with fish, but it is unlikely that the industrialization at Bervie would have proceeded with only this outlet.
13. D.G. Adams, *Johnshaven and Miltonhaven: A Social and Economic History* (Brechin, 1991), gives the number of active fishing boats in Johnshaven as increasing from 27 boats and 68 men to 59 boats and 120 men in 1881.
14. J.J. Waterman, *Aberdeen and the Fishing Industry in the Eighteen Seventies* (Aberdeen, nd), p. 35.
15. *AJ*, 6th Mar. 1867, p. 2. The builder was Robert Miller, Bervie, and the new establishment had a dining room, 3 parlours, 8 bedrooms, 2 wcs, a large kitchen, scullery, cellar etc. Stables and adjoining coach house were also provided. The building still exists, though now a retirement home.
16. *AJ*, 7th Jul. 1884, p. 4. The harbour was designed by Mr Willett of Aberdeen using sketches prepared for Hercules Scott's grandfather, Colonel Hercules Scott, by John Rennie.

Chapter 10

A North British Branch Line

North British Control (1881-1922)

It might have been expected that as a sleepy North British branch, the Bervie Railway would lead an uneventful life until the closures of the mid-twentieth century, and to some extent this appears to have been true; however this perception probably derives from the lack of detailed records of the line after the North British takeover. There were periods when the branch was anything but sleepy, especially when the Caledonian Railway decided to resurrect its running powers, and during the renewed campaign to build the Kittywake Line.

The Bervie & Stonehaven Line

It was clear that the North British Railway still had dreams of an independent route to Aberdeen, of which the Tay Bridge and the direct line between Arbroath and Montrose constituted important parts. Certainly when the latter opened in 1881, the *Evening Telegraph* thought that:

> *The North British own the line from Montrose and Bervie and it is believed that at no distant date they will apply for powers to extend the system to Aberdeen.*[1]

However, nothing had happened by September 1889, when Bervie Town Council decided to ask the North British to promote a line to Stonehaven '*and possibly Aberdeen and Peterhead*', with a letter of support from Hercules Scott.[2]

Things became a little more hopeful when the North British Chairman, the Marquis of Tweedmouth, was reported as talking to prominent Aberdeen citizens about an independent Aberdeen line. This route would have used the Montrose & Bervie, then a new line to Stonehaven and another new line west of the Caledonian main line, but then crossed the Dee from Torry to Aberdeen near the Victoria Bridge (which would have been east of the Caledonian line). He was quoted as saying this scheme would be considered when Walker (then the North British manager) was replaced.[3] Obviously encouraged by all this, Aberdeen Town Council promptly set up a sub-committee to examine a North British proposal for the line, which was now proposed to run via Bervie, Stonehaven, Netherley, Maryculter (Mill Inn) and Aberdeen, with a branch from the Mill Inn via Durris, Banchory, Potarch, Kincardine o'Neil to Aboyne and Tarland.[4] However, a few days later the sub-committee had decided that they had better just confine their consideration to the main line, and not the Deeside Branch. A meeting with the North British was set up for 10th September, but whether this meeting took place is not recorded.[5] Bervie and Stonehaven councils passed motions from time to time that they favoured such a scheme[6] but there was nothing further from the North British. The agitation for an extension of the Bervie line north continued until after the First World War, with proposals being put forward by Bervie Council in 1899 now to the Caledonian as well as the North British.[7] In 1913 a long article on light railway schemes for the north-east of Scotland was published in the *Aberdeen Journal*;[8] this included a map showing the Bervie–Stonehaven line as well as lines from Ballater to Braemar, Alford to Strathdon, Aberdeen to Newburgh, Udny to Methlick, Maud to Turriff and Peterhead to Fraserburgh. Stewart, the Great North of Scotland Chairman, in a carefully worded letter of support, said that the GNSR would be prepared to build such lines where they could see a 4% return, and would work lines laid by others for a fee. Perhaps the promoters, the Association for the Development of the Counties of Aberdeen, Kincardine and Banff, should have remembered an earlier GNSR response to the light railways question in 1906:

> *Owing to the comparatively sparse population of many of the district, the expense of making railways, even light railways, was out of the question, ... and that a service of motor omnibuses would largely solve the difficulty of providing convenience in poorly-populated districts.*[9]

The final effort was in 1918 when Kincardine County Council called on the Road Transport (Scotland) Committee to propose a light railway from Bervie to Stonehaven (as well as a line to

Very much an NBR scene at Bervie yard with Wheatley Class 'C' No. 267 of 1871 (as rebuilt by Holmes). It was one of two Class 'C' engines fitted with Westinghouse brakes. It was withdrawn in October 1923 without carrying an L&NER Class 'J31' number and scrapped in 1924. Oddly, it has an express headcode and a route indicator at the base of the chimney (fitted the wrong way round). The train is also interesting; behind the four-wheel inside spring tender are two three-plank open wagons, a fully-panelled 'break' van, a fruit and yeast van and more three-plank open wagons. Behind the locomotive can be seen the Bervie scotch derrick crane, while the cattle bank is on the left. It is thought the photograph dates from circa 1886.

Libraries, Leisure & Culture, Dundee: Alexander Wilson collection WC1031

This February 1964 photograph of Bervie station building shows the 'standard' extension built for the Caledonian in 1897 at all Bervie line stations. The original building was the section to the left of the vertical line right of the clock; the section to the right was clad in vertical clap-board (in contrast to the horizontal clap-board of the original). At Johnshaven a separate building end-on to the platform was built. *Norris Forrest*

Fettercairn). Given that motor buses were by then well established on the Stonehaven route, and steam and motor lorries were operating, this seems a forlorn hope.

CALEDONIAN TO BERVIE (AGAIN)

Although the Caledonian Railway had operated the Montrose & Bervie line until the North British takeover in 1881, it nevertheless was a notable event when the company announced that it would seek to enforce the running powers it still retained in August 1897, with a full service of passenger and goods trains.[10] This was apparently in retaliation for a North British incursion into Caledonian territory at Brechin.[11] To cater for the duplicate service, the Caledonian paid for building extensions at each Bervie line station where a building existed, and stationed its own staff there, although this was only after an angry letter from the Caledonian General Manager to his North British counterpart complaining that:

You surely cannot be aware that the office work of our staff has to be conducted at the Montrose and Bervie stations in lamp rooms and waiting rooms, and in one case in an old van.[12]

The resultant service was seven North British and four Caledonian trains a day each way, a ludicrous over-provision for the branch, and a shameful waste of shareholders' funds. It was also of dubious benefit to the travelling public, but then that was not the main point of the exercise. An editorial in *The Montrose Review* entitled 'Railway Eccentricities' demonstrated the confusion which arose.

The dual service on the Montrose & Bervie line, while it undoubtedly increases the facilities to the travelling public, is not without its drawbacks to the unwary traveller. The running powers which the Caledonian Company have over the line are hedged in by conditions that are puzzling and troublesome to passengers. The other day a gentleman travelled by Caledonian from Montrose to Johnshaven taking a return ticket. Having some time at his disposal he walked to Bervie intending to return by Caledonian train. When he asked for a ticket from Bervie to Johnshaven he was informed that one could only be given if he paid the full fare into Montrose, the Caledonian not having the power, it was said, to issue tickets to intermediate stations. The circumstance was explained but it was no use, the gentleman had to pay one shilling for the short journey from Bervie to Johnshaven.[13]

The animosity between the Caledonian and the North British also found expression in physical violence between their respective employees. At St. Cyrus in October 1897, a Caledonian Railway 'canvasser' (goods agent) was reported by a North British inspector for pushing the signalman out of the way and clearing the signals for

This turn of the century photograph of Johnshaven yard shows a Drummond 0-6-0 (possibly No. 560). The toolbox at the back of the tender was a typical feature of Drummond engines.
Benholm & Johnshaven Heritage Society

a Caledonian train to proceed. This gave rise to an angry exchange of letters between David Deuchars, the NBR Superintendent of the Line, and John Conacher, the NBR General Manager, as well as between him and the Caledonian General Manager.

To J Conacher, Esq, General Manager, North British Railway
29th October 1897

Dear Sir,

<u>Caledonian Servant interfering with Signals, St. Cyrus</u>

I beg to send you the enclosed report from Mr. Robertson, Dundee, and relative telegrams.

You will observe that this is a case where a Caledonian Canvasser forcibly removed our Agent and opened the signals to admit of a Caledonian train proceeding. I think we are perfectly justified in pressing for the removal of Dunbar [the canvasser] as we cannot be safe in the hands of such a man. If this is not done, then I would recommend that criminal proceedings be instituted against him.

There is no use in the Caledonian Company referring to obstruction as an answer to the complaint because for the last 20 years during which we have been running over their line, our trains have been delayed in many cases through gross obstruction, but our servants have never resorted to such an objectionable method as Dunbar adopted on the present occasion and which is condoned by his superiors.

You will notice from Mr. Robertson's letter that this man has been very officious, and no restraint appears to have been placed upon him, which is another reason why his transfer should be insisted upon.

Yours truly
David Deuchars

To J Conacher, Esq, General Manager, North British Railway
Nov 11th 1897

Dear Sirs,

<u>Interference with signals at St. Cyrus</u>

With further reference to your letter of the 29th ultimo, I have referred to the telegrams and letters exchanged between Mr. Deuchars and Mr. Kempt, and have enquired fully into the whole matter.

No doubt the Inspector [Dunbar] should not have interfered with the signal, but so far as I can find there was not the slightest risk or danger to any person through his action, and his action was brought about by a most needless and irritating obstruction on the part of your company's servants.

I may say that Dunbar and the other parties named have been suitably cautioned and dealt with.

I regret extremely that Mr. Deuchars should have used the language he does to Mr. Kempt, and I am not prepared to accede to your request to remove Dunbar or any other servant of this Company from the Bervie Section.

It is very strange that the reception which my Company's servants have received on the Montrose and Bervie Line is so very different from what my Company have at all times afforded to your Company in the exercise of running powers.

Neither you nor Mr. Deuchars have in letter or telegram taken the slightest notice of the complaint of the obstruction and delay to our traffic.

Yours faithfully,
James Thompson[14]

Although the North British was concerned enough to conduct a weekly survey of traffic on the competing trains to Bervie, it was

No. 241 with a train at Broomfield on its way to Bervie around 1910. The end coaches are three-compartment Brake Thirds, the second vehicle appears to be a First, or possibly a Composite, built by the Ashbury Railway Carriage & Iron Co. Ltd, Manchester, and the third vehicle seems to be a five-compartment Third, possibly also built by Ashbury. The station agent (and dog) are greeting the train. *Kenneth Hay collection*

Lauriston in 1906. Recently appointed Passenger Agent James Haxton stands in his new uniform on the left, while the 'Lad Porter' is to the right.
Brian H. Watt

noted that the passengers and goods consignors remained largely loyal to the North British, probably because they could see that this particularly egregious example of competitive testosterone could not last.[15] The *Evening Telegraph* noted that 'railway circles' were surprised at the decision, but that the service was a loss-maker and:

> in this instance the competition, although healthy, has not withdrawn the patronage of the traders and others from their opponents, the North British.[16]

The Caledonian and the North British eventually made peace on the issue of the Brechin trains, and the Caledonian service to Bervie was abandoned as quickly as it was introduced, giving one day's notice and making twenty staff surplus in the process.[17] The deal between the Caledonian and the North British provided that the Caledonian would withdraw from Bervie and the Bo'ness Branch, while the North British would withdraw from Blairgowrie, Laurencekirk (passenger and freight), Kirriemuir, Forfar and Brechin (freight).[18] The resultant outcry from consignors who had transferred to the Caledonian service forced the Caledonian to restore the goods service for a few months from October 1898, but that was withdrawn in June the following year.

Commercial Performance in the North British Era

The Bervie line was seen as a worthwhile acquisition by the North British, which had effectively purchased it at a 40% discount; it could be used as a strategic lever on the Caledonian Railway and the traffic levels of both passengers and goods were satisfactory. Although it had been announced that 'mixed' trains (passenger trains with freight wagons attached) would cease after the 1881 takeover, in fact the practice continued on some occasions. As late as 1920 a complaint from a passenger alleging that the 5.15pm from Montrose to Bervie on Fridays (Montrose Market Day) regularly had:

> farmers travelling on the Bervie Branch from Montrose in the first class with third class tickets. Now there is only one carriage and these farmers are more or less under the influence of drink, it is very disagreeable to the passengers who pay their way.[19]

The subsequent report to the General Manager said that the Montrose stationmaster had been reminded that additional carriages from the second train set were available for strengthening the train, but noted that:

> The train concerned is the 5-15pm Montrose to Bervie and is a mixed train for the purpose of taking cattle from the Market at Montrose to Stations on the Bervie Branch ...
>
> The full accommodation on the train is thirteen third and two first class compartments and when the working was watched on Friday last there were about 90 third-class and four first-class passengers, all seated in the proper class of accommodation.[20]

This indicated a well-used service, but it is interesting to see how the branch performed more generally. In the half-year ending January 1881, the last for which traffic figures are available for the independent company, 45,892 passengers and 9,926 tons of freight were handled. In the corresponding half-year to January 1900, the figures were 48,039 passengers and 16,509 tons of freight. Thus, while passenger numbers were broadly similar (and averaged around 39,000 to 40,000 until the First World War), freight had markedly increased. Significant numbers of livestock were also being transported, far more than the small numbers reported by the M&B. On one occasion in May 1909 it was reported that eighteen trucks, containing 600 sheep, were dispatched from Bervie.[21] In 1882 the North British had introduced a through fish train during the herring season to Edinburgh, to connect with the London

CHAPTER 10: A NORTH BRITISH BRANCH LINE

service, and thereby opening up the Gourdon fisheries to wider markets.[22]

Bervie accounted for about half the freight traffic in 1900, followed by Johnshaven and Gourdon. Passenger traffic was much more evenly spread, with Bervie, Johnshaven and St. Cyrus accounting for 20-25% each, and Gourdon and Lauriston at 12-15%. These figures remained broadly consistent until about 1906/07, after which there was a perceptible decline up to the First World War. Passenger revenue was £2,732 in 1900, and £2,506 in 1906, but had fallen to £2,521 in 1915, with fare increases pushing revenue up to £3,510 in 1921, though with 44% fewer passengers.

As working days (and weeks) became shorter and disposable

| TABLE 9: BERVIE BRANCH TRAFFIC 1900-1921 |||||||
| YEAR | PASSENGERS || FREIGHT ||||
	No.	REVENUE (£)	GOODS (TONS)	MINERALS (TONS)	COAL (TONS)	LIVESTOCK (HEAD)
1900	86,467	2,732	15,879	4,516	9,794	4,673
1901	83,828	2,820	15,753	6,712	8,292	4,656
1902	80,954	2,714	13,655	6,959	9,256	4,282
1903	80,856	2,744	13,542	8,165	9,517	3,272
1904	81,591	2,691	13,156	8,561	8,810	4,354
1905	80,312	2,634	14,153	7,915	8,785	4,742
1906	79,580	2,506	14,868	9,132	8,950	5,240
1907	84,173	2,625	14,185	9,417	9,119	6,675
1908	76,774	2,741	16,970	10,414	9,461	5,447
1909	76,236	2,617	14,564	9,123	8,602	5,476
1910	77,701	2,620	14,792	8,192	9,042	4,296
1911	72,119	2,478	14,007	9,371	9,246	5,993
1912	62,248	2,306	15,580	8,661	7,847	5,422
1913	78,187	2,642	20,815	3,187	9,417	6,772
1914	80,598	2,675	20,496	3,999	9,327	7,146
1915	77,918	2,521	22,319	2,988	9,046	5,412
1916	69,989	2,974	20,032	2,548	9,085	5,761
1917	50,820	2,456	21,577	2,741	8,779	4,099
1918	67,163	3,260	24,551	4,816	8,361	4,036
1919	68,376	3,806	27,432	5,125	8,069	2,806
1920	65,496	3,847	20,157	6,384	7,464	3,459
1921	43,708	3,510	17,422	3,450	5,054	3,200

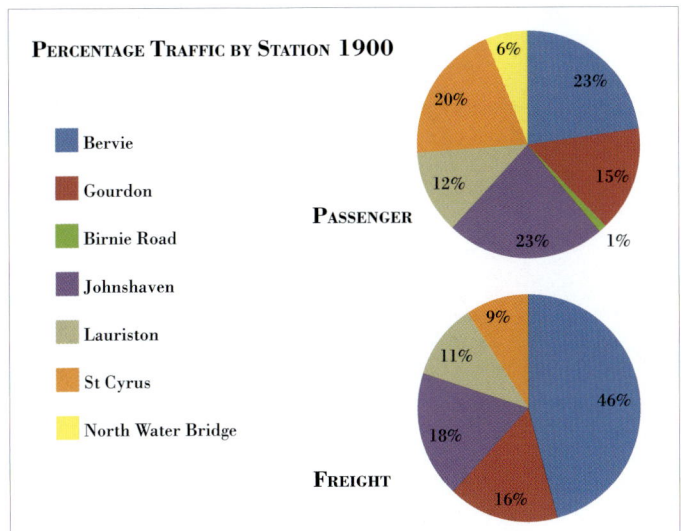

PERCENTAGE TRAFFIC BY STATION 1900

- Bervie
- Gourdon
- Birnie Road
- Johnshaven
- Lauriston
- St Cyrus
- North Water Bridge

PASSENGER: 23%, 15%, 1%, 23%, 12%, 20%, 6%

FREIGHT: 46%, 16%, 18%, 11%, 9%

L&NER Class 'G9' No. 9475 (NBR Class 'M') of 1909 with its one-coach train heading for Bervie over the North Esk Viaduct. The coach had a goods brake compartment for small goods and parcels. No. 9475 was withdrawn in November 1940. *Bill Lynn collection*

532 On the North Esk River, Montrose.

ABOVE: Bervie station in 1914 with Craig David headland behind. An interesting selection of North British rolling stock is on display, including the six-compartment coach parked on the west siding. Salmon fishermen occupied the cottages behind, and one of their boats can be seen beached at the mouth of the Bervie River. *Tom Valentine*

BELOW: A second view of Bervie in 1914. Stables, goods shed, coal shed, signal box and crane are all clearly visible. The wagons are a mix of North British Railway and private owner, and there are at least three horse-drawn carts in the station yard. *Brian H. Watt*

CHAPTER 10: A NORTH BRITISH BRANCH LINE

Another pre-First World War view of Bervie station, with Hallgreen Castle behind on the hill. There is a coach on the west siding behind the signal box, and the first engine shed (destroyed in 1914) is on the extreme left.
Brian H. Watt

income increased, excursion traffic was developing also, and apart from passengers from the local area as far as Aberdeen and Dundee using the line at Bank Holidays, there was a significant flow from stations in the Glasgow area to Bervie and Gourdon for people enjoying the new phenomenon of 'summer holidays'.[23]

However, even before the First World War there were signs of competition from road transport. While a Bervie–Stonehaven coach had run regularly on a couple of days a week ever since the railway had opened, and there had been a daily mail gig connection to Fordoun for many years, in 1907 a Bervie cycle shop owner, W.P. Davidson, started a daily motor bus on the Stonehaven route.[24] This probably diverted some traffic towards Aberdeen via Stonehaven which might have used the railway to Montrose and changed onto northbound services there, even though on occasions the use of the bus could be a risky business. In March 1914, for example, a Davidson bus was involved in a collision as it returned from Stonehaven. The driver was *'a young man named Laing'*. One passenger was thrown out of the bus and badly cut, but the *Dundee Courier* continued, reassuringly, that *'the motor bus is not much the worse for the accident'*.[25] The bus took one hour to get to Stonehaven station, having left Bervie at 8am. That meant that a passenger travelling to Aberdeen could do the 26-mile journey by bus in about an hour less than going via Montrose on the railway, besides departing from the centre of the town instead of down by the sea shore.[26]

In terms of operating costs, it is safe to assume that these were not markedly different to the levels achieved by the Montrose & Bervie; staffing was similar, and train working expenses would have been similar with a comparable number of train miles run. There are no references in the surviving records to any need for operational economies, indicating that the North British did not see any need to economise on a branch which was covering its costs from freight revenue and was earning over £2,500 from passenger traffic.[27]

Bervie in North British days. The locomotive is No. 241, a Drummond Class 'R' 0-6-0 of 1876 which carried the name 'Bervie' for a few years in the early 1880s.
H. Stevenson collection

Notes

1. *ET*, 1st Mar. 1883, p. 3, report of inspection of the Arbroath & Montrose
2. *DC*, 18th Sep. 1889, p. 3. It was not explained why Peterhead should be the ultimate destination, unless Bervie Council thought that through stopping fish trains would be likely.
3. *AJ*, 22th Jun. 1891, p. 4. It is possible, of course, that this was all said for the benefit of the Caledonian Railway, with whom the NBR were attempting to settle commercial terms of traffic to Aberdeen.
4. *EE*, 21st Aug. 1891, p. 3.
5. *EE*, 1st Sep. 1891, p. 3.
6. *DC*, 9th Sep. 1891, p. 4 (Stonehaven); *AJ*, 12th Jul. 1893, and *DC*, 6th Oct. 1893, p. 6 (Bervie).
7. *AJ*, 19th Oct. 1899, p. 7, reported Provost Gibb as saying a sub-committee of two Bervie Council members and two each from Dunottar, Kinneff and Stonehaven should approach the CR and the NBR and report back. Nothing happened.
8. *AJ*, 18th Jan. 1913, p. 3. The map also included a line from Ballindalloch to Tomintoul in Banffshire. Lord Aberdeen chaired the committee, but it seems to have been a loosely constituted pressure group rather than formally sponsored by the local authorities. The railway companies declined to pay for any surveys of these lines, but eventually the GNSR surveyed the Strathdon line. When the Association then decided another alignment (to Cairnie) might also be surveyed, the GNSR lost interest.
9. *AJ*, 28th Jul. 1905, p. 4. Statement by GNSR in support of Order promoting bus services. These comments were in respect to Ballater–Braemar, Culter–Midmar, Udny–Methlick and Huntly–Aberchirder lines, but they could easily have been taken as including the Stonehaven–Bervie line.
10. The CR service started on 2nd August 1897 and lasted to 30th September 1898.
11. D. Ross, *The Caledonian Railway*, op. cit., p. 152.
12. NRS file ref BR/NBR/8/1273, letter dated 23rd Aug. 1897.
13. *Montrose Review*, 9th Sep. 1898, quoted in A.F. Nisbet, 'The Montrose & Bervie Railway' in *Backtrack*, Nov. 2013, p. 677.
14. Both letters are in NRS file ref BR/NBR/8/1273.
15. NRS file BR/NBR/8/1273 has several copies of the census reports. On week ending 25th September 1897 the CR trains carried 62 singles and 25 returns from Montrose to all Bervie line stations, with many fewer bookings in the opposite direction. For the whole of August 1897 the figures from Montrose were 355 singles and 201 weekend tickets or returns. That meant an average load of up to six passengers in August, about three at the end of September from Montrose, and fewer on the return.
16. *ET*, 26th Sep. 1898, p. 2.
17. According to *DC*, 5th Oct. 1898, p. 5, the CR employed twenty men – six loco drivers, four guards, five porters and five stationmasters. The drivers were rapidly redeployed, but it took some time to find alternative work for the other staff.
18. *DC*, 29th Jun. 1899, p. 4. Nowadays such an agreement would be illegal under competition legislation, and the participants subject to heavy fines.
19. NRS file BR/NBR/8/1532. Edwin G. Gibb to James Calder, 30th Apr. 1920.
20. NRS file BR/NBR/8/1532. Report to James Calder, 20th May 1920.
21. *AJ*, 10th May 1909, p. 8. The sheep were dispatched by James Calder, Midtown of Barras.
22. *ET*, 27th Jun. 1882, p. 3.
23. This is evidenced by the ticket issues for stations on the North British system in NRS file BR/NBR/4.
24. In the *DC* round up of the year 1908, the newspaper commented that '*the success of the firm … is an up to date evidence of the enterprise and pushfulness of the good folk of Bervie*' (*DC*, 23rd Jan. 1909, p. 7).
25. *DC*, 7th Mar. 1914, p. 7.
26. This assumes that the bus reached Stonehaven in time to connect with the 8.55am local to Aberdeen (arr Aberdeen 9.35am). If the connection was with the later express, the saving was reduced to about 20 minutes.

A very grimy No. 9475, L&NER Class 'G9' (NBR Class 'M') waits for the departure signal at St. Cyrus with its one-coach train from Inverbervie on 16th April 1938.
Ken Nunn, by permission of the Science Museum

Chapter 11

The L&NER Years

The First World War and the L&NER

In common with every other employer, the North British Railway was faced with wage inflation as well as increases in the cost of materials during the First World War. Control of the railways was assumed by the Government and by 1918 passenger services had been reduced by 45% to conserve fuel and to allow diversion of resources to goods traffic. Road transport had also been severely curtailed, with motor vehicles and horses being requisitioned, so there was, if anything, an improvement in the railways' competitive position. After the war, however, the situation dramatically worsened. Large numbers of motor vehicles became available from military sales, and many returning servicemen now had the skills necessary to drive and maintain road vehicles. To make matters worse, the railways had undergone a disruptive reorganisation into four large territorial groups, and a number of damaging labour disputes had the effect of forcing customers (both passenger and freight) to look for alternatives to the train.

The Bervie line now became part of the London & North Eastern Railway (L&NER), which had absorbed the North British, while the Caledonian was now part of the rival London Midland & Scottish Railway (LM&SR).

During the war also, the Bervie line had lost a number of staff to the armed forces, and several of these either did not return or returned with serious injuries. A porter at St. Cyrus, Douglas Laing, was reported missing in May 1918, while Robert Jolly, a ticket collector at Bervie, was wounded in his left hand. Another member of staff at Bervie, clerk Alexander Young, was wounded by a shell and severely gassed.

Meanwhile, road services were recovering and developing. At the February 1919 North British AGM a Bervie shareholder had complained that the rail service to Aberdeen via Montrose was now so poor that one could scarcely get there and back in a day,[1] while it was reported later the same year that a motor charabanc had started running between Stonehaven and Aberdeen.[2] By October 1921 James Peter, a Bervie motor garage proprietor, trading as the 'Thistle Service', was running a bus between Montrose and Bervie,[3] while even the excursion traffic from Dundee was under attack by charabanc operators advertising runs from Dundee to Forfar, Brechin, Laurencekirk and Stonehaven, returning via Bervie and Montrose.[4] However, on the Dundee Holiday in 1926 it was noted that 9% of the trippers from Dundee Tay Bridge station (900) were heading for Bervie, said to have been the fifth most popular destination.[5]

The state of the roads was also improving; in the summer of 1921 the Montrose–Bervie road was tarmacadamed over its *'entire width'*, the first major improvement since the turnpike alterations.[6] Together with some bridge and culvert strengthening, the ability of the road to handle heavier and faster traffic was improved.

The earliest motor bus operator in Bervie was Davidson, a cycle shop owner who started operations in 1907. SU 79 was probably one of his vehicles and it is seen here in Johnshaven, possibly driven by the owner. This card, posted in June 1911, was published by a Laurencekirk bookseller, Archibald Taylor, although produced by Reliable. The writer says *'This is a view of the Ship Hotel. We are sailing pretty smoothly. The Captain and his wife asked to be remembered to you'*, so presumably she was taking a boat trip down the east coast. *Author's collection*

In the early 1920s, indeed, rail traffic levels increased significantly, with over 61,000 passengers travelling in 1925, though generating lower revenue. In April 1927, however, Scottish Clan Motorways started an Aberdeen–Glasgow service with stops at Montrose, Bervie and Stonehaven. Although this was a once-daily limited stop service, it was the forerunner of much more frequent local services. The report in the *Evening Telegraph* of the exodus for the 1928 Dundee Holiday showed a photograph of a queue over 100 yards long for the Montrose and Aberdeen bus, rather than a report of the numbers at Tay Bridge station.[7] The following year, a consolidation of a number of bus operators on the east coast route took place, when Progressive (Dundee–Arbroath), McFarlane (Arbroath–Montrose), J. Peter (Montrose–Stonehaven) and Clark (Stonehaven–Aberdeen) combined to form Northern General Motors Ltd with a capital of £50,000.[8] Northern General rapidly established a through hourly bus service from Dundee to Aberdeen via Montrose and Bervie.[9] In May 1930 Northern General Motors was acquired by W. Alexander & Sons Ltd, Falkirk.

The response of the railways to the bus threat was twofold; they instituted a '*fair play*' campaign designed to restrict bus operators, while seeking to reduce costs. The effect on the Bervie line was dramatic, as can be seen in Table 10.

ABOVE: SU 321, one of the first motor lorries in the area, makes its way south along the middle of King Street, Bervie, long before the main road was tarmacadamed. Comparison with the picture of the same street in Chapter 1 shows how much the town had changed since 1880. JV78407 is a 1914 postcard by J. Valentine of Dundee. *Brian H. Watt*

LEFT: SU 1575 was a splendidly named Thornycroft Boadicea with Strachan & Brown body, new in 1924. Within a couple of years buses with solid tyres were obsolete. It carries the number 40 on the small plate below the nearside window. This may have been a hackney licence number. *Brian H. Watt*

CHAPTER 11: THE L&NER YEARS

TABLE 10: BERVIE BRANCH TRAFFIC 1922-1932						
	PASSENGERS		FREIGHT			
YEAR	No.	REVENUE (£)	GOODS (TONS)	MINERALS (TONS)	COAL (TONS)	LIVESTOCK (HEAD)
1922	49,466	3,152	14,060	2,968	7,233	3,582
1923	56,574	3,002	13,949	3,449	7,902	4,069
1924	60,216	3,464	11,641	2,389	8,544	4,692
1925	61,814	3,019	10,589	4,213	7,393	4,427
1926	42,252	2,289	12,002	3,679	6,257	7,693
1927	37,625	1,939	9,598	2,739	7,916	10,323
1928	24,533	1,514	8,618	2,598	7,531	6,133
1929	18,240	1,233	6,477	4,116	7,380	4,883
1930	16,888	1,196	6,917	4,104	6,943	5,077
1931	17,916	1,199	4,301	1,761	6,446	3,885
1932	16,863	1,151	2,083	1,236	5,523	2,782

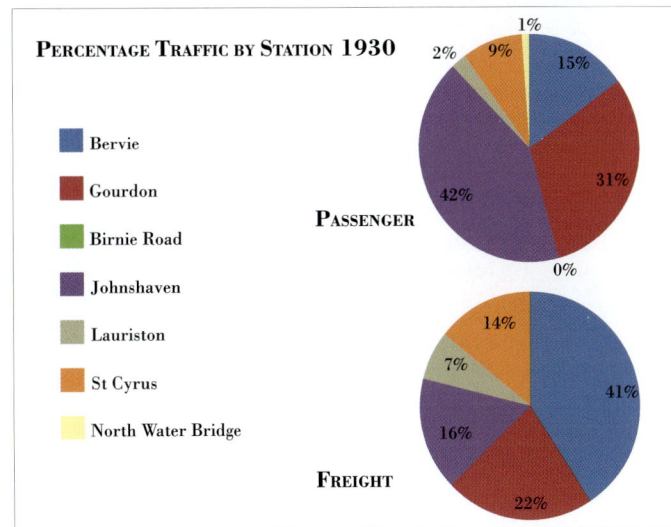

Between 1925 and 1930 passenger numbers had collapsed by 73% and revenue had reduced by 39%. The Bervie line stations were sometimes poorly located: Bervie was at the foot of Kirkburn, some 300 yards from the main street, Gourdon and Johnshaven were well-positioned in the middle of the villages, while St. Cyrus was a short distance from the main street. The two bus stops in Bervie served each end of the main street, and the stop in St. Cyrus was on the main road, while buses passing Gourdon and Johnshaven stopped at the respective road ends on what is now the A92. A bus passenger for Gourdon faced a 500 yard walk, while a Johnshaven resident faced a similar walk, but up a very steep hill. However, although Gourdon and Johnshaven passenger numbers showed more resilience than the other stations, the railway was in general competing with a low frequency service (between three and five trains each way) against

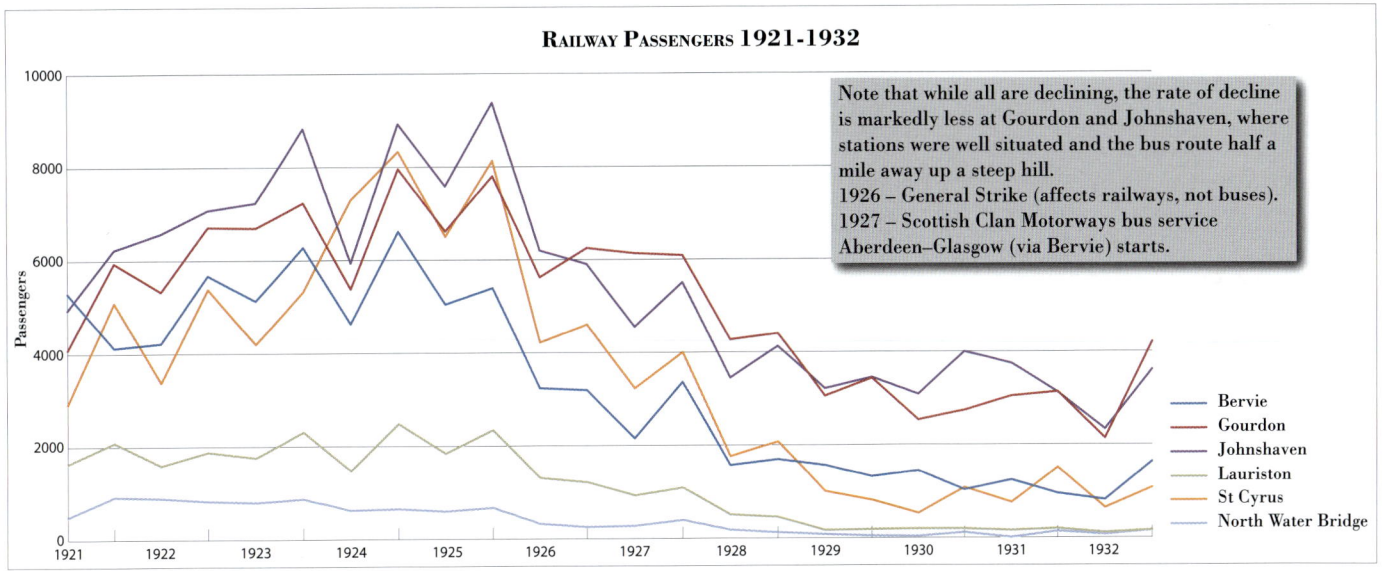

By the mid 1920s Peter's Thistle Service buses were fitted with pneumatic tyres (which allowed a higher speed limit) and were able to market themselves as '*safety coaches*' in contrast to what had occasionally occurred previously.
Graham Martin-Bates

RIGHT: No shortage of passengers at St. Cyrus. This crowd in the mid-1920s is probably waiting for the market day train to Montrose which is just approaching under the bridge, passing the signal protecting the yard. By this time much of the regular traffic had transferred to the buses. *Jimmie Davidson*

BELOW: No. 9475 at Inverbervie on 7th April 1939. The driver was David Pearson and fireman William Templeman is on the first step. The Class 'G9' locomotive had an interesting train of an LM&SR van, six-wheeler Third and four-compartment Brake.
W. Hennigan, Bill Lynn collection

an hourly bus service which also used newer, more comfortable (though less spacious) vehicles and a slightly faster service. In Montrose the bus delivered passengers to the High Street, while the railway delivered them to the station several hundred yards away. This was fine if passengers were making onward railway connections, but unsatisfactory for shoppers and commuters. It does not appear that fares were uncompetitive, however. Fares data in the surviving railway records in the National Records of Scotland is very sparse (unlike timetable data), but the comparable fares noted in 1938 when bus/rail interavailability was being considered by the Scottish Traffic Commissioners (the licensing authority for buses from 1931) showed a very comparable position between bus returns and railway cheap day returns, though railway standard returns were more expensive.

TABLE 11: BUS AND RAIL RETURN FARES – BERVIE BRANCH 1938		
MONTROSE TO	BUS	RAIL
St. Cyrus	10d	9½d
Johnshaven	1s 6d	1s 5d
Gourdon	1s 9d	1s 9d
Inverbervie	2s 1d	1s 11d
Taken from *Notices and Proceedings of the Northern (Scottish) Traffic Commissioners* issue 223 (10th Feb. 1938). The railway fares used were cheap returns.		

The relatively poor safety record of the early buses was not enough to dent public confidence in them. The brakes on these vehicles were poor, and a number of accidents were reported which could be attributed to this cause. In addition, their engines were prone to 'back-fire' and set the vehicle alight. In one such case, in January 1929, a Thistle bus caught fire on Charleston Road, Montrose, on its way to Stonehaven. However, it was reported that a bucket of water was thrown over the flames, the fire was put out, and the passengers got back in and resumed their journey.[10]

On the Bervie line the response was to reduce the need for signalling. When it opened, the Bervie line had used a 'one engine in steam' system, which meant that only one train could be on the entire branch at one time. After the North British takeover, this very restrictive system had been replaced by train staff and ticket arrangements, in conjunction with the absolute block system of working. A loop was installed at Lauriston in 1883 so that more than one train could be on the branch at one time. On 1st May 1927 the signal boxes at Lauriston and Bervie were closed and the line reverted to one engine in steam.[11] The problem with this solution was that while it saved staff and equipment maintenance, it also locked the branch into a very low frequency service.

The railway campaign to deal with road competition was instrumental in introducing quantity and quality licensing for buses in the Road Traffic Act 1930, a measure which allowed massive

CHAPTER 11: THE L&NER YEARS

railway investment in the large territorial bus companies. In effect, although railway spokesmen were at pains to point out that theirs was purely an investment, and not operational influence, the major bus companies were no longer seen as competitors by the railway companies, but as a solution to falling passenger numbers on expensive railway branch lines. Interavailable fares were promoted in the 1930s, while during engineering closures of the line, passengers were actively encouraged to use W. Alexander & Sons buses, the arm of the part railway-financed Scottish Motor Traction group operating in the area.[12]

Freight traffic, on the other hand, held up reasonably well in the inter-war period. Bulk traffic, including minerals and coal, remained reasonably steady until 1930, when the general economic situation saw a reduction, particularly in minerals.[13] One-off contracts boosted returns in specific years; for example, in 1929 gravel from Bervie beach was moved to Montrose for the new road bridge being built there by Sir Robert McAlpine & Son, necessitating a light railway being installed on Bervie shore.[14] General goods, however, which was much more vulnerable to road competition (and attracted higher rates) declined steadily over the period from a postwar peak of around 20,157 tons in 1920 to only 2,093 by 1932. It was becoming clear that the railway was handling only traffic which road transport was unable to deal with.

The trends were clear. The Black Isle and Strathpeffer branches were reported as under consideration for closure by the LM&SR in 1929. An L&NER spokesman was at pains to deny that his company was considering similar actions:

We are closing passenger stations in certain cases where they are not proving of public service, but so far as the north-east of Scotland is concerned there are no proposals that I know of for the whole or partial closing of branch lines to passenger traffic.[15]

However, internal L&NER correspondence in August 1930[16] makes it clear that a number of branch lines were being considered for withdrawal of passenger or all services. This included the Bervie line, but in the event some minor economies were made by centralising the management of all the stations under one agent in 1932, and a number of lower graded posts were left unfilled. Under the headline 'Inverbervie Rail Economies' the *Dundee Courier* reported that:

further economies are likely to be effected shortly through dispensing with the station agent at St. Cyrus and carrying on the line under the supervision of the present agent at Gourdon. There were formerly five stationmasters along the line – at Inverbervie, Gourdon, Johnshaven, Lauriston and St. Cyrus.[17]

The savings these changes made were probably inconsequential in terms of cash saved, but arguably made it easier for road competition to capitalise on a more remote and impersonal service. The harsh reality, of course, was that the economics of transport, and the emergence of a more responsive, more convenient and often cheaper alternative was making the branch ever more irrelevant to the transport needs of the area. After the Second World War, during which time the railways were again under government control, and consideration of closures would have been off the agenda, the figures had deteriorated even more. Traffic returns on the branch immediately after the war are shown in Table 12.

It was clear that passenger traffic was continuing to decline after the busier wartime period, with the three trains each way carrying an average of around six passengers by 1947, at an average revenue of about 14s. Indeed revenue from parcels now outweighed that from passengers by a considerable margin, although it only contributed about £4 per train.[18] While staff costs on the Bervie line (with ten station staff and three train crew) amounted to just over £2 per train, the line was likely to meet the direct costs of this traffic. Freight on the other hand was increasing both in volume and in revenue, the latter aided by price increases. By 1947 the average revenue per train was over £20 for originating traffic. The limited availability of lorries immediately after the war no doubt helped.[19]

Bus services had continued to develop. In addition to the hourly Dundee–Aberdeen Route 11 via Inverbervie, new Route 11H (Montrose–Johnshaven–Inverbervie) provided five additional return journeys on Saturdays and two at peaks Monday to Friday, while Route 42 (Gourdon–Inverbervie–Laurencekirk) also ran four Saturday journeys and two on Mondays.[20] The Alexanders bus timetable for 1929 shows twelve daily journeys and fourteen on Saturdays compared with a handful of railway journeys. The cost advantage of buses was also overwhelming for the operator; Lofts estimates that in 1950 operating costs for a train were 12½ times that of a bus.[21]

TABLE 12: TRAFFIC LEVELS 1946-1947 – INVERBERVIE BRANCH

STATION	BERVIE		GOURDON		JOHNSHAVEN		LAURISTON		ST. CYRUS		TOTAL BRANCH	
PASSENGER TRAFFIC	1946	1947	1946	1947	1946	1947	1946	1947	1946	1947	1946	1947
Season Tickets	0	0	0	0	12	17	0	0	0	7	12	24
Seasons Revenue £	0	0	0	0	22	26	0	0	0	7	22	33
Tickets Sold	2,761	1,883	7,778	4,941	3,937	2,762	300	212	1,661	1,210	16,437	11,008
Ticket Revenue £	305	241	446	360	465	391	23	21	353	322	1,592	1,335
Misc Forwarded tons	0	0	1,401	1,121	123	146	7	2	0	0	1,531	1,269
Misc Received tons	0	0	30	126	43	10	0	0	0	0	73	136
Other Revenue £	0	0	10	10	0	0	0	0	26	10	36	20
Parcels Forwarded	855	650	905	854	773	704	157	91	603	568	3,293	2,867
Parcels Received	2,085	1,726	908	888	1,756	955	139	147	673	757	5,561	4,473
Parcels Revenue £	127	155	7,203	6,412	934	1,023	21	9	214	127	8,499	7,726
Total Receipts £	432	396	7,659	6,782	1,421	1,440	44	30	593	466	10,149	9,114
GOODS TRAFFIC												
Goods Forwarded tons			7,202	8,688	Gourdon returned the goods figures for the whole of the branch.						7,202	8,688
Goods Received tons			2,394	2,574							2,394	2,574
Minerals Received tons			2,951	2,017							2,951	2,017
Coal Received tons			4,574	4,714							4,574	4,714
Goods Revenue £			12,135	19,425							12,135	19,425

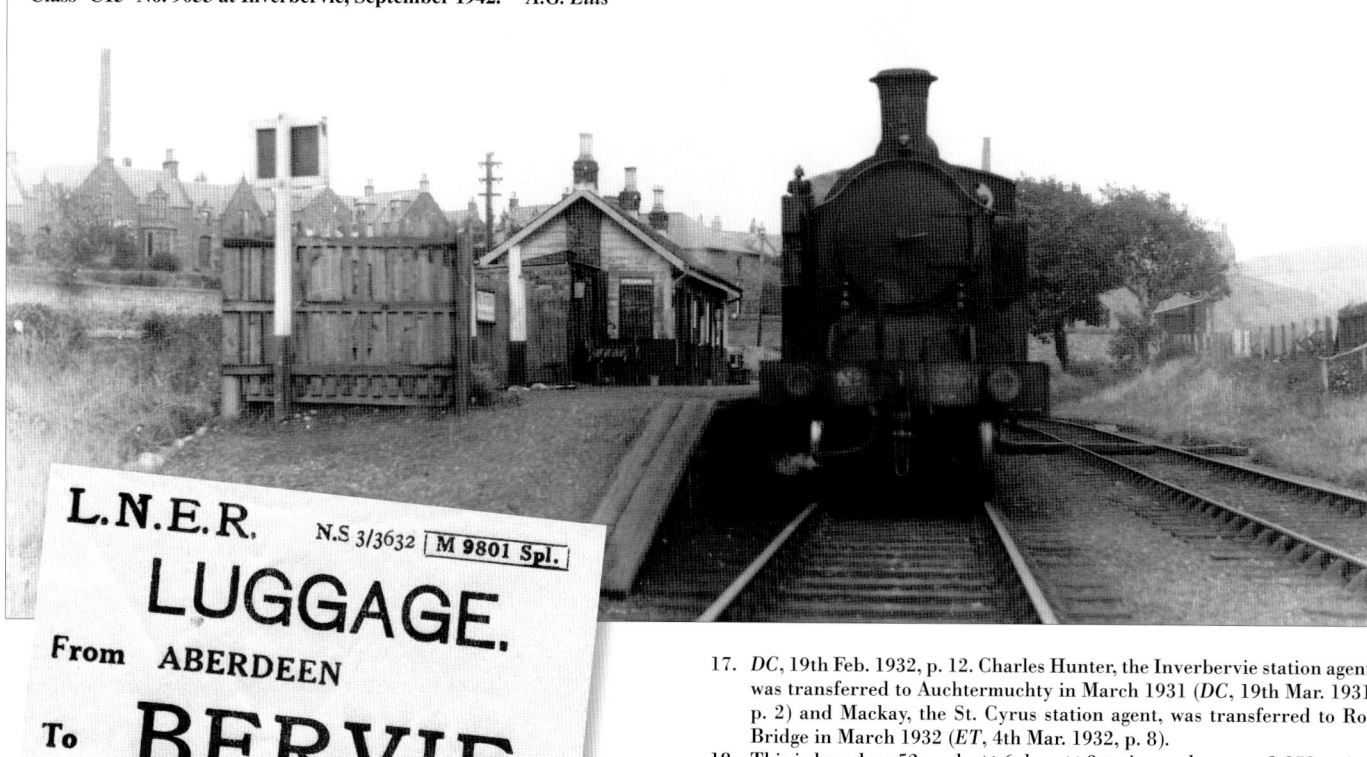

Class 'C15' No. 9053 at Inverbervie, September 1942.   *A.G. Ellis*

Notes

1. *AJ*, 22nd Feb. 1919, p. 5.
2. *AJ*, 1st Oct. 1919, p. 6.
3. *DC*, 28th Oct. 1921, p. 5. By 1924 J. Peter & Co had introduced services from Montrose to Forfar and Edzell (*DC*, 18th Jun. 1924, p. 5, and 18th Sep. 1924, p. 4).
4. *DC*, 19th Jul. 1921, p. 1. One of the operators was Will, Dundee.
5. *DC*, 13th Apr. 1926, p. 5. The others were Edinburgh (3,400), Tayport/Newport (1,300), St Andrews (1,200) and Aberdeen (1,100).
6. *DC*, 31st Aug. 1921, p. 6, and 21st Sep. 1921, p. 3.
7. *ET*, 23rd Jul. 1928, p. 1.
8. *DC*, 20th Apr. 1929, p. 2.
9. [Aberdeen] *Press & Journal* [*P&J*], 4th May 1929, p. 1. Buses left Aberdeen every hour from 6.30am to 9pm and Dundee at 7am to 10pm (11pm on Saturdays).
10. *DC*, 14th Jan. 1929, p. 6. Fourteen months earlier the *ET* (21st Nov. 1927, p. 1) had reported on another Thistle bus that suffered a brake failure on the way to Montrose – after the driver succeeded in steering into the ditch, the bus was towed back to Bervie.
11. Full details of signalling can be found in Appendix 3.
12. For example, in *ET* (23rd Aug. 1929, p. 9) an advert appeared by the L&NER for service suspensions on the Bervie line, and that Alexanders buses would run as near as possible to the train times.
13. NRS figures from traffic returns in files BR/LNE/4.
14. *P&J*, 7th Feb. 1929, p. 8. The Customs Committee of Inverbervie Town Council were empowered to '*take the necessary steps to for the protection of the public*' in connection with this light railway, though it was not specified what these steps were.
15. *P&J*, 1st Oct. 1929, p. 7. In fact the Strathpeffer Branch continued until closure to passengers at the end of 1946; the Black Isle (Fortrose) line closed to passengers on 1st October 1951. The L&NER branches to Boddam (Cruden Bay) and Oldmeldrum closed to passengers on 31st October 1932 and 2nd November 1931 respectively.
16. NRS file BR/LNE/23/361 (accountant's file on branch line closures) letter dated 12th August 1930, listed the following branches for possible closure: Leslie, Torrance, Port Carlisle, Lauder, Selkirk, Gifford (including Monktonhall–Ormiston), Glencorse, Penicuik, Invergarry & Fort Augustus, Inverbervie, Newburgh & North Fife, Old Meldrum, Alford, Banff, St Combs and Cruden. Detailed analysis was given for most of them, but that for the Bervie line has not survived.
17. *DC*, 19th Feb. 1932, p. 12. Charles Hunter, the Inverbervie station agent, was transferred to Auchtermuchty in March 1931 (*DC*, 19th Mar. 1931, p. 2) and Mackay, the St. Cyrus station agent, was transferred to Roy Bridge in March 1932 (*ET*, 4th Mar. 1932, p. 8).
18. This is based on 52 weeks × 6 days × 3 trains each way = 1,872 trains. Originating freight traffic is divided by outbound trains only (i.e., 936).
19. The latest traffic data available in the National Records of Scotland are for the years 1946 and 1947. Unfortunately no data has been found covering the subsequent years following nationalisation, and information on cost allocations is also lacking, so it has not been possible to establish the subsequent financial state of the branch other than by deduction from the reducing service and shorter trains.
20. *Scottish Bus Timetable* (SMT Group), Oct.–Dec. 1947.
21. C. Lofts, *Last Trains: Dr Beeching and the Death of Rural England* (London, 2013).

CHAPTER 12

BRITISH RAILWAYS AND CLOSURE

The inevitable closure of the passenger service nevertheless took four more years to implement. It was not until September 1951 that British Railways (Scottish Region) notified Montrose Town Council that the line was being considered for closure to passengers due to poor patronage. The expenditure on two passenger trains a day was *'out of proportion to the small receipts'*.[1] The closure submission to the British Transport Commission (BTC) gave the figures shown here.

TABLE 13: INVERBERVIE BRANCH CLOSURE SUBMISSION 1950			
TOTAL BRANCH: 1950 PASSENGER RATED TRAFFIC	£	£	£
Ticket revenue	2,578		
Parcels revenue	10,072		
Current passenger revenue			12,650
Less: Estimated loss of parcels receipts		1,500	
Less: Estimated additional road cartage costs		250	
Net revenue retained			8,322
Add: Train working savings			3,913
Net position after passenger closure			12,235

The BR submission claimed a *'net annual economy'* of £2,163, representing the train working saving less the loss of parcels receipts and additional cartage costs, whereas the estimate demonstrated that if the expectation that £1,750 lower parcels receipts and additional costs materialized, these and the loss of passenger receipts would actually exceed the train working savings. There was, however, a claim of further unquantified savings from maintenance. Revenue had increased since 1947 in both categories of passenger traffic, largely due to rate increases, but still amounted to only £1.38 per train from passengers and £5.38 for parcels. In the same time period costs were rapidly increasing as successive substantial wage settlements were agreed to. The government was anxious to avoid the threat of strikes in what was still a vital national transport network on which the country depended for the movement of heavy freight in particular. The BTC gave its approval for the passenger closure on 24th April 1951.[2]

A few months later, in September, BR announced that the passenger service would be withdrawn.[3] The reaction among the local authorities was interesting. The Provost of Montrose said that while there was a *'reasonable'* bus service, the withdrawal would not have been necessary if the railway provided a better service and cheaper fares. However, since all the stations were in Kincardineshire, it was not a matter for Montrose! Inverbervie Town Council merely noted at their meeting on 18th October 1951 that the passenger service was being withdrawn and that W. Alexanders had sent them a new timetable.

The last regular passenger train from Inverbervie ran on Saturday 29th September 1951, hauled by Class 'J39/2' locomotive No. 64790, with virtually no notice being taken of it by the inhabitants. The *Dundee Courier* carried a brief report, with a picture of the train at St. Cyrus, where its departure was marked by the local postman, in full piper's regalia, playing *'Will ye no come back again'*. There were fourteen passengers on the two-carriage train, *'the busiest for months'* according to the *Courier*. One loyal passenger, Herbert Hay of St. Cyrus, who had used the service twice a day, six days a week, since 1919, told the reporter:

I'm terribly disappointed that it had to be taken off. I'll miss it very much. It's so much quicker and more comfortable than the bus, but there's nothing else for it now. I have made this trip thousands of times before, but I just want to have a last kick. There's been a big drop in passenger traffic since I first began to use the train. And the fares are so high. Once my monthly return cost 18s and before that it was even cheaper. Now it's over 27s.[4]

RIGHT: The last regular passenger train from Bervie, headed by Cowlairs Class 'J39/2' No. 64790, at St. Cyrus. *Kenneth Hay*

FACING PAGE: Flowers for the driver of No. 64790 at St. Cyrus. *Kenneth Hay*

Ex-NBR Class 'J37' 0-6-0 No. 64624 heads the goods trip to Montrose through Gourdon in the early 1960s. No. 64624 was introduced into service in January 1921 and was finally withdrawn in January 1966.
Kenneth Hay

CHAPTER 12: BRITISH RAILWAYS AND CLOSURE

ABOVE: On another bright day in summer 1964, No. 64624 awaits departure at Bervie. *Les Moffat*

LEFT: Several rail tours were operated in the late 1950s and 1960s, usually using one of the Tay Bridge Class 'J37's. This one was unusual in using No. D8028, one of the then nearly new Class '20' English Electric 1,000hp Bo-Bo locomotives. Here it is leaving Inverbervie on 22nd April 1962, on a 'Scottish Rambler' tour.
Stuart Sellar

Mr Hay would have found that the bus fare to Montrose was 10d return, with a monthly ticket around £1.

Freight services lasted a few years longer. The increase in goods seen after the war reversed as road haulage increased and some traders obtained their own transport. The daily freight trip worked by the Montrose Station pilot engine in the 1952 timetable soon became a twice-weekly trip, latterly conveying half a dozen wagons at most. Coal for the merchant at Inverbervie (Smith Hood & Co.) was often the only consignment by the late 1950s, though sometimes vans of fish or parcels for the Bervie and Gourdon mills would appear, and at seed potato time vans would be required in some numbers. This could not continue, of course, and the line closed completely with effect from Monday 23rd May 1966. The only surprise was that it lasted as long as it did.

In contrast to the passenger closure in 1951, however, the final closure received a massive public send-off. A Johnshaven lady, Mrs Mary Officer, who wanted to give her young son an opportunity to travel on the line before it closed, took the unprecedented step of hiring a train from BR to do a last run.

This was well before the days when such arrangements were normal, and she was conscious that she was taking a big financial risk with a hire charge of £200, a considerable sum in 1966.[5]

In the event, even though the weather was poor, so many people came to ride on the last train that many passengers had to stand in the corridors of the six-coach train on its two runs to Bervie, Class 'J37' locomotive No. 64547 having to be assisted up St. Cyrus bank by a diesel shunter (No. D3343) when it stalled on the first run.

This evocative description of the last day's events was written for the *Montrose Standard* by Robert Kennedy:

I was ticket collector on the last train from Inverbervie, last Sunday afternoon. Even the sky wept a deluge on the late lamented train. And seldom has a Bervie train been so lamented or so late. It was due to start off at 1.30 from Montrose for the

MARY OFFICER

Mrs Mary Officer may have seen herself as an ordinary housewife and mother. But when British Railways 35 years ago attempted discreet closure of a little branch line, she proved more than a match for them.

The formal legal notice early in 1966 by BR that the goods-only railway from Montrose to Inverbervie would close drove her to lay aside household duties and pester railway brass until officials were persuaded enough to lay on a last train. Aged 29 and with a young family, Mary could not mask her distaste that such a distinctive part of the local community was being put to rest without so much as a fond farewell.

This was no Beeching closure, for the century-old line had given up on its last passenger train in 1951. But trains were part of Mary's life; each weekday she watched the daily goods train rumble past her home adjacent to Johnshaven station.

What Mary didn't realise when rallying family and friends to market the train was the tiger she had by the tail. Orders for tickets flooded in from all corners of the UK, as far away as the south coast of England. The train grew from two coaches to six, the maximum number the line could accommodate. With a growing waiting list, she partially solved the problem by having the train make two runs up and down the 12-mile line, and over 700 tickets were sold.

The energetic Mrs Officer and her troops insisted on a gala spirit for Sunday 22nd May 1966. The vintage North British 0-6-0 tender loco that saw local duties in Montrose was specially cleaned up, and flags and bunting decorated each of the five stations along the line ...

Mary Officer in front of the train she hired.   *Aberdeen Journals*

Platform pipers and guards of honour supplied by Brownies and Guides were matched by support from the provosts of Montrose and Inverbervie. For the occasion Provost William Johnston of Montrose insisted on wearing full civic regalia complete with top hat, and being accompanied by his scarlet-jacketed Halberdier George Davie. The crowds at Montrose were enough to have the station bookstall opened for the first time on a Sunday in a quarter of a century ...

The train cost Mrs Officer £200 to hire. '*To her, it was worth every penny*' said her husband David. '*She couldn't bear to let the occasion of the last train pass*'. The event proved a one-off, and she never again ventured into the world of railways.

She was born in London within the sound of Bow Bells, daughter of an expatriate Scots Guardsman. On his discharge from the regiment, the family returned to Kincardineshire. An enthusiast for plants and flowers, she was a founder member of Johnshaven Horticultural Society.

Mary Elizabeth Officer nee Myles, born 7th May 1937 in London, died 22nd October 2001 at Johnshaven, Kincardineshire, aged 64.

SOUVENIR TICKET

The bearer of this ticket is permitted to travel on the

LAST TRAIN

on the Montrose-Inverbervie Branch Line on Sunday, 22nd May, 1966

One return journey — 5/-.

Gordon Casely

double journey. When zero hour arrived the six coaches were there, waiting at the small bay platform with N.B. steam engine No. 64547. But there was not a soul on board. The platform was empty too.

Behind locked glass doors, in the entrance hall and waiting room, the station officials were still struggling to transform a milling crowd of about five hundred would-be travellers into an orderly couple of lines to get their tickets punched. There were to be no gate-crashers on this trip. There was no room for them. As I tried to elbow my way through the crowd, there were moments when I wondered whether I would ever reach the glass doors, to punch their tickets before they got on to the platform. But eventually the last ticket was punched and I ran madly through the rain to be last aboard the bulging train. That second last trip to Inverbervie and intermediate stations started twenty minutes late. And just because it was pouring and the rails were going to be slippery, a diesel engine was slipped on at the back at the last moment.

One advantage of being last aboard is the fact that, no matter how crowded the train may be, you always have a window to lean out of. I had that as far as St. Cyrus—and those first six miles were the most exciting part of the journey.

All along the lineside, people were waving handkerchiefs or flags, ringing bells or blowing trumpets. Bunting was hanging over the line at Kinnaber Farm. The rain ran down my nose as I watched the long line of cars drawn up to see us crossing the North Water Bridge [sic]. There must have been hundreds of snapshots taken as the train puffed proudly across. The carriages were gaily decorated with streamers. The engine had its buffers painted white and on the headboard was painted the

CHAPTER 12: BRITISH RAILWAYS AND CLOSURE

ABOVE: The last train waits to leave Montrose. The Montrose Provost's Halberdier and Town Officer, George Davie, stands guard. *Gordon Casely*

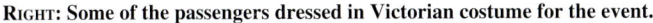

ABOVE: The Montrose Provost William Johnson, at Bervie. His counterpart Provost R.A. Baker of Bervie was also present. *Gordon Casely*

RIGHT: Some of the passengers dressed in Victorian costume for the event. *Norris Forrest*

Approaching Gourdon from the south. *Mike Stephen*

No. 64547 leaving Bervie. Note the Second World War pillbox and tank traps on the right. *Author*

legend 'Last Train to Inverbervie', made by Andrew Kennedy. He still has it, as a souvenir.

In pouring rain the elderly steam engine led the way up the hill north of the bridge, by far the steepest gradient of all. A few weeks ago a special train stuck on that gradient and had to reverse back down. This time too the engine was slipping a lot. But the banking diesel at the back pushed her on.

All along the Aberdeen road we could see a long line of slow-moving cars, sounding their horns and keeping pace with the train.

Though originally it was hoped that this would be the main line to Aberdeen, the country stations were never planned to cope with anything as big as a six-coach train. The train was too long for the stations, even though the railway officials had sealed off the first three carriages.

CHAPTER 12: BRITISH RAILWAYS AND CLOSURE

Leaving Gourdon. *Mike Stephen*

A policeman was on duty at St. Cyrus—and at every other station along the line—to make sure that only the ticket-holders got through. The doors were locked, just in case anyone might fall out, and with a chorus of whistles and cheers we were on our way again. There was no risk of me falling out. A farmer and his wife from St. Cyrus were leaning out of my window now.

Still more people, came on at Johnshaven, Gourdon and Inverbervie. It was becoming very difficult to get along the corridors to clip the tickets and to make matters worse, some people almost panicked at the thought that I might not give them back their souvenir tickets after I had clipped them. I finished up chasing one old lady in and out along the crowded corridor, before I finally got her ticket punched. I carried on to the end of the train. As I was coming back, she swiped at me with a rolled up newspaper.

Eventually we reached Inverbervie. It had not been a fast run by any means. Even with the aid of the diesel shunting engine, banking in the rear, we took over an hour to make the northward journey. Coming back, we knew what it was like to be in a crowded train. There were fourteen passengers in one compartment and seventeen in another. It is wonderful how many you can squeeze in, when teenagers are willing to sit in the luggage racks!

I spent the homeward journey, punching tickets with a vengeance. There was inside information that some people had pushed past the police at the little stations, and got aboard without tickets. But the inside information was wrong.

There was not a single stowaway to be seen. And in these days when we hear so much about vandalism, it is pleasant to record that there was not a trace of vandalism, though eight hundred passengers of all ages made the sentimental journey that afternoon.

The weather was better for the second run but not so many people made the journey this time and I got a seat at last. Mrs Officer, the organiser of the trip, was up in front, in the engine. The diesel had been left at Montrose. Provost Peter of Inverbervie and the members of the Council were in the train. So was Provost Johnston, with Montrose town officer Mr. George Davie, the one in his robes and the other in his scarlet uniform.

Tape recorders were in evidence. There was a battery of whirring cine cameras at the North Water and the hill beyond.

At Inverbervie a man brought his bicycle aboard for the last run down. The Provosts of the two Royal Burghs shook hands in farewell and 64547, with a long-drawn-out whistle, pulled out of the northern terminus.

The train was only half full now. There was time to lean out of the window, and wave to the people of the coast who had come to say goodbye. Some sheep had come as well. A stop was made to chase them off the line. There were flags and bunting at the level crossing gates beside the line, and handkerchiefs waving from the carriage widows, as the train came down the hill and over the bridge and across the fields to Montrose for the last time.

The track was lifted soon afterwards, and most of the wooden station buildings disappeared within a few years. Today the course of the line is a walk and cycleway between Inverbervie and Johnshaven, and over the North Esk Viaduct, which still exists. Between Johnshaven and St. Cyrus most of the line has been ploughed into the fields, with only the stone overbridges and the well-hidden Den Finella Viaduct as reminders of the line.[6]

ABOVE: At Gourdon Bay. *Mike Stephen*

BELOW: Emerging from Lauriston Bridge. *Author*

CHAPTER 12: BRITISH RAILWAYS AND CLOSURE

ABOVE AND LEFT: Crossing the Montrose Links.
Author

BELOW: Arriving at Montrose. Here the John Menzies bookstall opened on a Sunday for the first time in a quarter of a century. *Gordon Casely*

THE MONTROSE & BERVIE RAILWAY

The Line in Retrospect

In many respects the Bervie Branch was a typical railway branch line. It enjoyed a relatively profitable existence until the emergence of road transport after the First World War, when the greater convenience and frequency of competing bus services rapidly eroded its passenger traffic. Freight traffic took longer to disappear, with road lorries initially taking the general goods traffic and, after the Second World War, the minerals and coal traffic. By the mid-1930s the line had become irrelevant for passenger traffic, and an anachronism for freight by the late 1950s.

The Montrose Provost felt that better service and lower fares would have prevented the passenger closure, but given the location of Inverbervie and Montrose stations, even a more frequent service operating later into the evening would have been unlikely to have prevented the decline, and would have been uncompetitive with the buses in cost terms. In other cases the arrival of modern diesel multiple unit trains helped reduce costs and provide a more attractive service, but in all these cases in the rest of north-east Scotland this was a temporary reprieve.

It must be asked why the L&NER and then British Railways took so long to react to what was a very clear and probably irreversible

ABOVE: At Bervie the site of the station still exists, though apart from a section of platform wall and the outline of the turntable, nothing now remains to indicate its former use. The housing development on the left of the station wall is recent. *Author*

LEFT: The old trackbed is now a public walkway from Bervie to Johnshaven, but from there to the North Esk Viaduct most of it has disappeared into the farmland it was built on. This is the scene from Lauriston overbridge looking toward St. Cyrus. *Author*

FACING PAGE TOP: One or two stone overbridges still remain … *Bob Reid*
FACING PAGE BOTTOM: … and the North Esk Viaduct is now part of a walk and cycleway, having been fitted with safety barriers. *Author*

decline. It seems inconceivable in today's world that a line clearly losing its passenger business would be allowed to carry on for several years with a full passenger service carrying handfuls of passengers without either positive action to restore the situation, or closure. It was not because railway managers were unaware of the position; detailed returns of traffic were submitted regularly by local agents, and the Montrose stationmaster commented in 1951 that *'for days on end'* only two or three passengers used the service.[7] The

financial position of the L&NER, and later of BR, was such that both organisations should have been eager to remove costs where they could, but this did not happen at anything like the speed expected by a business today. Partly it seems to have been the delay in obtaining permission to close the passenger service from the BTC, but that is only part of the cause, as it still took until 1950 before a closure submission to them was made. Perhaps it was the sheer scale of the task, and the fact that the Bervie Branch was a very small part of the operation. Perhaps also it was because decisions on closures, inevitably, were centralised and taken at very senior level, where many other concerns were present. The Montrose stationmaster may well have been aware of the position of the branch, but it was not within his power to do anything about it.

This is not the place to discuss the wider issues of railway network contraction. The reader is instead referred to the excellent study of railway closures and the impetus behind them in Charles Loft's *Last Trains: Dr Beeching and the Death of Rural England'*. Despite the fact that the Bervie Branch was in Scotland, his conclusions are nevertheless relevant. In particular he quotes a Southern Region Commercial Superintendent, who responded to demands for more closures with the complaint that:

no machinery exists within the commercial department for the ascertaining of revenue on a branch or at an individual station and this results in all such information having to be obtained from the accountant, in whose department all cases fell to be assessed by one group of staff who have their ordinary work to do … A somewhat similar position exists on the expenditure side.[8]

The Bervie line probably lasted as long as it did because of similar issues.

It is tempting to consider whether the line might have developed a new role as a 'heritage railway' had it lasted into the 1970s or '80s. Certainly the scenery is attractive enough, with the run out over the Montrose Links, the dramatic crossing of the North Esk Viaduct and the cliff-foot run through Johnshaven and Gourdon to Inverbervie past the stately homes of Brotherton and Hallgreen being at least as good as most other 'preserved' lines. At twelve miles long (thirteen if the NBR connection to Montrose station is included) it was not over-long, and was well-situated, being about thirty miles from the two major cities of Aberdeen and Dundee. Perhaps it might have been an alternative to the nearby relatively pastoral line from Bridge of Dun to Brechin which is less scenic (and shorter) but has a much more impressive terminal station building in the city of Brechin. Crucially, however, the Brechin Branch remained open later and thus survived into the 'preservation era'. Had the Bervie line survived in a new role as a 'pleasure ride' it might have been able to contribute to the economy of east Kincardineshire in a way its builders would never have envisaged.

NOTES

1. *DC*, 13th Mar. 1951, p. 4.
2. The National Archive file AN13/1740 contains the closure submission, although the branch does not appear on the file description in the National Archive catalogue. At this time the level of financial analysis required was minimal, but even then the delay between submission and decision was lengthy. Lofts, op. cit., discusses the part played in the early post-nationalised railways by government interference in wages policy.
3. *DC*, 5th Sep. 1951, p. 3.
4. *DC*, 1st Oct. 1951, p. 2.
5. *P&J*, 23rd May 1966. By comparison, a substantial house in Aberdeen at the time cost around £1,000. She arranged printing of the tickets and was reported to be '*very pleased*' (and no doubt relieved) that over 800 people travelled at 5 shillings each, exactly covering her outlay on the train hire.
6. The connecting lines at Broomfield Junction closed as follows: Broomfield–Montrose CR (passenger), 30th April 1943 (trains from Brechin diverted to Montrose from Montrose (East); Broomfield–Dubton–Brechin (passenger), 4th August 1952; Broomfield–Dubton (freight), 20th June 1963; Montrose East–Broomfield and Broomfield–Montrose (freight), 19th June 1967.
7. *DC*, 1st Oct. 1951, p. 2.
8. National Archive file AN177/2, Mepstead-Hopkins, 13th June 1951, quoted in Lofts, op. cit., endnote 48.

Above: Stuart Sellar photographed Montrose East in its last days.

Right: Happily a new use was found for this imposing building and it now forms the award-winning centrepiece of a sheltered housing development. *Author*

Chapter 13

A Summer Holiday on the Bervie Line

In July 1964, Michael Mensing spent a few days photographing the goods trains on the branch while on holiday in the area. These beautiful photographs capture the atmosphere of the line, as its ancient Class 'J37' locomotives moved the odd van of fish and wagon of coal along the coast north of Montrose in the final years of the line. All the photographs in this chapter are by Michael Mensing.

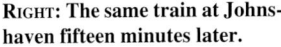

ABOVE: No. 64558 heads the daily pick-up freight from Montrose off the North Esk Viaduct on 6th July 1964.

RIGHT: The same train at Johnshaven fifteen minutes later.

ABOVE: The return working was due out of Bervie at 3pm. The driver was Willie Smith.

BELOW: No. 64558 is seen running round Gourdon Bay towards Johnshaven.

CHAPTER 13: A SUMMER HOLIDAY ON THE BERVIE LINE

ABOVE: A couple of days later, on 8th July 1964, No. 64608 running tender first is about to pass under the Lauriston overbridge while a surfaceman scythes the grass. In the background a competing lorry heads in the same direction.

BELOW: A short distance later, No. 64608 pauses at Lauriston. Latterly the station building was curtailed to only the 'CR' extension.

ABOVE: At Gourdon …
BELOW: … and awaiting return at Bervie. The Karrier railway lorry is transferring freight to the van.
FACING PAGE TOP: Running along the shore at Gourdon Bay, one of the most spectacular stretches of the line.
FACING PAGE BOTTOM: A couple of days later, on 8th July, No. 64608 leaves St. Cyrus to descend the 1 in 50 incline towards the North Esk Viaduct and Montrose. The St. Cyrus camping coach can be seen in the siding. Camping Coach No. DM SC12 was originally built by the Caledonian Railway in 1913 as a Composite Lavatory to Diagram 113, in its previous identity it carried number SC19956 before being converted in May 1953.

CHAPTER 13: A SUMMER HOLIDAY ON THE BERVIE LINE

THE MONTROSE & BERVIE RAILWAY

CHAPTER 13: A SUMMER HOLIDAY ON THE BERVIE LINE 87

FACING PAGE TOP: On 10th July, No. 64624 had just crossed Den Finella Viaduct with a couple of empty vans for Bervie.
FACING PAGE BOTTOM: No. 64624 is running round its train at Bervie, the fireman standing just about where the water tower was.
ABOVE: No. 64624 just south of Johnshaven.
BELOW: Approaching St. Cyrus …

ABOVE: Crossing the North Esk Viaduct.
BELOW: Michael's final visit to the line in 1964 was on 16th July to see No. 64624 crossing the North Esk Viaduct on its way to Bervie.
FACING PAGE TOP: Just north of Johnshaven.
FACING PAGE BOTTOM: Leaving Bervie, having dropped off the coal wagon.

CHAPTER 13: A SUMMER HOLIDAY ON THE BERVIE LINE

ABOVE: Between Bervie and Gourdon …

BELOW: … and coasting past the Broomfield caravan site into Montrose.

Appendix 1: Turnpike Road Finances

Table A: Turnpike Road debt in Kincardineshire in 1859

Trust	Length (Miles)	Toll Gates	£ In Hand	£ Debt etc*	£ Accum. Interest	Comments
Consolidated	58	6	3,647	0	0	Regulated by 1795 Act, renewed in 1816 and 1838. Previously four trusts. Original debt £12,000.
Slug	16	3	0	1,852	5,212	Regulated by Acts of 1800, 1820 and 1842. Debt purchased by Consolidated Trust @ £9,825 for £750.
South Deeside	14	2	0	11,550	5,758	Regulated by Act of 1837. Paid interest at around 3½%.
Netherley	11	1	922	161		Regulated by Act of 1820.
Marykirk Bridge	na	na	0	6,250	719	Act of 1811.
Wellington Suspension Bridge	na	na	0	9,815	0	Act 1829; £9,815 subscribed. None paid off, but 3% paid per annum.

* The debt figure includes personal loans.
SOURCE: *Royal Commission on Roads*, 1859.

Table B: Turnpike Road Expenditure in NE Scotland in 1859

Trust	Length (Miles)	Toll Gates	Average Revenue £	Average Maintenance £	Average Admin. £	Total Costs £	Average Revenue £ per mile	Average Costs £ per mile
Consolidated	58	6	761	544	50	594	13.12	10.24
Slug	16	3	290	111	15	126	18.35	7.97
South Deeside	14	2	304	118	10	128	21.71	9.14
Netherley	11	1	51	29	5	34	4.64	3.09
Marykirk Bridge	na	na	256	5	11	16	na	na
Wellington Suspension Bridge	na	na	484	70	12	82	na	na
Kincardineshire								9.50
Aberdeenshire								14.37
Forfarshire								27.09

SOURCE: *Royal Commission on Roads*, 1859, Appendix A.

Table C: Kincardineshire Toll-Houses (South of Stonehaven) 1801-1879

Turnpike Section	Dates	Notes
Stonehaven–Laurencekirk		
Invercarron	1802-1879	Dual toll-house. In use as private residence on A957.
Mondynes–Drumlithie	1801-1857	Still in existence at Bridge of Mondynes just west of A90.
Laurencekirk 1	1801-1832	Possibly just south of school on A937.
Laurencekirk 2	1832-1879	Just north of Spurryhillock turn on A937.
Inglismaldie–Upper North Water Bridge	1832-1878	Still in existence, half a mile east of A90.
Stonehaven–Bervie–Montrose		
Invercarron	1801-1879	Dual toll-house. In use as private residence on A957.
Fawside (Kinneff)	1814-1824	West side of road ½ mile south of Fawside. Demolished.
Bridge of Bervie	1801-1879	North side of old bridge; demolished when new bridge built in early 1930s.
Brotherton	1813-1837	Location uncertain. Possibly at at Brotherton Bridge. Demolished circa 1838.
Lower North Water Bridge	1813-1879	North end of bridge. Still in existence 2015 but ruinous, on A92.

TABLE D: TOLL REVENUES FROM TOLL ROUPS 1801-1878 ON BERVIE AND MONTROSE ROADS

	1801	1802	1803	1804	1805	1806	1807	1808	1809	1810
Invercarron (B)*	No data	106	50	50	No data	203	144	157	120	124
Bervie Bridge		125	56	56	112	200	169	120	161	130
Total	223	519	368	368	374	836	650	637	803	696

	1811	1812	1813	1814	1815	1816	1817	1818	1819	1820
Invercarron (B)*	120	176	150	152	Not let	154	151	No data	*143	*128
Fawside		Tollbar erected 1813		51	90	74	68		48	45
Bervie Bridge	141	131	189	121	139	128	136		80	
Brotherton	Toll bar erected 1812		123	85	70	111	108		112	116
Lower North Water Bridge	Toll bar erected 1812		268	255	230	218	249		218	218
Total	711	768	1,303	1,196	679	1,237	1,199	0	719	667

	1821	1822	1823	1824	1825	1826	1827	1828	1829	1830
Invercarron (B)	*123	*120	*125	86	75	81	75	65	75	75
Fawside	40	52	50	Toll bar removed						
Bervie Bridge	118	110	107	86	100	130	100	100	144	144
Brotherton	109	116	115	98	91	115	100	70	77	77
Lower North Water Bridge	229	259	250	243	188	227	232	247	290	290
Total	657	781	522	936	943	1,073	1,006	902	1,006	1,006

	1831	1832	1833	1834	1835	1836	1837	1838	1839	1840
Invercarron (B)	No data	73	74	74	78	55	62	60	*94	*80
Bervie Bridge		146	126	126	145	130	180	150	152	131
Brotherton		99	60	60	70	64	Toll bar removed 1837			
Lower North Water Bridge		295	223	223	Not let	170	176	192	221	195
Total		1,508	1,045	1,045	831	930	1,008	1,627	1,476	1,320

	1841	1842	1843	1844	1845	1846	1847	1848	1849	1850
Invercarron (B)	*85	*83	*100	*103	*112	*119	*148	*139	*117	*56
Bervie Bridge	146	142	129	130	140	131	160	165	118	80
Lower North Water Bridge	195	184	200	216	216	220	234	249	180	100
Total	1,443	892	1,417	1,461	1,490	1,470	1,799	1,824	1,422	749

	1851	1852	1853	1854	1855	1856	1857	1858	1859	1860
Invercarron (B)	*70	*52	*46	*52	*48	*33	*54	*48	*58	*52
Bervie Bridge	112	91	80	104	139	76	64	59	67	77
Lower North Water Bridge	151	153	123	121	90	170	154	146	189	179
Total	835	749	633	670	623	662	632	561	526	463

	1861	1862	1863	1864	1865	1866	1867	1868	1869	1870
Invercarron (B)	*52	*50	*41	*39	*39	*52	*39	*49	*48	*16
Bervie Bridge	69	66	50	74	81	91	79	75	70	20
Lower North Water Bridge	133	136	122	155	101	73	73	80	70	25
Total	376	363	306	379	366	396	348	361	338	131

	1871	1872	1873	1874	1875	1876	1877	1878
Invercarron (B)	*16	*25	*29	*24	*28	*29	*36	*36
Bervie Bridge	22	34	20	20	40	36	31	50
Lower North Water Bridge	51	30	25	25	25	30	48	51
Total	191	186	146	174	170	188	167	217

* Trustees apportioned bids at Invercarron 60/40 Laurencekirk/Bervie roads in 1816 and 1817. Where combined bids placed and not apportioned, the same ratio has been applied.
SOURCE: Minute books of Kincardineshire Turnpike Trustees (figures in £).

TABLE E: KINCARDINESHIRE CONSOLIDATED TURNPIKE TRUSTS FINANCIAL RESULTS 1838-1879														
	1839	1840	1841	1842	1843	1844	1845	1846	1847	1848	1849	1850	1851	1852
Brought Forward	1,092	1,142	1,028	655	205	460	1,310	3,149	0	0	0	0	0	0
Interest Paid	110	401	448	483	457	394	469	283	253	223	153	31	0	0
Road and Bridge Repairs	1,245	2,429	2,667	1,229	1,850	1,520	772	1,258	1,427	805	931	946	603	574
Salaries	15	90	90	85	136	120	80	140	120	160	123	127	133	105
Operating Expenses	4,646	3,200	2,710	3,754	2,675	2,329	1,259	1,811	1,923	1,086	2,831	1,231	855	841
Roup of Tolls	1,627	1,710	1,520	1,655	1,518	1,718	1,667	1,773	1,768	2,170	2,000	1,715	889	1,011
Coach Payments	1,379	1,376	1,441	1,414	1,388	1,441	1,389	1,656	846	1,774	1,623	1,336	81	1
Carried Forward	1,142	1,028	655	205	460	1,310	3,149	0	0	0	0	0	0	0
Operating Income	3,094	3,086	2,991	3,304	2,930	3,179	3,475	1,812	2,614	4,156	3,623	2,788	1,096	1,133
Cash in Bank	580	624	680	59	465	1,522	3,264	4,927	5,619	8,411	792	2,350	2,591	2,883
Bank of Scotland Bond	8,000	8,000	8,000	8,000	8,000	8,000	8,000	8,000	8,000	8,000	0	0	0	0
Mr Wood's Bill	2,000	2,000	2,000	2,000	2,000	2,000	2,000	2,000	2,000	2,000	0	0	0	0
Net Debt	9,420	9,376	9,320	9,941	9,535	8,578	6,736	5,072	4,381	1,589	0	0	0	0
Investments	0	0	0	0	0	0	0	0	0	0	0	0	750	0
														4,365

	1853	1854	1855	1856	1857	1858	1859	1860	1861	1862	1863	1864	1865	1866
Brought Forward	0	0	0	0	0	0	0	0	0	0	0	0	0	0
Interest Paid	0	0	0	0	0	0	0	0	0	0	0	0	0	0
Road and Bridge Repairs	555	480	488	487	430	500	500	494	494	574	590	536	529	590
Salaries	155	130	130	130	100	106	106	113	106	106	106	106	110	110
Operating Expenses	1,754	1,023	881	653	602	711	654	630	624	702	738	679	666	1,611
Roup of Tolls	879	748	799	748	793	728	728	682	672	593	506	487	408	465
Coach Payments	0	0	0	0	0	0	0	0	0	0	0	0	0	0
Carried Forward	0	0	0	0	0	0	0	0	0	0	0	0	0	0
Operating Income	1,204	1,031	1,199	1,063	1,026	990	990	932	882	919	782	733	673	1,482
Cash in Bank	2,243	2,251	2,569	2,913	3,368	3,647	3,647	622	622	881	897	868	747	588
Net Debt	0	0	0	0	0	0	0	0	0	0	0	0	0	0
Investments	750	750	750	750	750	750	750	0	0	0	0	0	0	0
	4,365	4,365	4,365	4,365	4,365	3,565	3,565	3,565	3,565	3,565	3,565	3,565	3,565	3,565

	1867	1868	1869	1870	1871	1872	1873	1874	1875	1876	1877	1878	1879
Brought Forward	0	0	0	0	0	0	0	0	0	0	0	0	0
Interest Paid	0	0	0	0	0	0	0	0	0	0	0	0	0
Road and Bridge Repairs	533	593	590	596	523	506	479	458	545	526	524	No Data	516
Salaries	110	110	110	110	110	62	67	65	71	72	75		75
Operating Expenses	671	762	733	769	674	946	757	734	645	1,095	625		918
Roup of Tolls	526	447	484	462	171	232	250	218	232	240	260	257	287
Coach Payments	0	0	0	0	0	0	0	0	0	0	0	0	0
Carried Forward	0	0	0	0	0	0	0	0	0	0	0	0	0
Operating Income	635	646	613	623	1,221	946	360	587	468	1,095	531		805
Cash in Bank	537	399	229	24	0	396	147	177	0	94	0	111	0
Net Debt	0	0	0	0	0	0	0	0	0	0	0	0	0
Investments	3,565	3,565	3,565	3,565	2,665	2,665	2,365	1,865	1,865	1,865	1,865	500	0

NOTES:
  Initial £10,000 loans were used to pay off all road trustee individual loans.
  1850: toll revenue was after allowing rebates to toll keepers of £379 due to loss of revenue from Aberdeen Railway.
  1852: instruction to surveyors to reduce expenditure to set targets (£410 in aggregate).
  1853: income received from debt of Slug Road Trust (£5,260 of debt purchased for £750) (£100 in 1853).
  1854: arrears of tolls had become a problem: £44 outstanding from 1852; £91 from 1853, and £89 from 1854. In 1855 £100 was written off as irrecoverable. By 1857 the total arrears had been reduced to £66.
  1861: payments made to Commutation Districts of £494 and most of cash balance invested to produce returns.
  1866: Upper Deeside road transferred from Aberdeenshire Trustees for £885.
SOURCE: Minute books of Kincardineshire Turnpike Trustees (figures in £).

ABOVE: **No. 64598 with a train of vans at Bervie in the 1960s.** *Hugh Davies*

BELOW: **No. 64608 passes Johnshaven yard on its way to Bervie on 22nd February 1964.** *Mike Stephen*

Appendix 2: Railway Infrastructure

Line opened: 1st November 1865.
Line closed: (passenger) 1st October 1951, (freight) 23rd May 1966.

Except where otherwise noted, all stations opened on the first day and closed with passenger and freight closures.

Stations and Structures

All station booking offices were built to the same design, consisting of a wooden frame clad with horizontal planking and with brick chimney stacks at each end. They were built by John Gordon, Montrose. When the Caledonian Railway extensions were added in 1898, these were also wooden framed, but with vertical planking. These extensions were effectively a lengthening of the existing structure, except at Johnshaven where a separate building was constructed, gable end to the railway. The original buildings had a small office and a waiting area, while the CR extension was later used as a store. None of the station buildings survive. Stone-built station agents' houses were provided at St. Cyrus, Lauriston, Johnshaven and Gourdon, but not Bervie (John Elliot lived at 12 Kirkgate); all of these survive. Platforms were initially 150 feet long, but the NBR lengthened them by 1884.

Bervie line stations featured regularly in the 'Best Kept Stations' awards, first on the NBR and then in L&NER days:

St. Cyrus	1892; 1894: 1898; 1913; 1919; 1926; 1930; 1931; 1932; 1933
Lauriston	1894; 1895: 1898; 1919
Johnshaven	1894; 1913; 1926; 1928; 1933
Gourdon	1894; 1895; 1898; 1926; 1927; 1928
Bervie	1894; 1895; 1898; 1902; 1903; 1905; 1913; 1919; 1926; 1927; 1928

Stations were graded into first to fourth class and received a small cash payment accordingly.

NOTE: Distances, in miles and chains, are taken from the February 1884 (NBR) timetable and would be from Montrose NB station.

Broomfield [NO717592] [67ch]

Broomfield was the junction with the SNER and entry to the Montrose & Bervie Railway. Initially a simple junction from the SNER single line from Montrose to Dubton was supplemented by a siding leading from the M&B behind the signal box, which was shown on the east side of the line. It was actually built on the other side of the line. A loading bank was added in 1866.

As built, the layout had gained a facing crossover at the south end, allowing a train to be held at the junction while another accessed the branch. The eastern side of the loop was termed an exchange siding. When the signalling was simplified in May 1927 a buffer stop was erected at the north end of this siding and the northern connection removed.

An 'Aerodrome Siding' just north of Broomfield was installed in 1919 to serve Montrose Airfield. Montrose was the first operational military airfield in Britain when it opened in 1913 to No. 2 Squadron, Royal Flying Corps, at Upper Dysart, just south of Montrose. In early 1914 the RFC moved to Broomfield. It closed in 1920 and the siding was removed in May 1927. RAF Montrose reopened as a training base (though later also with operational aircraft located there) on 1st January 1936, closing for good on 2nd June 1952.

As early as 1867 consideration was being given to closing Broomfield; after the resolution of the access charges dispute with the CR there was little need for it, and therefore it was closed on 1st February 1869. A campaign by Montrose Town Council in 1894 to have it reinstated as a joint station was rebuffed by the NBR.

The wreckage of RAF Airspeed Oxford L9654 lies beside Broomfield Junction signal box on 17th October 1939. Part of one of the aircraft's propellers was made into a clock, and this is on display at the Montrose Air Station Heritage Centre.
Montrose Air Station Heritage Centre

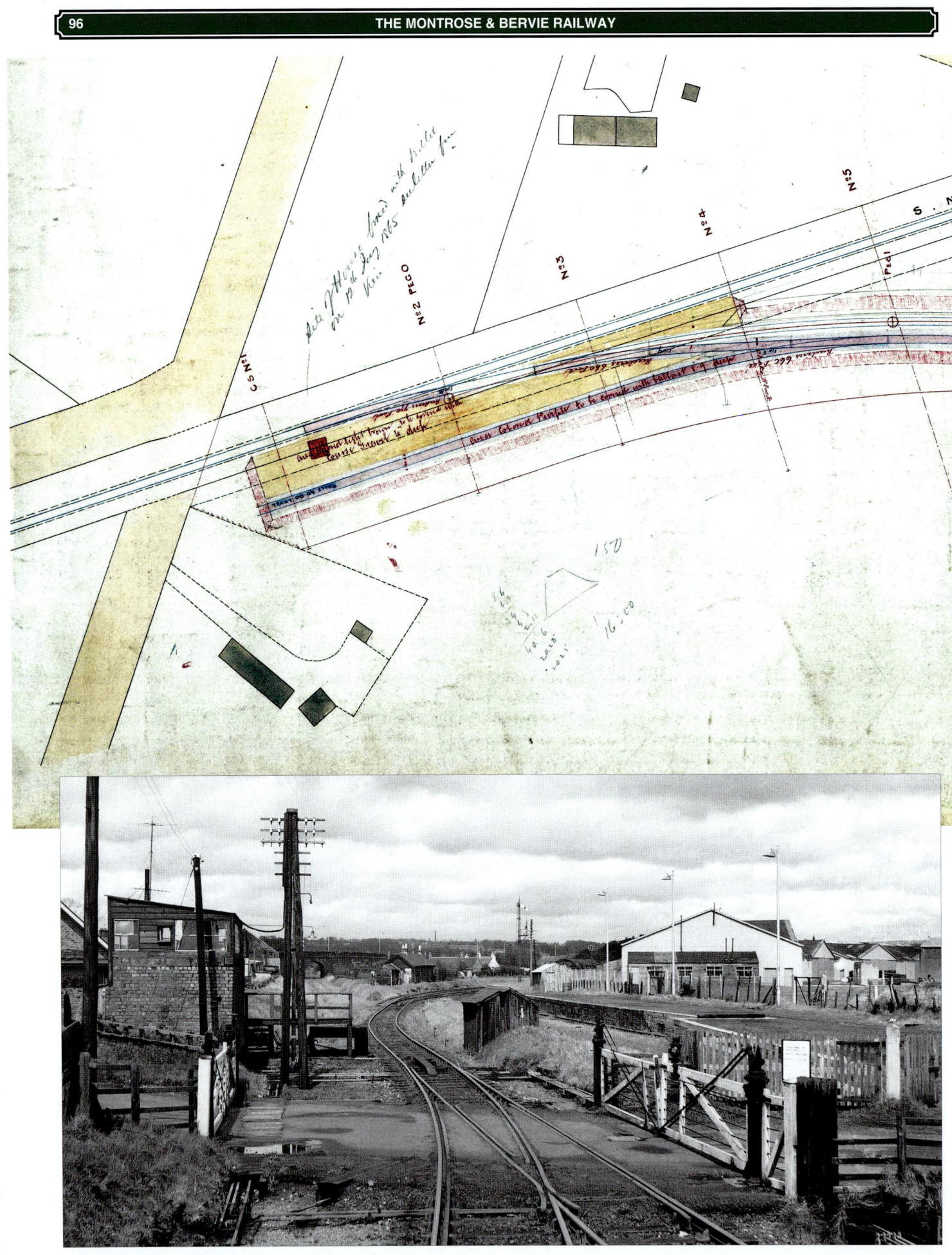

On 17th October 1939 an Airspeed Oxford RAF training aircraft hit the signal box on take-off and demolished it; a *'temporary'* lean-to shed-like structure was put up on the brick substructure, and this remained until the end.

The LM&SR passenger service from Brechin to Montrose LM&S was diverted to Montrose L&NE on 30th April 1943, and Montrose LM&S was closed to passengers. The Brechin–Dubton–Montrose NBR service was withdrawn on 2nd August 1952 and the line from Broomfield to Dubton was closed for freight on 20th June 1963. Montrose (East) (as the LM&SR station had become) to Montrose via Broomfield was closed on 19th June 1967. The line from Broomfield to Dubton was lifted by 1966.

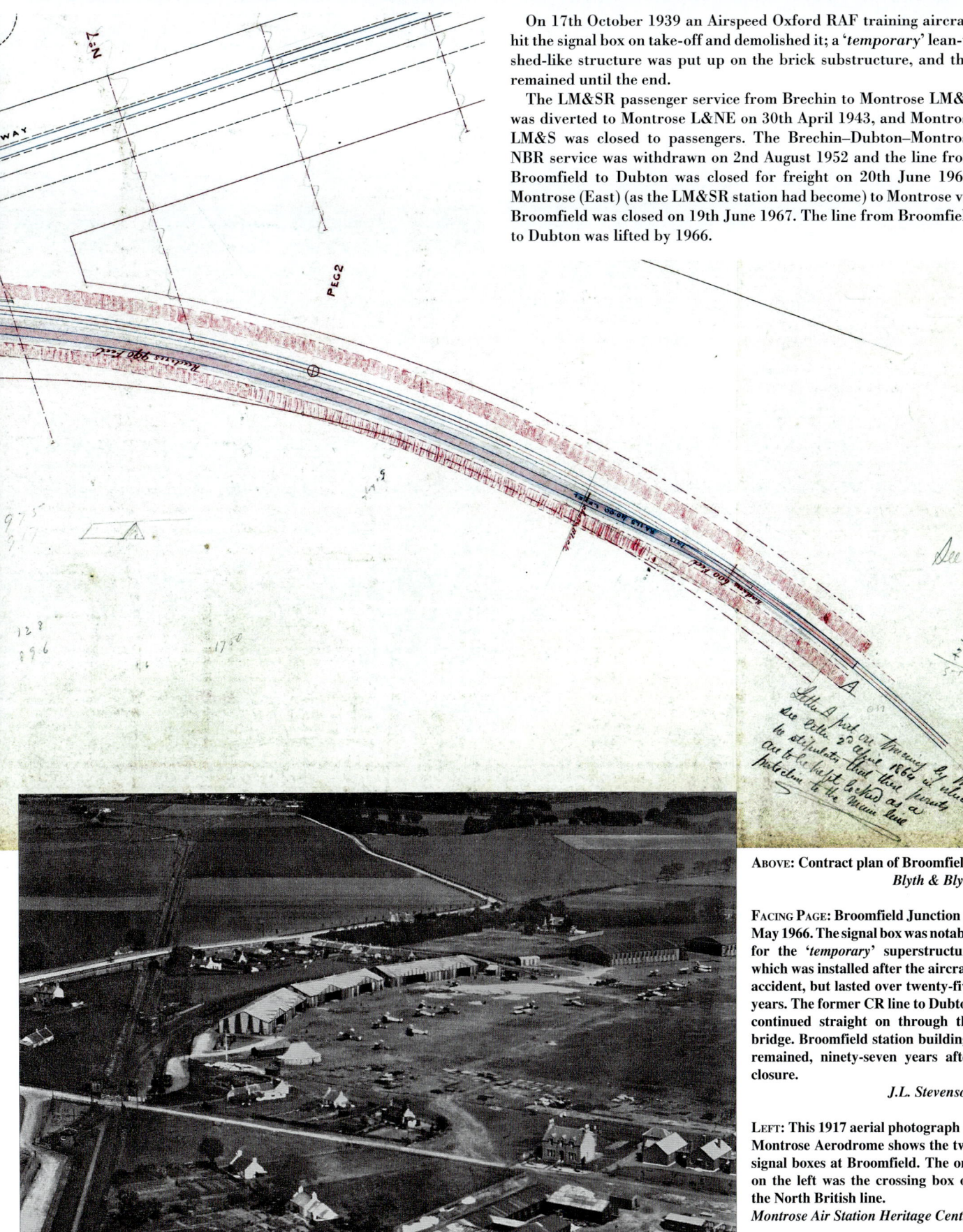

ABOVE: Contract plan of Broomfield.
Blyth & Blyth

FACING PAGE: Broomfield Junction in May 1966. The signal box was notable for the *'temporary'* superstructure which was installed after the aircraft accident, but lasted over twenty-five years. The former CR line to Dubton continued straight on through the bridge. Broomfield station buildings remained, ninety-seven years after closure.
J.L. Stevenson

LEFT: This 1917 aerial photograph of Montrose Aerodrome shows the two signal boxes at Broomfield. The one on the left was the crossing box on the North British line.
Montrose Air Station Heritage Centre

The railway viaduct was the North Esk Viaduct, while the road bridge just upstream is the North Water Bridge (correctly, the Lower North Water Bridge, to differentiate it from the Upper North Water Bridge on the A90 south of Laurencekirk). *J.L. Stevenson, June 1957*

North Esk Viaduct [NO725621]

This is the largest viaduct on the line, and is a major structure built of local stone. It is 200 yards long and around 75 feet high. There are twelve arches – five skew arches of 50 feet span the river, while five arches to the north and two to the south, complete the structure. The 3 mile post (from Montrose CR) was at the south end of the bridge. Repairs were made to the viaduct by British Rail Property Board in 1992/93 at a cost of £200,000. The structure now belongs to Angus and Aberdeenshire councils and it has reopened as a footpath. This was extended three miles to Montrose in 2011.

North Water Bridge [NO725624] [3m 7ch]

North Water Bridge (opened Friday 1st June 1866) was almost invariably referred to by the M&B in official documentation (and the opening press announcement) as a 'station', although it was never staffed. It consisted of a wooden platform on the west (outside) of the curve from the North Esk Viaduct. A flight of wooden stairs led to the main road.

Warburton [NO725623] [3m 8ch]

Warburton appears in the construction plans dated 1864, but was not built, presumably as a cost saving measure. The halt at North Water Bridge was provided in response to pressure from local farmers.

Warburton was to have been built slightly nearer St. Cyrus than the halt which was eventually opened at North Water Bridge; unlike the halt, Warburton would have had goods facilities. *Blyth & Blyth*

RIGHT: Warburton station would have been located about here, and the wider fence line indicates the land it would have occupied. More or less the same site (but slightly nearer the viaduct) was occupied by the North Water Bridge halt. By 1955 the platform and hut had been removed, but it is still possible to see the approach path fencing by the third telephone pole on the right.
J.L. Stevenson, May 1955

BELOW: The North Water Bridge halt. *Lens of Sutton Association*

St. Cyrus [NO748648] [5M 21CH]

St. Cyrus as built had a single line through the station, with a 150-foot platform on the west side only. There were two sidings facing Montrose just before the station, one of which (to the east) led to a goods shed and the other to a 100-foot loading bank. Interestingly, the overbridge at the north end of the station was shown as an underbridge on the initial plan.

Pencil alterations to this plan show a further connection between the goods shed road and the loading bank siding. This loop was used latterly to stable a camping coach (DM SC12). This was last used in 1964 but was still there in May 1965. A cattle pen was added in 1866.

St. Cyrus was a very pretty station with a well-kept station garden, frequently winning Best Kept Station awards. *Lens of Sutton Association*

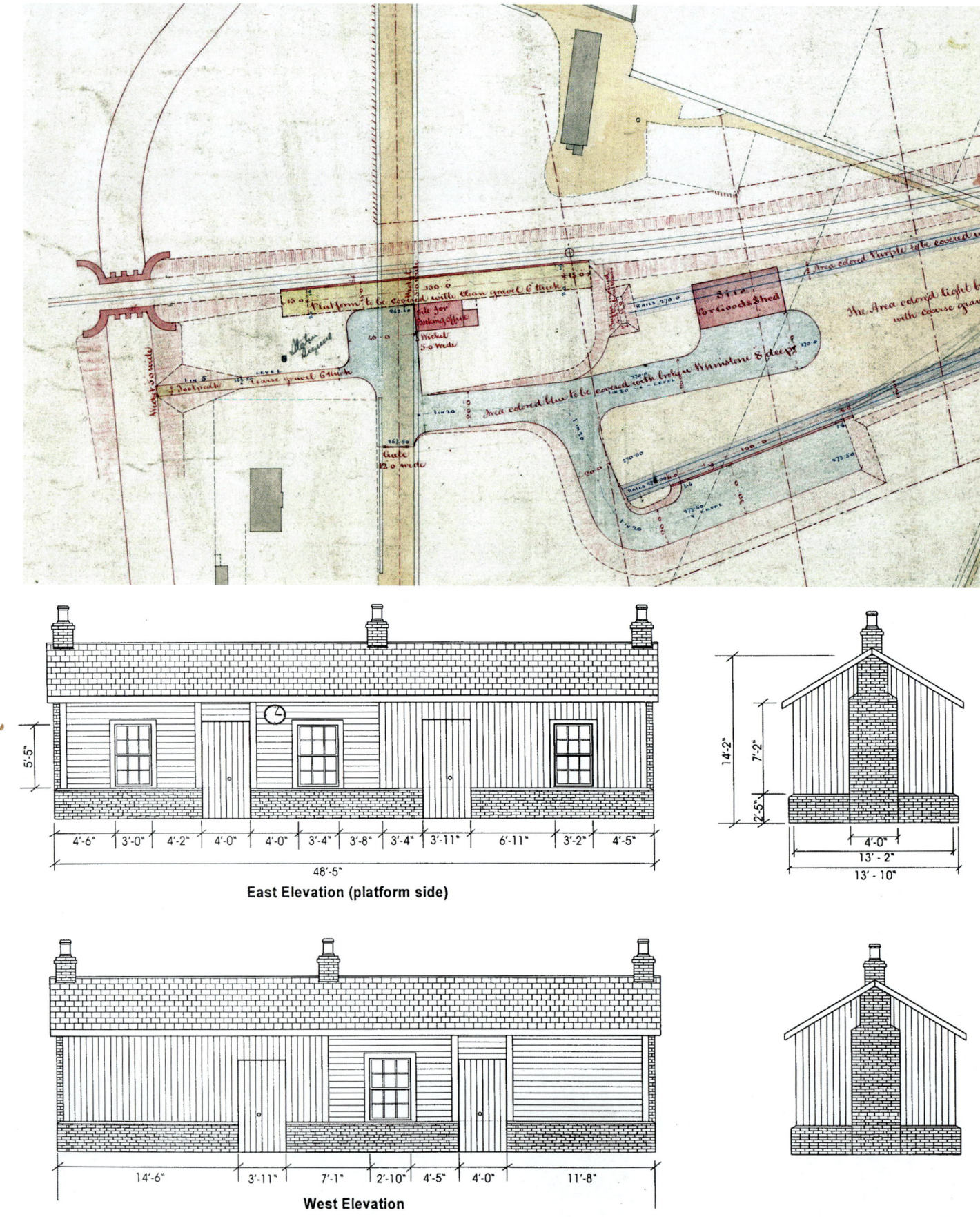

St. Cyrus station building. The vertical-boarded section was the extension requested by the Caledonian Railway for its staff while the running powers dispute was current. The stations at Lauriston, Gourdon and Bervie were identical, but the extension at Johnshaven was in the form of a separate building to a similar design.
Drawing by Allan Rodgers

APPENDICES

LEFT: Contract plan of St. Cyrus. Note the pencil alterations.   *Blyth & Blyth*

BELOW: Planning drawing for St. Cyrus station house.
National Records of Scotland RHP81621

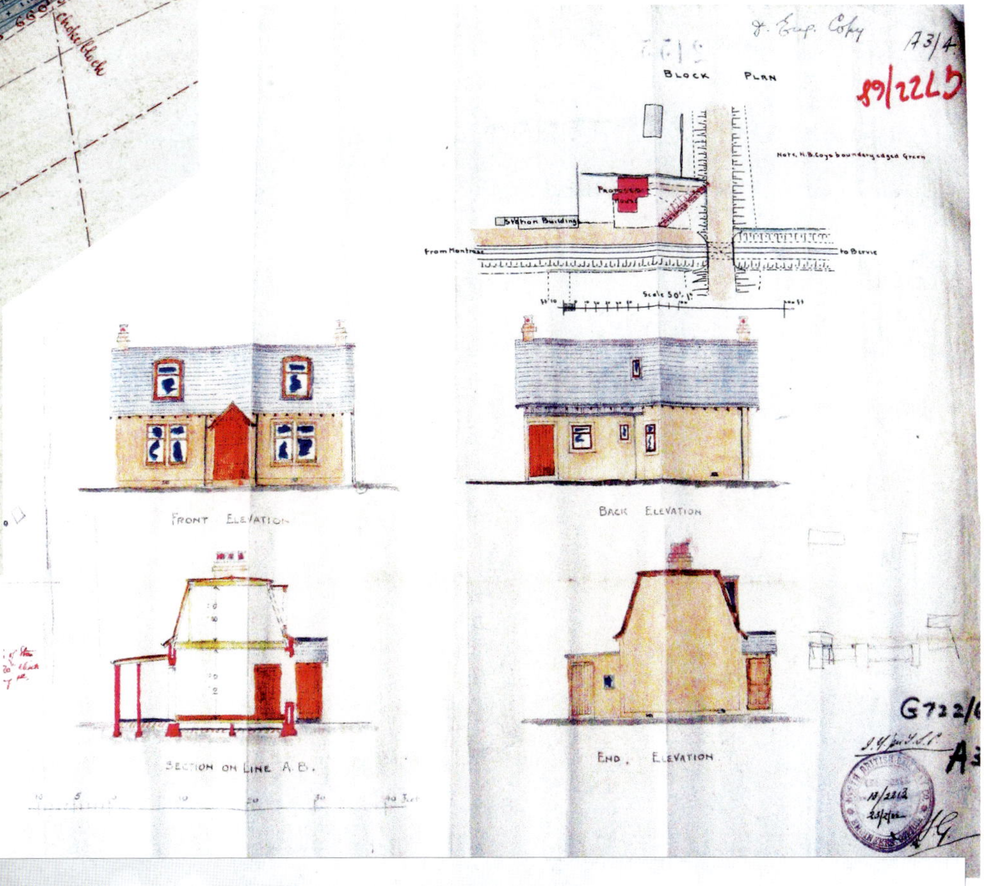

BELOW: A J.B. White postcard of St. Cyrus. The photograph – probably taken about 1935, although this postcard was not posted until July 1961 – shows the station in the middle distance. A camping coach was located there in summer 1934, and was joined by a second vehicle in 1936. The contract for the new council houses behind the station was let in 1935.
H. Stevenson collection

Lauriston [NO759656] [6m 18ch]

Lauriston was designed as a passing loop, with two 150-foot platforms, and station buildings on the west (Down) side. The loop was not built, however, as the train service did not require it in M&B days. After the NBR takeover in 1881 steps were taken to improve the train service and the siding to the west of the through line was converted to a loop in 1883 to accommodate the crossing of the first Up and first Down trains. Like St. Cyrus, there were two sidings facing Montrose, the right (east) one leading into a goods shed, while there was a short 40-foot loading bank on the left siding which terminated at the goods shed wall. A cattle pen was added in 1866.

Pencil alterations to the contractor's plan show the loading bank in a different position, west of the down platform and accessed by a trailing connection from the goods shed road. This was never built.

The Up platform was abandoned in May 1927 when the signal box was abolished, and the loop converted to a siding with catch points at each end.

The north end of the goods shed was converted to accommodate an L&NER delivery lorry in 1932, the buffer stops being moved a few feet to allow this. By 1939 all the buildings on the Down (west) platform had been removed, except for the 'Caledonian extension' which became the waiting room.

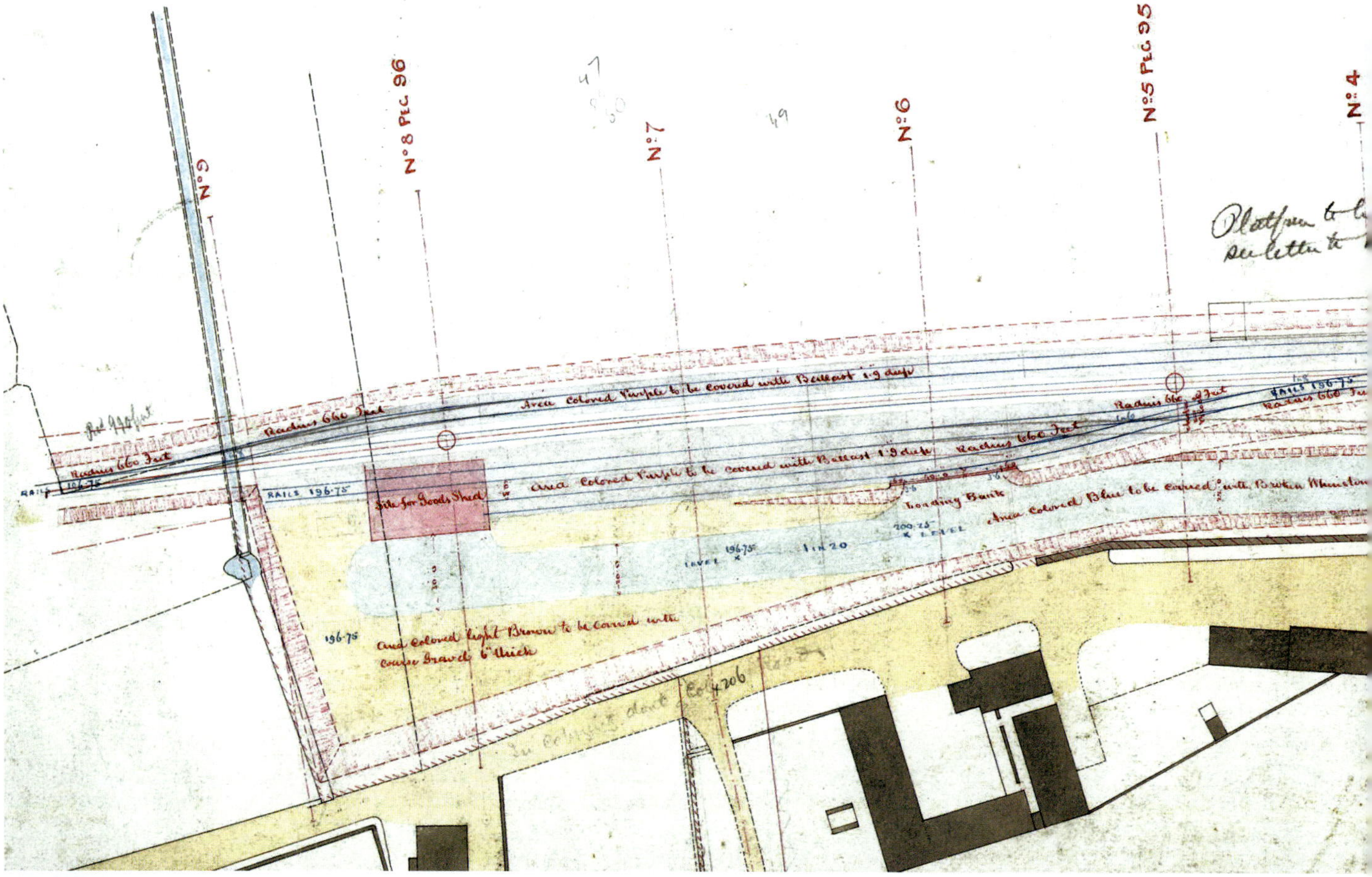

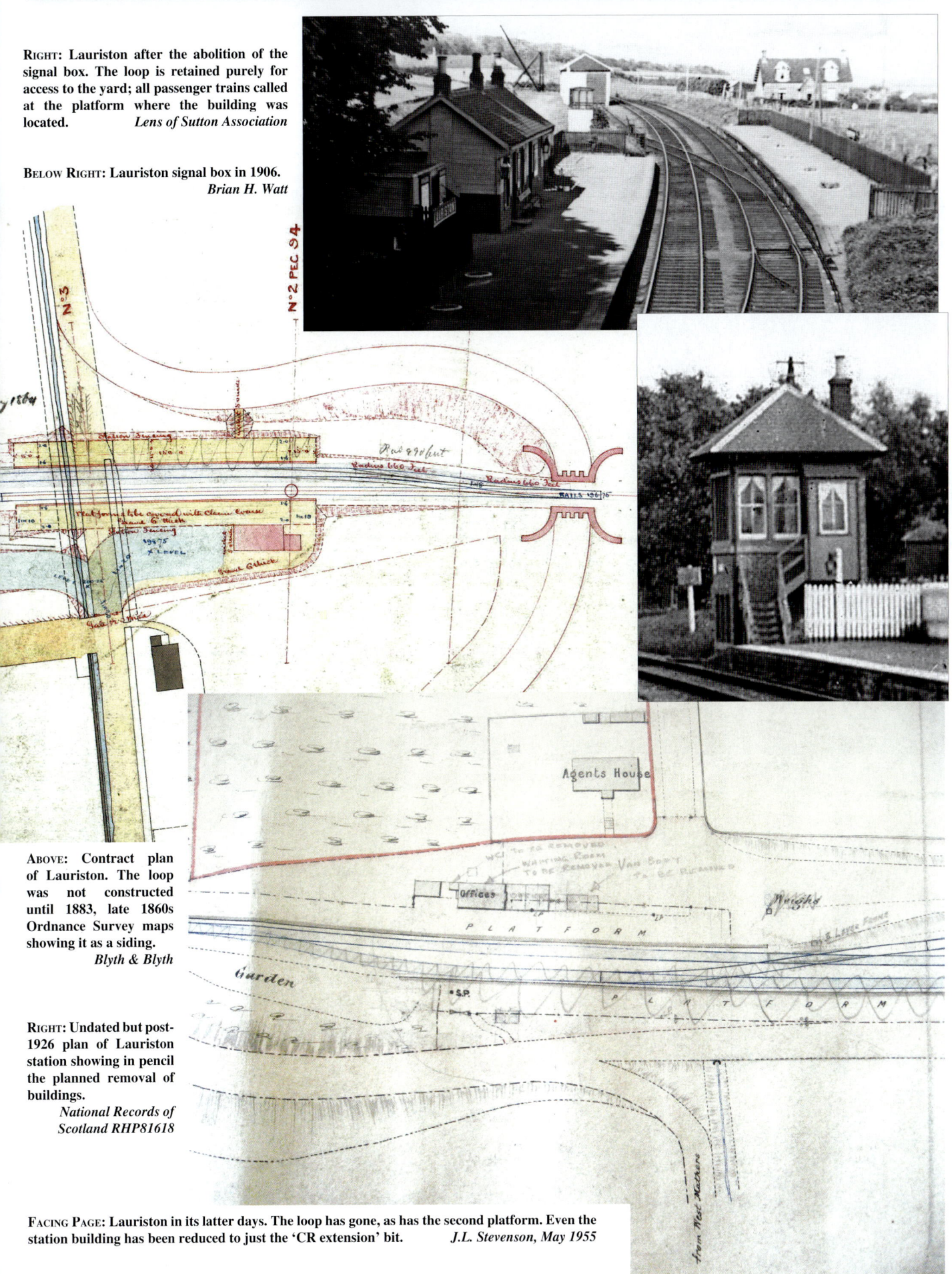

RIGHT: Lauriston after the abolition of the signal box. The loop is retained purely for access to the yard; all passenger trains called at the platform where the building was located. *Lens of Sutton Association*

BELOW RIGHT: Lauriston signal box in 1906. *Brian H. Watt*

ABOVE: Contract plan of Lauriston. The loop was not constructed until 1883, late 1860s Ordnance Survey maps showing it as a siding. *Blyth & Blyth*

RIGHT: Undated but post-1926 plan of Lauriston station showing in pencil the planned removal of buildings. *National Records of Scotland RHP81618*

FACING PAGE: Lauriston in its latter days. The loop has gone, as has the second platform. Even the station building has been reduced to just the 'CR extension' bit. *J.L. Stevenson, May 1955*

Den Finella Viaduct [NO772663]

This is a structure with three spans of 40 feet and one of 20 feet, constructed in local stone and 130 feet above the water. It still exists.

Johnshaven [NO794671] [8m 44ch]

Johnshaven had a single 150-foot platform to the east of the line, and slightly further north there was a standard layout of goods shed and loading bank sidings, with access from the Bervie end. The 50-foot goods shed was on the west siding. The loading bank was 100 feet. A cattle pen was added in 1866.

LEFT: Den Finella. *Author*

BELOW: Contract plan for Johnshaven. *Blyth & Blyth*

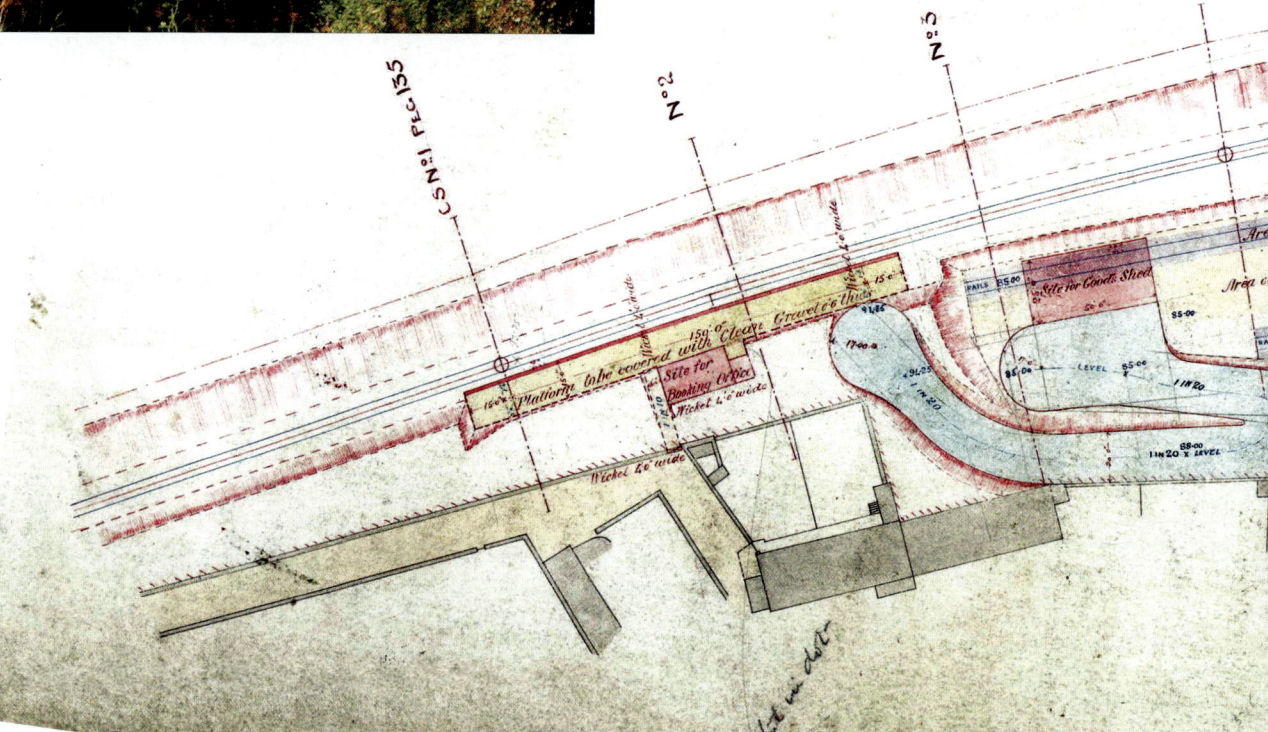

APPENDICES

Johnshaven station buildings were a little south of the yard and were unusual in that the 'CR extension' was a separate structure, gable end to the line.
J.L. Stevenson, May 1955

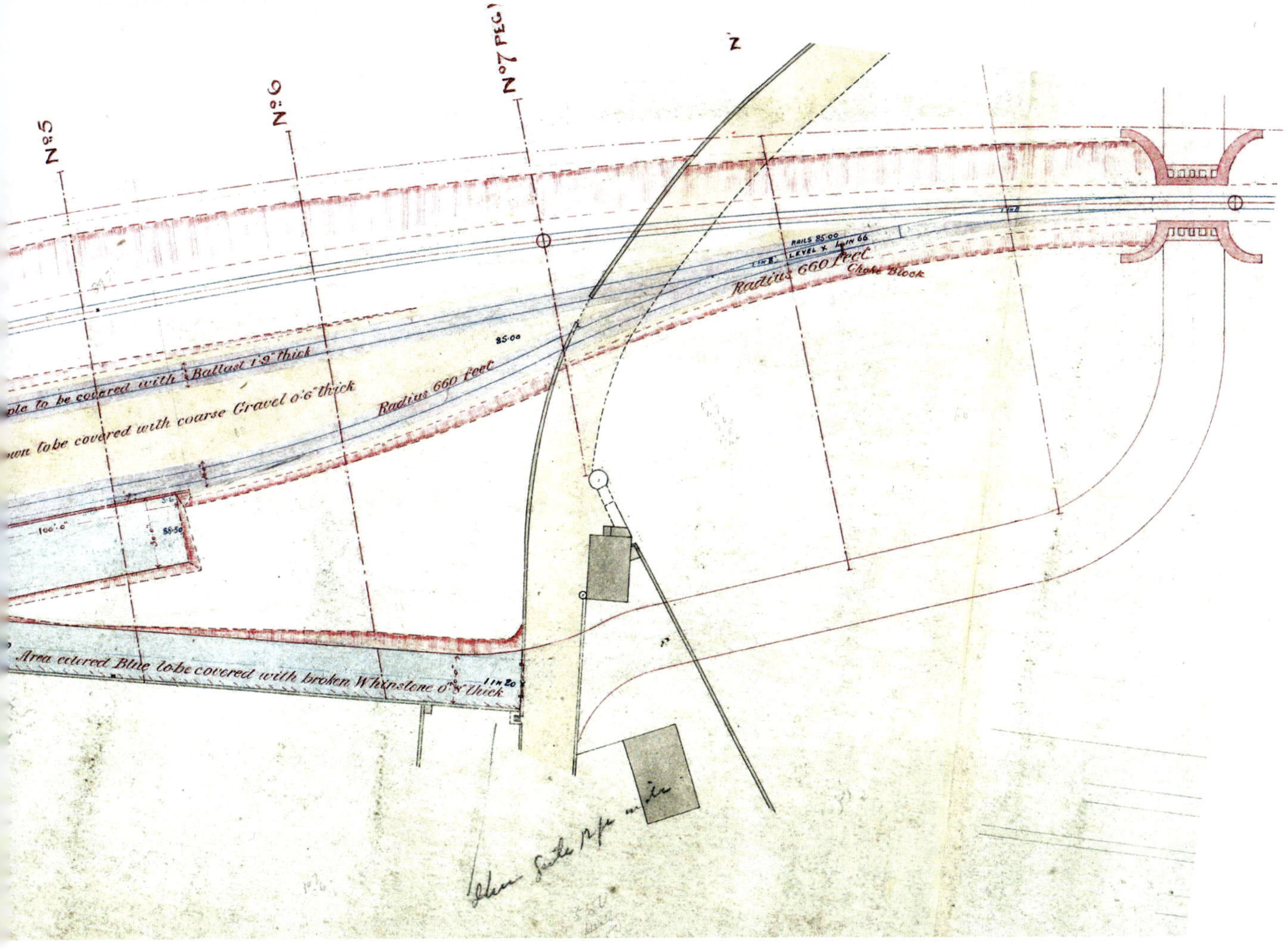

The yard at Johnshaven. The chimneys of the station building are just visible above the goods shed roof. *J.L. Stevenson*

BROTHERTON (PRIVATE) HALT [NO805675]

Brotherton had a single wooden platform on the west side of the line, accessed by a set of wooden steps. The location was almost exactly opposite No. 1 Beach Road, Johnshaven.

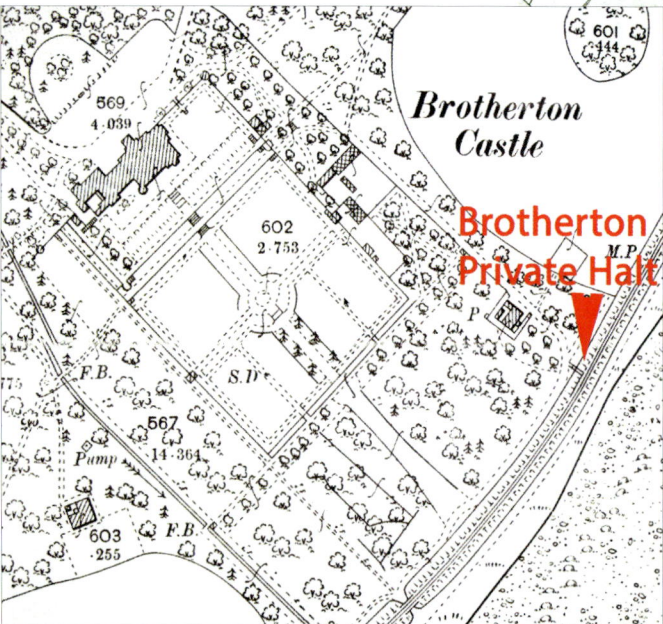

Brotherton estate in 1925, showing the location of the private halt for the Scott family. There are no known photographs of this halt, which was probably similar to that at Birnie Road (opposite).
By permission of the National Library of Scotland

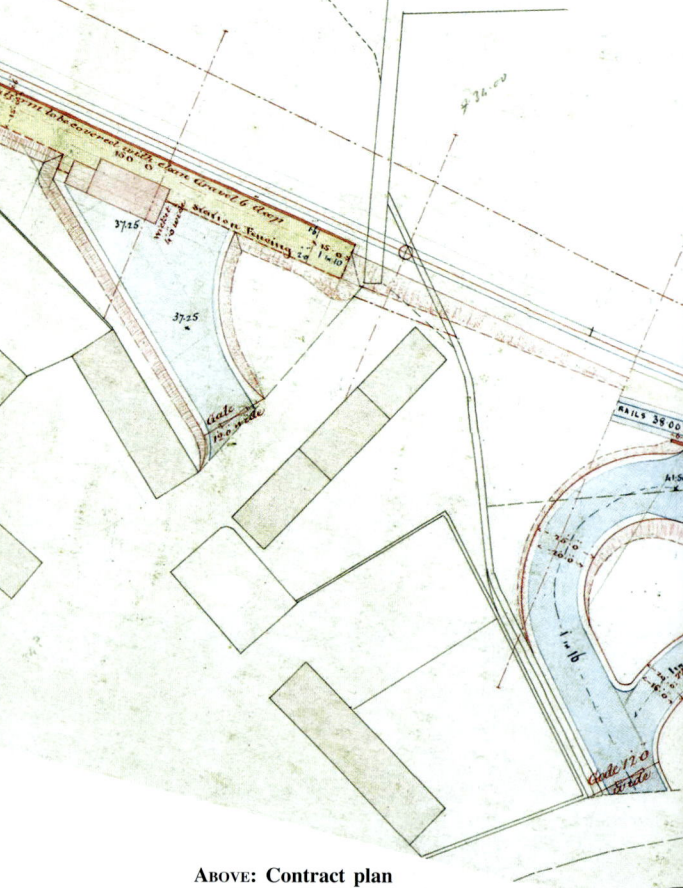

ABOVE: Contract plan for Gourdon. *Blyth & Blyth*

BIRNIE ROAD SIDING [NO809683] [9M 74CH]

Birnie Road Siding opened on Friday 10th August 1866 and had a single wooden platform on the west side of the line. Trains called on Fridays only and tickets were issued by the guard. Despite its official title, there was never a siding here.

GOURDON [NO718596] [11M 65CH]

The layout at Gourdon was similar to that at Johnshaven, except that the goods shed road was the seaward of the two sidings. The loading bank was 80 feet and the platform 150 feet.

The loading bank siding was later extended to rejoin the main line, thus making a goods loop. This had been lifted before final closure. There was also a short loading bank on the east side of the goods shed road, and the only (lattice steel) footbridge on the branch was here.

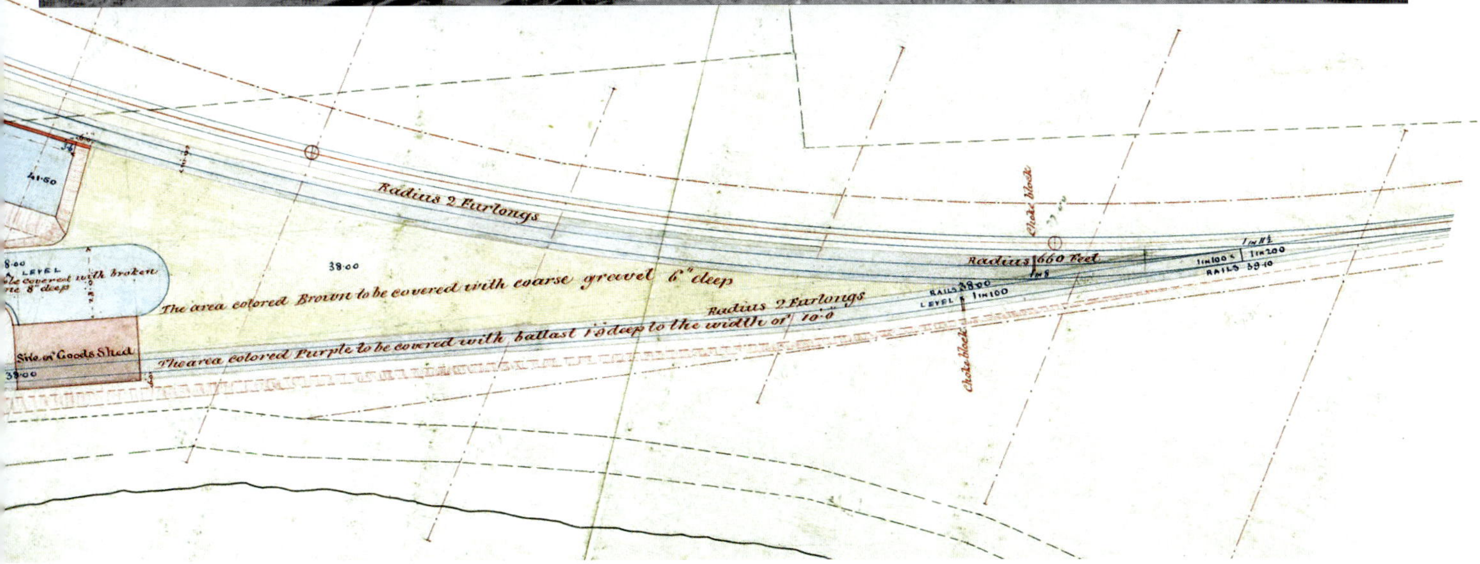

ABOVE: Birnie Road. The platform was on the west side. *H. Stevenson collection*

BELOW: Gourdon was the only station on the branch to have a footbridge. The yard was just to the north. *J.L. Stevenson, May 1955*

Bervie (Inverbervie from September 1926) [NO832723] [12m 75ch]

At the south end of Bervie there was to be a facing lead to the engine shed, which was to be a 50 foot long single road through structure built by Alexander Whishart, St. Cyrus, with a '*buffer bank*' at the rear. A '*tank house*' was to be installed on the seaward side of this siding, just in advance of a 40-foot radius Ormerod & Greerson turntable (cost £255). The Inspecting Officer did not approve of the facing connection to this siding, and a trailing connection was built instead.

Pencil alterations to the original plan show the trailing lead to the turntable and a slightly different siding layout, with the two sidings diverging from each other further north.

The wooden engine shed was destroyed by fire in January 1914 and the wooden replacement was a most unusual design, with a cantilevered sliding door (like an aircraft hangar) and a '*belfry*' type ventilator in the roof. The engine shed was photographed intact in summer 1939, but was removed around 1940.

On the west side of the line there was a siding accessed from the north (the 'west siding') and a 100-foot carriage shed was planned but not built. A run-round loop and a 150-foot platform on the west side were supplemented by two sidings, the western of which ended at a 100-foot loading bank and the other in a 50-foot goods shed. The 13 mile post (from Montrose CR) was at the end of the platform. A cattle pen was added in 1866. The platform was extended in 1884 by the NBR.

The loading bank had three different heights to cater for different wagon floor levels, there being two increases in height along its length. By 1892 there was a stone-built stable block facing onto Kirkburn, while an open-sided coal handling shed (built post 1924) was located on the same siding as the goods shed. On the platform, alongside the station building, was a fish store. A scotch derrick type crane was provided in 1866 to replace a lower capacity model, located between the two sidings, and a small NBR-style water tower and water crane was located at the buffer end of the platform, where there was also an ash pit. The water tower was removed some time after 1955. The west siding was removed in May 1927 when the signal box was abolished.

During the Second World War a concrete pillbox was built to the north of the turntable on the site of the engine shed. Concrete tank traps were also placed along the beach. All these were removed in the 1970s, though examples of both pillbox and tank traps may still be seen (2015) across the Bervie River from the site of the station.

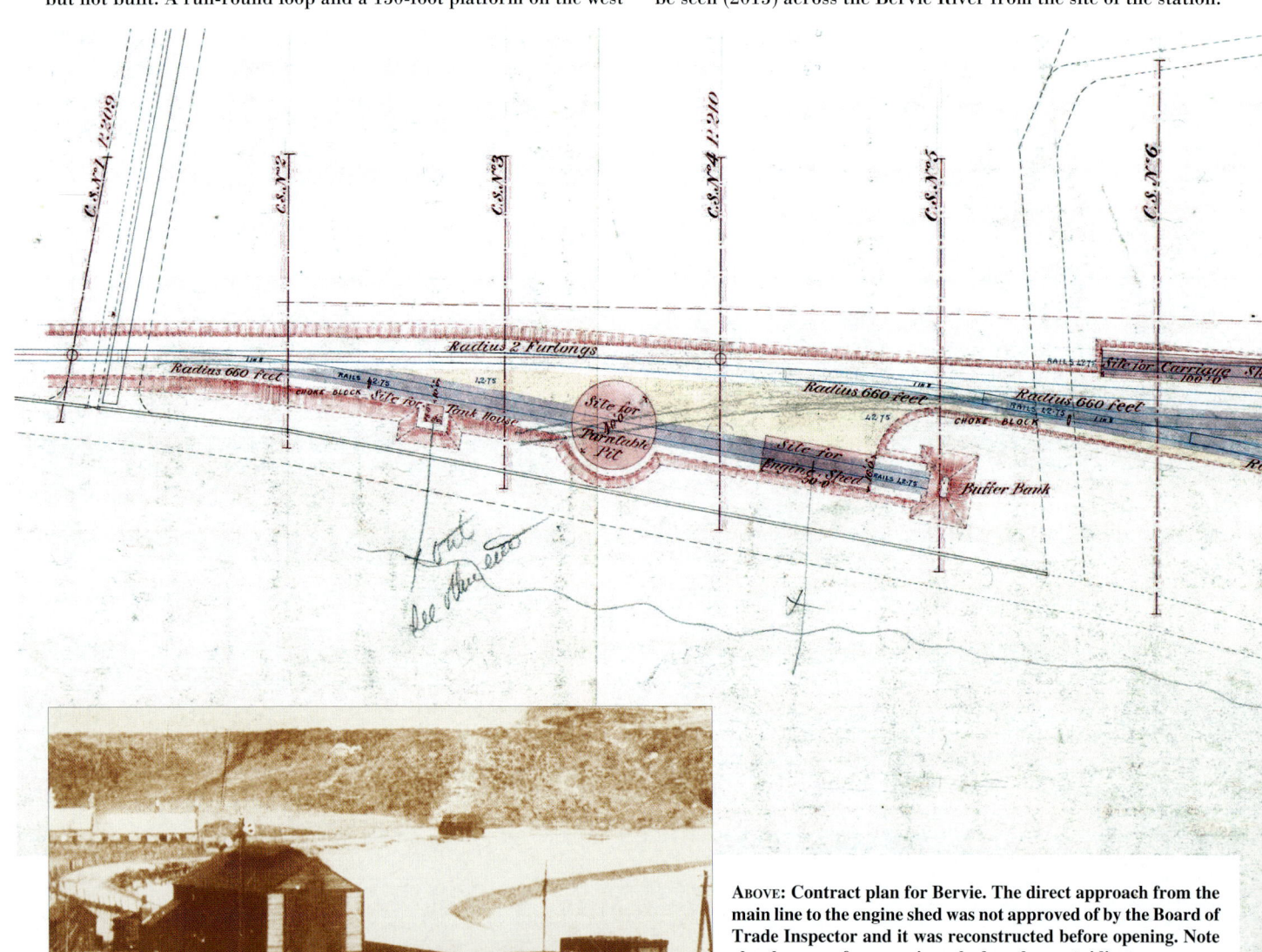

ABOVE: Contract plan for Bervie. The direct approach from the main line to the engine shed was not approved of by the Board of Trade Inspector and it was reconstructed before opening. Note also the space for a carriage shed on the west siding.
Blyth & Blyth

LEFT: Photographs of the engine sheds at Bervie are very rare. This is the first one, which was a conventional structure.
Brian H. Watt

Bervie often won Best Kept Station awards. Here the staff proudly show off the name picked out in sea pebbles in the garden opposite the station building in 1931.
Margaret Gray

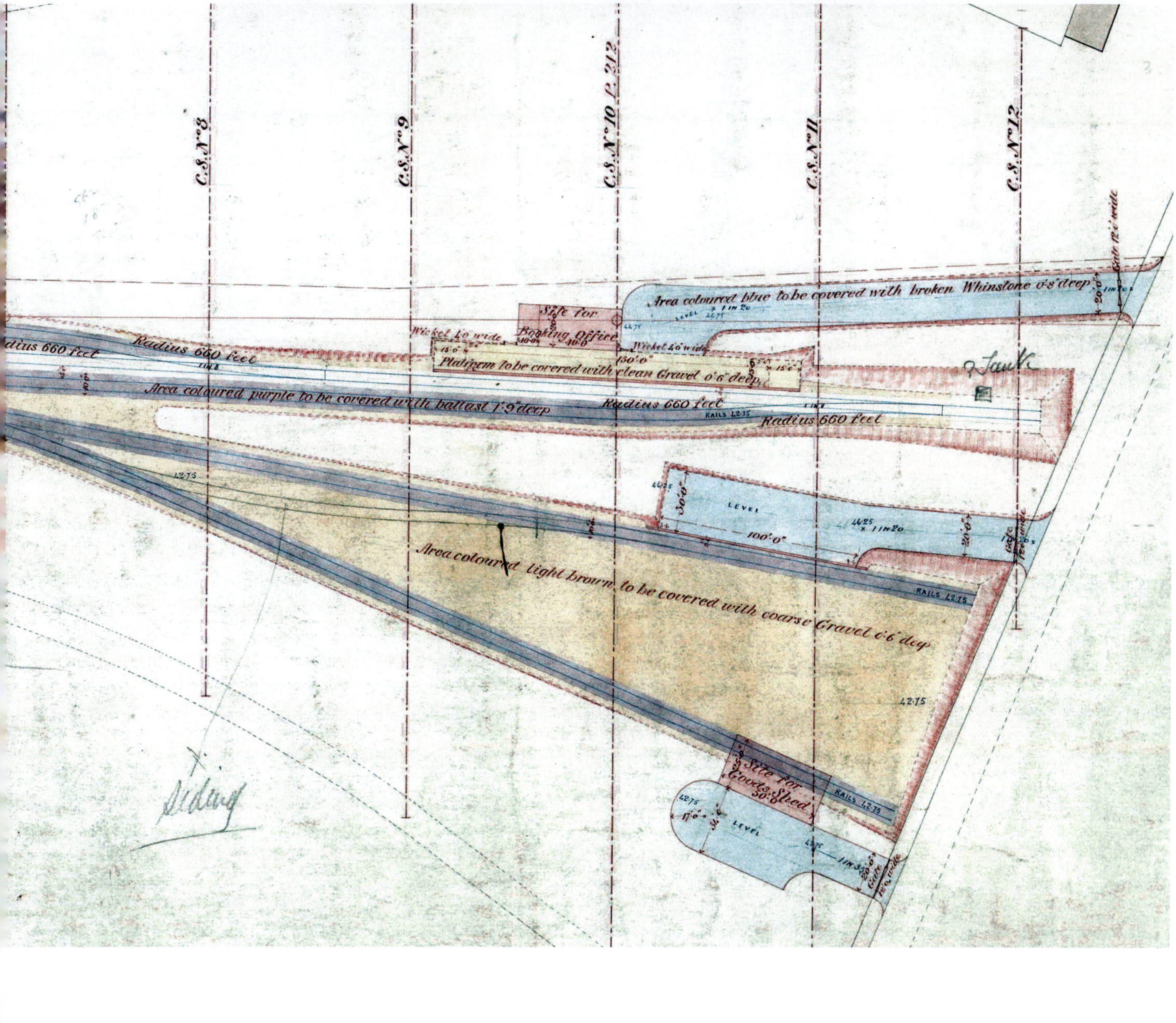

Photographs of Bervie signal box are also rare. This one shows the immaculate station and four of the staff. *Allan Rodgers*

A later view from the same end of the station. The platform extension carried out by the NBR can be seen, as well as the brick fish store next to the wooden station building. *H. Stevenson May 1955*

The replacement engine shed, which lasted from circa 1914 to circa 1940, was quite unusual both in having a 'belfry' type smoke outlet, and an 'aircraft hangar' door, which must have been a challenge to operate in windy conditions. L&NER Class 'G9' 0-4-4 tank No. 9475 is passing on a train to Montrose on Friday 7th April 1939.
W. Hennigan collection, courtesy Bill Lynn

Bervie around 1900; the locomotive is probably No. 241, a Drummond 0-6-0.
Margaret Gray

This photograph, taken from the buffer stops at Inverbervie, shows the water tower as well as the collection of sheds which served the freight traffic. The large pitched-roof shed on the left is the coal handling shed. There was also a short maintenance pit in the headshunt. In the left distance can be seen the Second World War pillbox, roughly on the site of the engine shed.
H. Stevenson, May 1955

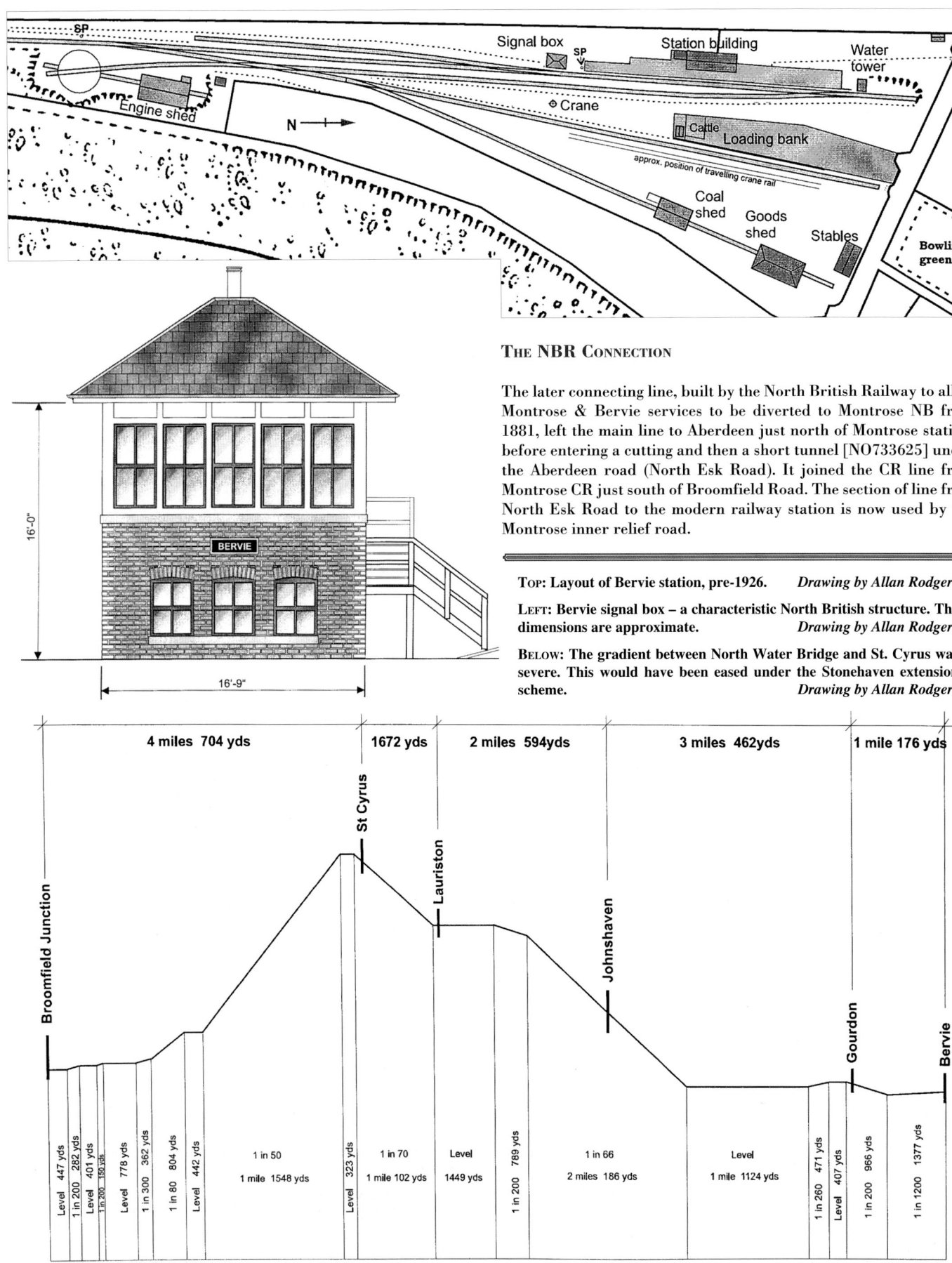

THE NBR CONNECTION

The later connecting line, built by the North British Railway to allow Montrose & Bervie services to be diverted to Montrose NB from 1881, left the main line to Aberdeen just north of Montrose station, before entering a cutting and then a short tunnel [NO733625] under the Aberdeen road (North Esk Road). It joined the CR line from Montrose CR just south of Broomfield Road. The section of line from North Esk Road to the modern railway station is now used by the Montrose inner relief road.

TOP: Layout of Bervie station, pre-1926.   *Drawing by Allan Rodgers*

LEFT: Bervie signal box – a characteristic North British structure. The dimensions are approximate.   *Drawing by Allan Rodgers*

BELOW: The gradient between North Water Bridge and St. Cyrus was severe. This would have been eased under the Stonehaven extension scheme.   *Drawing by Allan Rodgers*

Bervie Branch Gradient Diagram   (Broomfield Jct to Bervie: Total distance = 12 miles 88 yds)

APPENDIX 3: SIGNALLING AND OPERATIONS

The intended method of operation at the opening of the line was Train Staff and Ticket; however, because the signals were not complete at the date of the Board of Trade inspection, for a short period after opening the Company was obliged to use the very restrictive 'one engine in steam' system, which meant that only one locomotive could be on the line at one time.[1] An electric telegraph line was provided by the SNER from about 1866, with instruments at Montrose station, Lauriston and Bervie, but this does not appear to have been used for signalling purposes.[2]

The Train Staff and Ticket system allowed more than one train to be in a section at a time, but prevented trains running in opposite directions being in that section; it was also flexible enough to deal with unbalanced train movements – where two or more trains might move in one direction before a train was required to move in the other direction. The train staff authorised a driver to enter the section. If two trains were timetabled over the line before a train in the other direction, the first train was issued with a coloured ticket from a box whose lock was controlled by the presence of the Train Staff. On seeing the staff, the driver was authorised to proceed on the assurance that the staff was at his end of the section, and therefore no train could be coming towards him. The next train could be allowed to leave with the staff once the first train had departed.[3]

In fact, the working timetables for the Bervie line during the time it was operated by the Caledonian Railway show that the service could be operated by one locomotive, so there was no need either for a loop at Lauriston, or signals, even though it is clear from the Inspecting Officer's report that signals were provided.[4] In 1883, after the North British takeover, among the line improvements made were the installation of a loop at Lauriston, which allowed an enhanced service to be operated. Timetables for the period 1883-93 show that the first trains in each direction crossed here, and this necessitated the employment of a Signalman-Porter from June 1883. During this period the intermediate stations with sidings (St. Cyrus, Lauriston, Johnshaven and Gourdon) were provided with fixed signals. It is not known how these signals were operated; it is possible that the 'auxiliary' or distant signals were worked by wire from the appropriate home signal and the points worked by local hand levers, probably without any interlocking.[5]

In 1889, however, considerable public concern over the absence of a block system permitting only one train to be in section had been raised as a result of a major accident at Armagh, where a second train had collided with the rear section of a preceding train which had been issued with a ticket.[6] This resulted in the Regulation of Railways Act 1889, which gave the Board of Trade the power to enforce the adoption on Britain's railways of a method of working where only one train would be allowed to occupy a section at a time.

On 30th June 1893 the branch was converted to Tyer's Block Telegraph and Train Staff and Ticket, with new signal boxes at Lauriston and Bervie, and ground frames at St. Cyrus, Johnshaven and Gourdon. The ground frames controlled all the signals and points in the station yards and were fully interlocked, being released by an Annett's key. As will be seen below, special instructions covered the use of Brotherton (Private) Halt, as no fixed signals were provided there.

In 1897 the North British decided that the Electric Train Tablet Block System, Tyer's No. 6 tablet, should replace Tyer's Block Telegraph and Train Staff and Ticket, and a new signal box at North Water Bridge be provided to give greater capacity on the branch. This was to be installed during 1898. However, when the Caledonian Railway trains ceased running on the branch and there was no longer a need for a major capacity increase the scheme was dropped.

Initially, after the resignalling of 1893, ticket working appears to have been retained, but since the Annett's key was fixed to the train staff, only trains holding the staff (rather than a ticket) could shunt the intermediate yards. Possibly the debate over conversion to Electric Token Block in 1897 delayed the removal of the fixed signals which were no longer needed to protect a train calling to shunt the yards. The General Appendix to the Working Timetables issued in March 1898 states that:

> *Arrangements have been made for controlling some of the points leading to and from Sidings on Single Lines by means of a key affixed to the Train Staff, which renders the provision of fixed signals unnecessary.*[7]

Gourdon, Johnshaven and St. Cyrus were specifically mentioned.

In the 1901 General Appendix the instruction had been changed to specify that the key was *not* attached to the staff for these stations, presumably because the previous arrangements were too restrictive. As a result, the fixed signals were now required again and remained until 1927.[8]

The fixed signals and special instructions at Brotherton also remained in the General Appendix to the Working Timetable until the signalling simplification of 1927, though the nominated person issuing the instruction had by then changed from Mrs Hercules Scott to her daughter.[9]

Just how ready North British management were to penny-pinch is illustrated overleaf.

Ex-Edinburgh & Glasgow Railway No. 332 was reputedly the first North British locomotive on the Bervie line in 1881, though if this is correct it would probably have been used on goods trains. This photograph shows it before rebuilding by Holmes in 1892.   *John Alsop collection*

Early Days on the Montrose & Bervie Branch

Deuchars [the North British traffic superintendent] in 1897 had instructed Inspector Alex. Hogg to report on the working of the Bervie branch after the Caledonian had exercised its running powers over that piece of line, and this Hogg did on 7th August as follows. He stated that he had visited all the stations on the branch, and found that the trains were often running late, in which case the use of the system of train staff and ticket did not give the same elasticity as the block telegraph. In his opinion it would be necessary to substitute either the electric train staff or Tyer's No. 6 tablet system. The Broomfield Junction to Lauriston section was too long and ought to be divided in the vicinity of North Water Bridge station. There was also a shortage of staff, which would have to be increased if the existing train service was to be maintained. The Caledonian Railway had a stationmaster and porter at every station, although little traffic fell to them except at Gourdon.

On 12th August, Deuchars advised Conacher, the North British General Manager, that the No. 6 tablet should replace the train staff and telegraph. The costing of this change became the responsibility of Clement, the Electric Telegraph Engineer, and he reported on 28th August that the cost would be £630 to provide the No. 6 Tablet Telegraphs between Bervie and a new cabin to be provided at North Water Bridge and the Caledonian Company's class of tablets between North Water Bridge and Montrose North signal cabin. He also pointed out that the Caledonian cabin at Broomfield was at present working to Montrose North and Lauriston, and therefore CR class tablet instruments would be required, unless the Caledonian agreed to accept the No. 6 instruments. Deuchars thought that this proposal was too expensive, and suggested the substitution of train staff instruments. To this Clement replied that the saving would be a mere £20.

On 3rd December, Deuchars, still keeping at it, advised Conacher that electric staff instruments worked on a single wire, and that there was already a single wire in existence for working the Tyer's Block Telegraph on the Bervie branch. The instruments cost £36 approximately, so how was Clement's £630 made up? To which Clement replied on 11th December that electric staff instruments were worked by two wires as a precaution against the effects of lightning, thus doing away with earth connections as approved by the Board of Trade.

Eleven days later back came Deuchars to the effect that the Great Western Railway used a single wire and if they were not affected by lightning, then there was no reason why the Bervie branch should be. He still wanted a breakdown and this was duly sent to him.

On 3rd January 1898, after digesting the breakdown, Deuchars stated that Clement allowed for eight instruments, including the proposed North Water Bridge box, but he wanted only four at £36 each, two at Lauriston and one each at Bervie and Broomfield Junction. Ultimately, on 19th January 1898, Clement conceded that Deuchars had allowed only for instruments and not for staffs and bells. If there was to be no new box at North Water Bridge, the cost would be £255 and, obviously fed up with the whole matter, he added if Deuchars preferred the staff instrument, so be it.

If Clement thought that would be the end of the matter, he underestimated his General Manager. On 24th January he was back to the niggle disputing the number of instruments required and persisted that in Edinburgh the cost of the instrument with eight staffs and bell was £36. On 11th February, Clement again detailed his costs and again averring that eight staffs were too few, requiring fifteen with double column instruments at an additional cost of £22.

Correspondence flowed on and on until 24th May, when Deuchars wrote to Conacher to the effect that the costs were required only from Broomfield Junction to Bervie, and that there was no need for Clement to include the section from Broomfield Junction to Montrose North. He was satisfied the branch should be worked by electrical staff instead of the present system, and he did not anticipate delay if only eight staffs were provided, since the trains in each direction practically balanced each other. He continued to disagree with Clement's estimate, stating that fifteen staffs were unnecessary and that two wires were not required while the expense of poles, etc. should be charged to 'renewals'. And then apparently oblivious to the fact that any delay had been caused by himself when he ignored the advice of his experts, Hogg and Clement, he ended the battle by pointing out that the work should be proceeded with to obviate delay, which was serious at that time, and would increase as the summer advanced.

From an article by Ed. Nichol in North British Study Group Journal, *Issue 49, pp. 25-27*

Drummond 4-4-0 tank No. 103 showing off its 'Montrose' name. Likewise, No. 241 would have displayed 'Bervie' as its name in its early years working the Bervie Branch around 1881, when it was transferred from the Roslin Branch (and renamed from 'Roslin'). No. 241 would have been based at Bervie and No. 103 at Montrose.
W. Hennigan collection, courtesy Bill Lynn

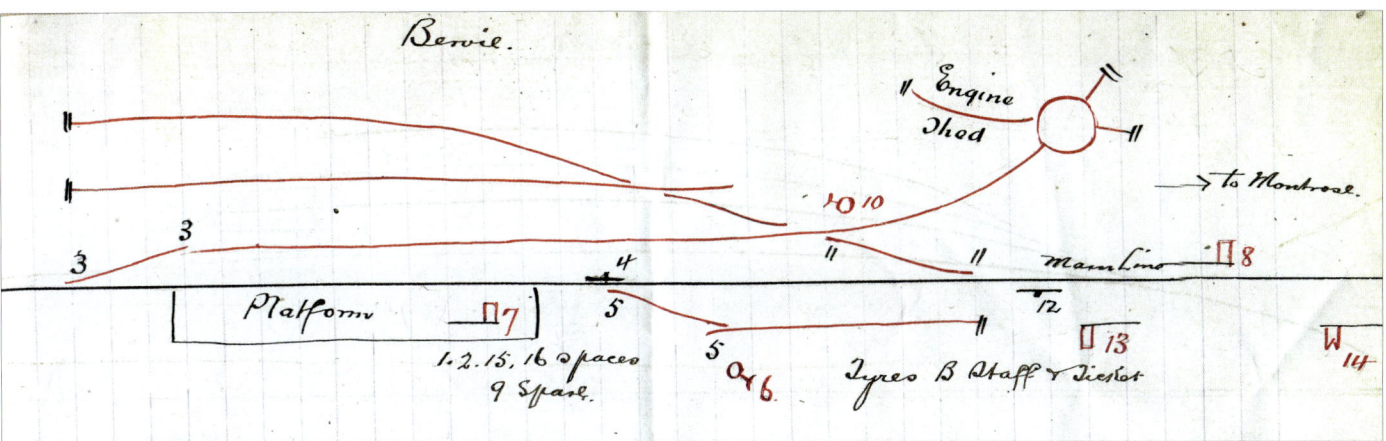

It was common for signalling inspectors and control staff to keep notebooks with details of signalling at individual stations, and we are fortunate that one of the Kirkcaldy controllers retained his Bervie line plans.
Courtesy R. Hollingworth

Bervie Signal Box Lever Frame

- 1 space
- 2 space
- 3 north end loop points
- 4 west siding points lock bar
- 5 west siding points
- 6 disc signal west siding exit
- 7 Up home signal
- 8 Up starting signal
- 9 spare
- 10 disc signal yard exit
- 11 south end loop points
- 12 south end loop points lock bar
- 13 Down home signal
- 14 Down distant signal
- 15 space
- 16 space

The Down distant was shown on the 1926 plan as '*Stationary*' but nevertheless appears to have been on the lever frame. A worked distant would seem to be superfluous for a terminal station.

Signalling Changes in 1927

In 1926, as part of an attempt to reduce costs, it was decided to remove the signal boxes at Bervie and Lauriston, reintroducing one engine in steam working, and carrying out other simplifications. The signalling and track layout at each station which existed prior to these new arrangements being implemented are shown on these plans, reproduced courtesy of Allan Rodgers. The changes were to be as follows:[10]

Bervie: All signals and signal box equipment to be removed as well as telegraph in booking office. An Annett's key on the train staff would unlock two ground frames, one with five levers (lock, west loop points, bolt and bar, west siding points, bolt and bar) and one with two levers (lock, north end loop points). Telephone to be moved from signal box to office.

Lauriston: All signals and signal box equipment to be removed. Catch point to be provided each end of [Up] loop. Ground frames with three levers (lock, loop and catch points, bolt and bar) and four levers (west end of loop) (lock, loop and catch point, bolt and bar, sidings connection).

At a subsequent site meeting it was agreed that 45 feet or so of the Up platform would be removed to accommodate the run-off for the new catch points.[11]

The Army's Scottish Command asked that the aerodrome siding be retained, but the L&NER South Scottish Area Superintendent recommended this should only be done if the military paid for it, and he added that the exchange siding at Broomfield should also be removed '*in view of the fact that it is never used nor is it likely to be required.*'[12] By late October it had been concluded that the Bervie west siding could also be removed.[13] On 13th March 1926 it was confirmed that the War Office did not require the aerodrome siding.[14]

The final plan was then produced and this proposed the changes to the signalling shown against the following track diagrams.

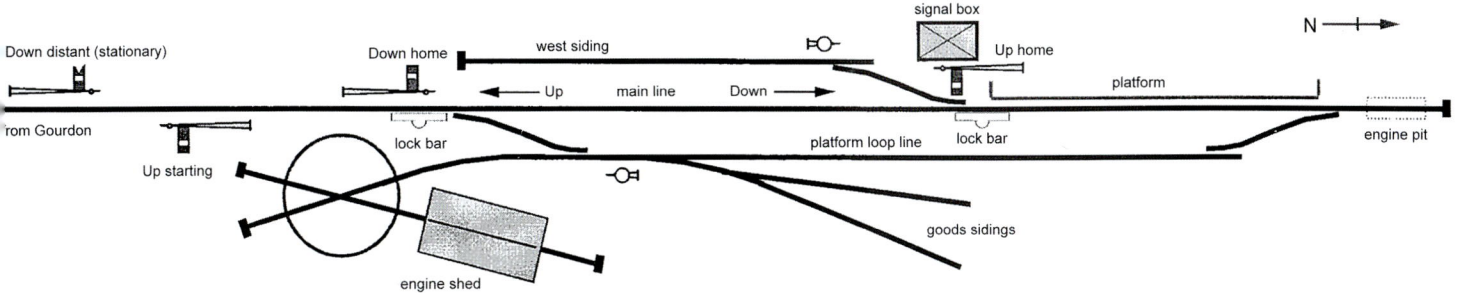

Bervie: Signal box to be closed. Installation of two lever ground frames for (1) goods siding connection and (2) platform line to loop. West siding to be removed.

116 THE MONTROSE & BERVIE RAILWAY

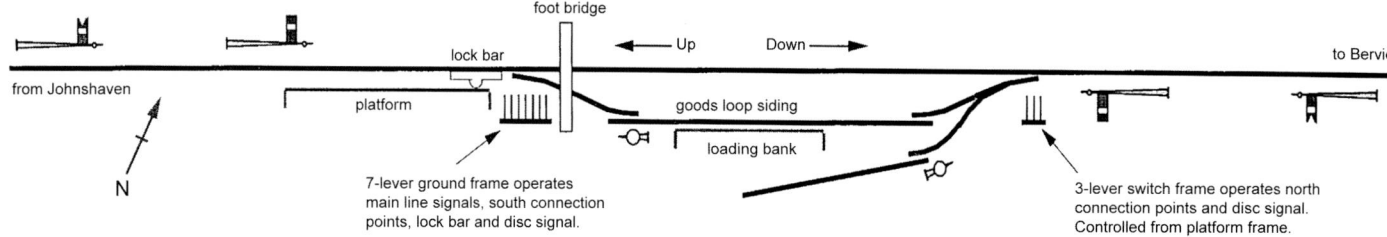

Gourdon: Present seven-lever frame (operating four main line signals, disc and lock bar) to be removed and replaced by a two-lever frame to operate connection to sidings.

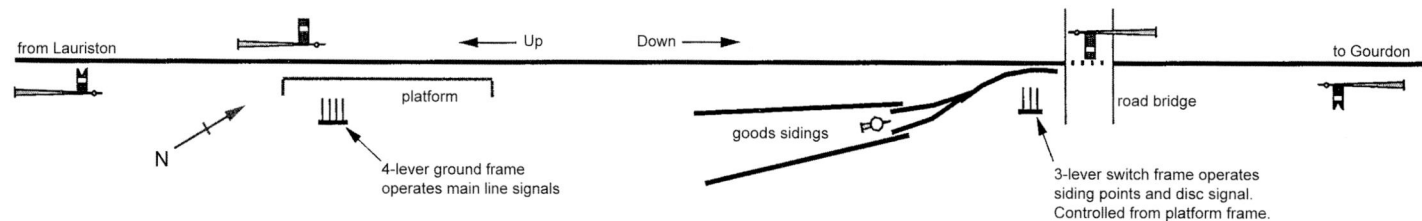

Johnshaven: Present three-lever frame (operating connection to sidings and disc signal) to be removed and replaced by a two-lever frame. The four-lever frame on the platform (operating the four main line signals) to be removed.

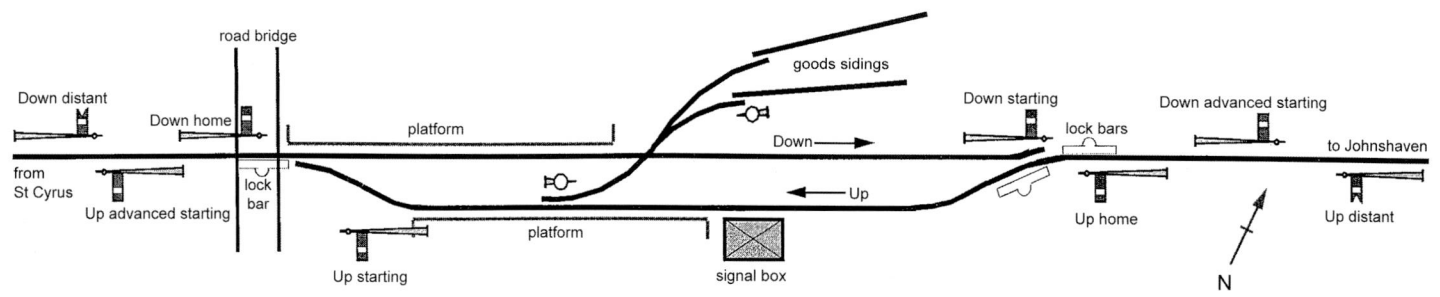

Lauriston: Signal box to be closed. Down platform line to become running line. Three-lever frame to be provided at east end of Down platform. Catch points to be provided at west end of Up platform line, and 45 feet of Up platform to be removed. Two-lever frame to be provided for east end connection, along with catch points.

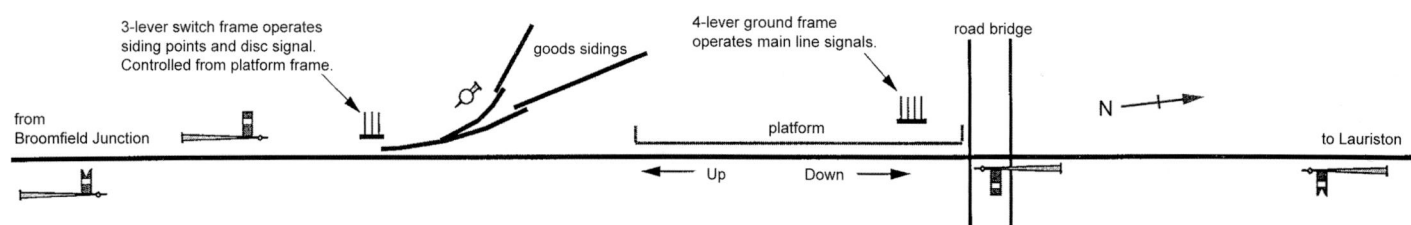

St. Cyrus: Present three-lever ground frame for operating the sidings to be removed and five-lever frame provided. New catch points to be provided 215 yards east of the new frame (which was to be 100 yards nearer the station), and clear of the overbridge. Four-lever frame (operating the main line signals) to be removed.

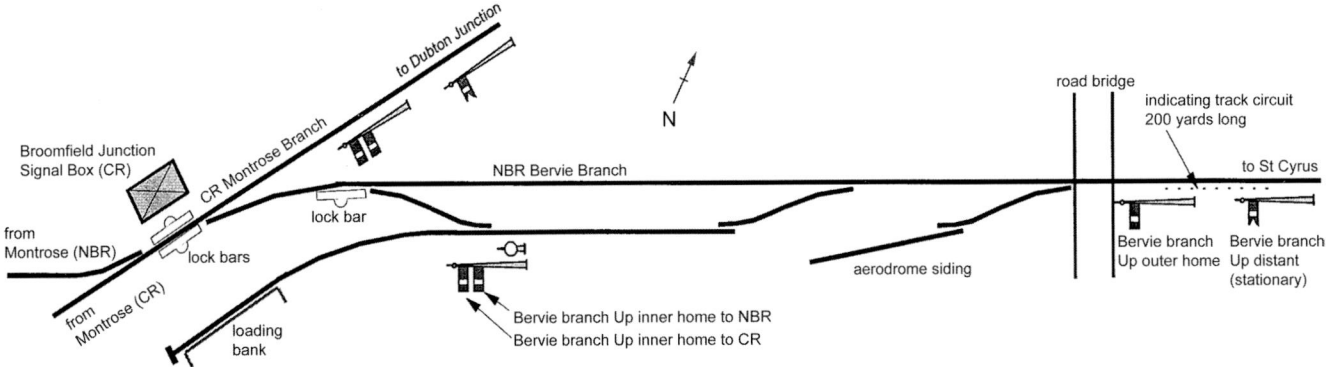

Aerodrome: Siding provided '*temporarily in 1919*' no longer required.
Broomfield: East end loop connections to be removed. Single lever in Broomfield (LM&SR) signal box to be made spare.[15]

On 24th April 1927 the new arrangements were to be brought into force. The new train staff for one engine in steam was lettered '*Broomfield Junction and Inverbervie*'.[16] However, because the Superintendent objected to the short notice for producing the staff circular, the actual implementation was delayed until 1st May. It had therefore taken just short of two years to develop the scheme.

Timetables

Working timetables exist for many of the years of operation of the branch, and are to be found in the National Records of Scotland. Apart from the brief period when the Caledonian Railway operated a competing service in 1898, the train service was relatively consistent

Operating Arrangements for Brotherton (Private) Halt

1. The Station Masters at Johnshaven and Gourdon are authorised to order passenger trains to call at Brotherton (situated between Johnshaven and Gourdon), either upon the personal request of Mrs Hercules Scott, or for persons presenting a printed order signed by her, and made out on the form of which is subjoined.

    It must be distinctly understood that the order to stop at Brotherton is to be given only by the Johnshaven Station Master, or by the Gourdon Station Master as the case may require (see clauses 2 and 3) – no other servant on the Montrose and Bervie branch having that authority – and that these two Station Masters will only do so on the personal application of Mrs Hercules Scott, or, upon the presentation to them of the printed order duly filled up and signed by Mrs H Scott.

    [There was an example of this printed in the appendix. All Mrs Scott, or more likely her staff, had to do was fill in the name of the station – Gourdon or Johnshaven – the time of the train, where from, and date it.]

2. In all cases where Passengers are to be set down or taken up by Trains from Montrose, previous intimation must be made to the Station Master at Johnshaven, whose duty it will be to instruct the Driver to stop at Brotherton, and the Driver will only stop on receiving that Station Master's instruction. The Station Master will at the same time inform the Guard and, in addition, he will caution the Driver of any train following within fifteen minutes of the previous Train having to call at Brotherton.

3. In all cases where Passengers are to be set down or taken up by Trains from Bervie, previous intimation must be made to the Station Master at Gourdon, whose duty it will be to instruct the Driver to stop at Brotherton, and the Driver will only stop on receiving that Station Master's instruction. The Station Master will at the same time inform the Guard and, in addition, he will caution the Driver of any train following within fifteen minutes of the previous Train having to call at Brotherton.

4. In the event of Passengers requiring to be taken up or set down at Brotherton before sunrise or after sunset, the following regulations (in addition to the foregoing) must be strictly adhered to:-

    1st. The Train by which Passengers are set down or taken up must only be a Train the Driver of which is in possession of the Lauriston and Bervie Train Staff, and the Station Masters at Johnshaven and Gourdon will be held responsible for satisfying themselves as to this before giving an Order for any Train to call at Brotherton.

    2nd. The Station Masters at Johnshaven and Gourdon will respectively see that the signals protecting any Train which may be authorised to stop at Brotherton after dark are kept at 'Danger' for at least fifteen minutes after departure of the Train.

5. The Guards of all Passenger Trains stopping at Brotherton to set down or take up Passengers must report all such stoppages in their Train Journals, and must also attach the printed orders (which will be handed to them by the Station Masters) to their Train Reports before sending them to the Office of the Superintendent of the Line.

6. Passengers to be set down at Brotherton by Trains from Montrose or taken up by Trains from Bervie, will pay the Gourdon fares; and in the case of Passengers to be taken up at Brotherton by Trains from Montrose or set down by Trains from Bervie, they will pay the Johnshaven fares.

    As regards the collection of Tickets of Passengers alighting, it will be the duty of the Station Master at Johnshaven to collect the Tickets of Passengers by trains which he orders to stop; and the Gourdon Station Master will in like manner collect the tickets from Passengers by Trains which he orders to stop. With respect to Passengers to be taken up, these must previously possess themselves of Tickets before the Trains arrive.[17]

Extract from March 1898 NBR
General Appendix to the Working Timetable

RIGHT AND FACING PAGE: Caledonian Railway Working Timetable for May 1876. It is notable that the train service could be operated with one engine, and that there was therefore no need for crossing facilities on the line. All trains on the branch ran mixed freight and passenger, giving a journey time on the trains to Montrose of 45-60 minutes and to Bervie of 50-60 minutes.

National Records of Scotland BR/TT/S/54

before the First World War, with only minor changes from time to time.

The February 1884 timetable showed three passenger trains from Montrose, at 10.18am, 12.55pm and 5.20pm, with mixed trains at 8.0am, 3.15pm and 8.05pm, and goods trains at 10.32am (to Lauriston) and 12.05pm. The 8.00am mixed and 5.20am passenger trains ran through from Arbroath. From Bervie trains departed at 8.05am (passenger – to Arbroath), 9.15am (mixed), 11.10am (mixed), 1.35pm (passenger), 1.50pm (goods), 4.30pm (passenger) and 6.45pm (mixed). The Lauriston goods train departed at 11.00am. None of the mixed trains attached or detached goods vehicles at intermediate stations; this was left to the two goods trains. Birnie Road Siding was served by the 11.10am from Bervie and the 8.15pm train from Montrose on Friday only.

By June 1903, the service consisted of five passenger, one mixed and two goods trains (to Arbroath) daily, whereas in July 1913 an additional passenger train had been added. Forced reductions during the First World War produced a service in April 1917 of only two passenger, one mixed and two goods trains daily, with one of the passenger trains also being mixed on Tuesday only. In October 1922 an additional passenger train was run, and in September 1927 the service still had only three passenger trains, at 6.35am (mixed), 11.00am, 4.57pm (from Arbroath) and a 7.38pm on Saturday only. The goods service was now daily at 1.15pm with a Friday only train at 8.20am. From Bervie the trains were 7.38am (passenger), 9.18am (mixed – Friday only), 12.35pm passenger, 3.40pm (goods), 5.45pm (mixed – wagons from Bervie and Gourdon), and 8.20pm (passenger – Saturday only).

The service in summer 1948 consisted of passenger trains from Montrose at 6.42am (mixed), 11.30am, 1.30pm and 5.09pm and from Inverbervie at 7.38am, 12.39pm, 3.15pm and 6.00pm (mixed). In addition a Fridays only Livestock train ran from Montrose at 11.30am.

After the closure to passengers in 1951, a daily goods was scheduled at 3.15pm Monday-Friday and 11.20am on Saturdays.

NBR WORKING TIMETABLE 1901
Allan Rodgers, in his 1999 article in the *North British Railway Sudy Group Journal*, set out how the branch was probably operated, based on the 1901 working timetable.

Train services on the branch were provided Monday-Saturday,

MONTROSE and BERVIE TRAINS.

Miles fr. Bervie.	From BERVIE and MONTROSE.	1 a.m.	2 Mx'd. a.m.	3 a.m.	4 Mx'd. a.m.	5 a.m.	6 Mx'd. a.m.	7 p.m.	8 p.m.	9 M'd. p.m.	10 p.m.		
	Bervie ....leave	...	7 30	...	...	...	11 0		...	5 25	...	...	...
1	Gourdon............ ,,	......	7 33	......	......	......	11 6		......	5 31	......	......	......
4¼	Johnshaven....... ,,	...	7 43	...	...	...	11 20		...	5 45	...	...	...
6¾	Lauriston .... ,,	......	7 52	......	......	......	11 28		......	5 53	......	......	......
7¾	St. Cyrus......... ,,	...	7 57	...	...	...	11 39		...	6 4	...	...	...
9¾	N. Water Bridge ,,	......	8 4	......	......	......	11 48		......	6 13	......	......	......
11¼	Broomfield Road. ,,	...	8 10	...	...	...	11 56		...	6 21	...	...	...
13¼	Montrose.........arrive	......	8 15	......	......	......	12 0		......	6 25	......	......	......
				†									
	Montrose......leave	7 25	8 30	9 15	9 25	10 50	1 30p	2 15	5 10	6 45	8 50	...	...
13½	Dubton..............arr.	7 35	8 40	9 22	9 35	11 0	1 40	2 25	5 17	6 55	9 0	......	......
52¾	Aberdeen.......... ,,	...	10 35	...	...	12 40	...	4 5	...	9 0	10 30	...	...
20¼	Brechin.................. ,,	8 15	......	9 46	......	11 35	2 40	......	5 50	7 30	......	......	......
64¼	Perth.................. ,,	10 10	...	...	11 40	1 35	3 48	...	7 15	9 40	...	...	...
127¼	Glasgow, Bu. St. ,,	1p25	......	......	2 15	4 35	6 5	......	10 30	......	......	......	......
	Edinburgh, Wav. ,,	1 50	...	...	2 25	5 0	6 25	...	10 4	...	...	...	...
215½	Carlisle............. ,,	......	......	......	5 5	7 18	8 39	......	12 20	a ...	......	......	......

NOTES.

On Fridays, the 11.0 a.m. Train from Bervie calls at Birnie Road Siding.

† Connection to Brechin on Tuesdays and Fridays only.

there being no Sunday service. Reference to the working timetable for 1901 gives a good idea of how the branch was operated by the NBR. The following description of train operations has been compiled from examination of the timetable and goods operation records in the National Records of Scotland. Whilst the description of the goods train operation is accurate, being taken from the 1898 census, it should be said that the passenger train operation described is Allan's conclusions, deduced from the timetable, and is not based on more definitive evidence.

Passenger Train Operation

The branch appears to have been served by two passenger train sets, one stabled overnight at Montrose and the other stabled at Bervie.[18] The passenger service connected Bervie, Montrose and Arbroath and the operation of each set is deduced from the timetable to have been as follows below. The timetable makes mention in some cases of mixed trains only handling goods traffic to/from Bervie and not from any of the intermediate stations (for example No. 1 Up on Tuesdays only). It is probably reasonable to assume that this applied to most mixed trains, although there may well have been exceptions, for example, No. 22 Up.

Passenger Train Set No. 1 (Montrose Based)

a) The Montrose-based set formed the first passenger train of the day (No. 2 Down) which left Montrose at 6.56am, arriving Bervie 37 minutes later at 7.33am.
b) It returned from Bervie at 7.38am (No. 1 Up) and took 38 minutes for the journey to Montrose, arriving at 8.16am. It then departed at 8.17 for Arbroath, arriving there 35 minutes later at 8.52am. On Tuesdays only, this train was a mixed train which took goods traffic from Bervie only and not from any of the intermediate stations and it is assumed that it ran forward to Arbroath as a mixed train.
c) It appears this train then returned from Arbroath at 9.33, arriving Montrose after 33 minutes at 10.06. It then formed the 10.31 departure from Montrose (No. 8 Down), arriving Bervie 37 minutes later at 11.08.
d) It returned from Bervie at 11.40 as a mixed train (No. 9 Up), except on Tuesdays when it was not a mixed train, arriving

BERVIE BRANCH. Feb. 1884. 48

Down Trains.

Stations and Sidings.	Distance from Montrose. Miles	Chains	1 Mixed Pass. 1 2 3 Class.	2 Pass. 1 2 3 Class.	3 Montrose Pilot.	4 Montrose Pilot.	5 Pass. 1 2 3 Class.	6 Mixed Pass. 1 2 3 Class.	7 Pass. 1 2 3 Class.	8 Mixed Pass. 1 2 3 Class.	9
			a.m.	a.m.	Goods	Goods	a.m.	p.m	p.m.	p.m.	
Edinburgh (via Bro'ty) dep.			...	6 30	a.m.	p.m.	9 30	...	1 15	4 0	...
Dundee Tay Br. Stn.... ,,	...	...	......	9 0	......	......	11 45	......	4 10	6 25	......
Do. East Stn. ... ,,	...	...	5 50	...	...	...	p.m.	...	...	...	...
Arbroath ... ... ,,	...	...	7 15	9 44	......	......	12 27	12 40	4 52	7 20	......
Montrose ... ... dep.	...	...	8 0	10 18	10 32	12 5	12 55	3 15	5 20	8 5	...
Broomfield Junction ... ,,	...	67	8 2	10 20	10 35	12 10	12 57	3 17	5 22	8 7	......
North Water Bridge ... ,,	3	7	8 9	10 25	10 42	12 17	1 3	3 24	5 29	8 14	...
St Cyrus ... ... ,,	5	21	8 15	10 31	10 50	12 25	1 9	3 30	5 35	8 20	......
Lauriston ... ... arr.	6	18	8 19	10 34	10 55	12 30	1 12	3 33	5 38	8 23	...
Do. ... ... dep.	6	18	8 25	10 35	Stop.	12 35	1 13	3 34	5 39	8 24	...
Johnshaven ... ... ,,	8	44	8 31	10 41	......	12 45	1 18	3 40	5 45	8 30	......
Gourdon ... ... ,,	11	65	8 40	10 51	...	1 10	1 26	3 50	5 55	8 40	...
Bervie ... ... arr.	12	75	8 45	10 55	......	1 15	1 30	3 55	6 0	8 45	......

No. 1 Down.—Runs through from Arbroath. Does not lift or leave Goods Wagons at any Intermediate Station. *Meets at Lauriston No. 1 Up.*

No. 3 Down.—Engine turns out at 7-30 a.m. Takes full load for Lauriston and beyond, the latter to be lifted at Lauriston by 12-5 p.m. *ex* Montrose.

No. 5 Down.—Does not wait arrival of 11-45 a.m. Train from Dundee if likely to be more than five minutes late.

No. 6 Down.—Does not lift or leave Goods Wagons at any Intermediate Station. The 3-15 p.m. Train from Montrose must call at Birnie Road Siding on *Fridays*.

No. 7 Down.—Runs through from Arbroath, leaving there at 4-25 p m.

No. 8 Down.—Does not lift or leave Goods Wagons at any Intermediate Station.

Left and Facing Page: One of the earliest North British timetables for the line was this one issued in February 1884. No. 1 Up and No. 1 Down trains were scheduled to pass at Lauriston, which had just been provided with a loop. Journey times had been improved to 40 minutes for most trains, with the 10.18 from Montrose scheduled to do the trip in 37 minutes. ***National Records of Scotland BR/TT/S/52***

MONTROSE and BERVIE.

	a.m.		a.m.		a.m.		p.m.			a.m.		a.m.		p.m.		p.m.
Glasgow (Buch. St.) leave	4d20	...	7 15	...	10 0	...	2 0		BERVIE ....leave	6 44	...	9 50	...	12 53	...	4 52
Edinburgh (Prin. St.) ,,	4 0	...	6 45	...	9 40	...	1 35		Gourdon ,,	6 47	...	9 53	...	12 56	...	4 55
Dundee (East) ,,	6 40	...	9 10	...	1230p	...	5 5		Johnshaven ,,	6 56	...	10 2	...	1 5	...	5 4
Aberdeen ,,	6 45	...	9 15	...	1 10	...	5 25		Lauriston ,,	7 2	...	10 8	...	1 11	...	5 10
MONTROSE .....leave	9 0	...	11 4	...	3 40	...	6 4		St. Cyrus ,,	7 6	...	10 12	...	1 15	...	5 14
North Water Bridge ,,	9 8	...	11 11	...	3 48	...	6 4		North Water Bridge ,,	7 11	...	10 17	...	1 21	...	5 20
St. Cyrus ,,	9 14	...	11 17	...	3 54	...	6 54		MONTROSE ....arrive	7 19	...	10 25	...	1 29	...	5 28
Lauriston ,,	9 19	...	11 21	...	3 59	...	6 59		Aberdeen ....arrive	9 30	...	1 0p	...	3 52	...	8 10
Johnshaven ,,	9 25	...	11 27	...	4 5	...	7 5		Dundee (East) ,,	9 15	...	12 2	...	3 50	...	7 30
Gourdon ,,	9 32	...	11 34	...	4 12	...	7 12		Edinburgh (Prin. St.) ,,	11 2	...	2 15	...	5 56	...	9 35
BERVIE ....arrive	9 35	...	11 37	...	4 15	...	7 15		Glasgow (Buch. St.) ,,	10 45	...	2 0	...	6 0	...	9 25

The Caledonian Railway competitive public timetable for June 1898. The trains were scheduled to complete the trip in as little as 33 minutes.

National Records of Scotland BR/TT/S/55

Montrose at 12.20pm after 40 minutes. As there was no timetabled early onward movement to Arbroath or a return to Bervie for this train, it is assumed that the goods wagons were shunted off at Montrose and the train then awaited its next turn of duty.

e) On Fridays only, Montrose market day, it appears this train departed Montrose as a mixed train at 2.50pm (No. 14 Down), arriving Bervie 38 minutes later at 3.28pm. It was booked to stop at Birnie Road Siding. It returned from Bervie as a passenger only train (No. 16 Up) at 3.40pm, arriving after 38 minutes at Montrose at 4.18pm.

f) Other than the Fridays only return movement to/from Bervie described above, it appears this train set remained at Montrose from its previous arrival from Bervie[21] at 12.20pm until the next scheduled departure to Bervie at 4.55pm on Tuesdays and Fridays only (No. 20 Down). This train was not booked to stop at North Water Bridge and took 33 minutes, arriving Bervie at 5.28pm. Except on Tuesdays and Fridays, this train normally departed Montrose at 4.05pm (No. 17 Down) arriving Bervie 38 minutes later at 4.43pm.

g) The final movement for this train was to form the 5.35pm departure from Bervie (No. 20 Up) which took 40 minutes to Montrose, arriving at 6.15pm. This train was required to carry mailbags for drop off at Broomfield Junction at 6.12pm for the Caledonian 6.15 train from Montrose to Dubton.

PASSENGER TRAIN SET NO. 2 (BERVIE BASED)

a) The first tour of duty for this train was the 10.30am departure from Bervie which took 38 minutes, arriving at Montrose at 11.08am (No. 7 Up). This train was booked to stop at Birnie Road Siding on Fridays only, Montrose market day. It is assumed that the branch engine at the time, Drummond 0-6-0 tank number 241, normally stabled at Bervie, would work this train.

b) The arrival at Montrose at 11.08 allowed a connection with the 11.18 departure for Dundee and Edinburgh. The branch train

This was the timetable in October 1912.

National Records of Scotland BR/TT/S/52

The 1943 timetable. Note the 'QFO' (if required, Fridays only) livestock train which was controlled by the Inverbervie Station Master.
National Records of Scotland BR/TT/S/50

then followed on at 11.26am from Montrose, arriving at Arbroath 35 minutes later at 12.01pm.

c) The return from Arbroath was at 12.13 as a mixed train, taking 38 minutes to Montrose, arriving at 12.51. (This train provided a connection with the 11.35am Dundee–Aberdeen train which was due at Arbroath at 12.04pm, although the branch train would not wait if the Dundee–Aberdeen was more that 30 minutes late.) The train departed Montrose at 12.53pm arriving at Bervie 37 minutes later at 1.30pm (No. 12 down).

d) The train shunted its goods wagons at Bervie then departed as a passenger train only at 1.35pm, taking 40 minutes on the journey to Montrose, arriving at 2.15pm (No. 11 Up). On Saturdays only, this departure was 10 minutes later, arriving Montrose at 2.25pm (No. 13 Up). It left Montrose at 2.36pm, arriving after a 42 minute journey at Arbroath at 3.18pm.

e) The return from Arbroath was not until 4.55pm, arriving at Montrose at 5.33pm, 38 minutes later. It left Montrose for Bervie at 5.34pm, taking 40 minutes on the journey before arriving at 6.14pm (No. 22 Down).

f) It then formed a mixed train departure from Bervie at 6.30pm, taking 50 minutes on the journey to Montrose, arriving there at 7.20pm (No. 22 Up). This timing is some 10 minutes longer than normal and the timetable shows 5 extra minutes being spent at both Gourdon and Johnshaven. It could be assumed that this was to allow time for the train to shunt goods wagons at these stations. However, whilst this is quite possible at Gourdon, which had a goods loop, it could present a challenge at Johnshaven where there was no loop and the siding points were in the facing direction for Up trains with the station being in the middle of a 1 in 66 climb from sea level up to Lauriston! It is more likely that the extended stop at Johnshaven was to allow goods to be loaded directly from the station platform.

g) The final movement of the day for this train set was the return journey from Montrose as a mixed train (except on Fridays when it was not a mixed train), departing at 8.45pm and taking 39 minutes to arrive at Bervie at 9.24pm (No. 25 Down).

Goods Traffic Operation – Goods Only Trains

In addition to the mixed trains described above, the branch was served by a regular daily goods working which started out from Arbroath in the early morning, then completed two return trips between Montrose and Bervie, before finally returning to Arbroath in the late afternoon. Considering the direction of the siding points at each station, it is assumed that it would have been normal practice for Down goods trains to shunt at Johnshaven and Gourdon, where the siding points would be trailing in the Down direction, and Up goods trains to shunt at Lauriston and St. Cyrus where the siding points are trailing in the Up direction. This would mean that goods traffic to or from intermediate stations would always travel via Bervie.

The goods train movements for the day were as follows:

a) The engine crew booked on at Arbroath at 5am for the daily goods which left Arbroath station at 5.45am and arrived at Montrose at 7.40am.

b) It then departed Montrose at 8.15am for the first trip to Bervie, arriving there at 9.05am after 50 minutes (No. 5 Down).

c) Having shunted the necessary wagons at Bervie, the re-marshalled train left Bervie at 9.33am, taking 51 minutes to travel to Montrose, arriving there at 10.24am (No. 4 Up).

d) After another period shunting at Montrose, the train departed again for Bervie at 11.25am, taking 55 minutes this time, to arrive at Bervie at 12.30pm (No. 10 Down).

e) Replenishment of coal and water was no doubt called for before the train's next departure from Bervie at 1.55pm (2.05pm on Saturdays), when it set out once again for Montrose, arriving there at 2.50pm after a journey of 50 minutes (No. 14 Up).

f) The final movement of the daily goods was a departure from Montrose at 3.00pm for the journey back to Arbroath, arriving at 4.17pm. After shunting at Arbroath and disposing of the engine, the crew finally booked off at 5.30pm having completed a working shift of 12.5 hours.

On Thursday 20th October 1898 the NBR carried out a detailed census of all goods trains operating across its entire system. The records for that day still exist in the Scottish Records Office and they give a fascinating insight into the NBR's goods traffic operation at the turn of the century. For the Bervie Branch, we see that the daily goods was in the charge of engine No. 560, a 'Wee Drummond' 0-6-0 tender locomotive. The engine travelled a total of eighty productive miles executing the various trips described above and, in addition, travelled a further six miles on shunting operations.

During the period January to March 1901, the NBR commenced running a cattle train which left Bervie for Montrose at 6.00am on Tuesdays only. This train took 41 minutes on the journey, arriving at Montrose at 6.41am. The engine for this train left Montrose for Bervie at 5.05am. It is assumed this would have necessitated the signal boxes at Lauriston and Bervie being manned earlier than usual. Presumably Tuesday was the day for the local cattle market. The traffic for this train proved not to be sufficient as it was discontinued in April and it is assumed that the first passenger train from Bervie at 7.38am (No. 1 Up), which was designated as a mixed train on Tuesdays only, carried the cattle traffic after this time.[19]

A remarkable survival in the records held at the National Records of Scotland are two guard's daily journals which list the activities of the branch goods train during 1894 and 1902. The entry for 12th May 1902, reproduced below, is typical.

LOCOMOTIVES

The locomotive used to open the branch in 1865 was the '*very powerful engine*' SNER No. 47,[20] but the branch engine was soon complained of as being '*too weak*', Porteous noting that all it could manage was six wagons and the passenger carriages.[21] No. 47 was a 2-4-0 built in 1855 by Brassie, Jackson, Betts & Co.[22] It may have been sent away for remedial work, for the Directors noted that the replacement was '*too slow in reverse*' and decided to enquire when the previous engine would be repaired.[23] Possibly the replacement engine was SNER No. 43 (CR No. 510), an 1862 Vulcan Foundry 0-4-2 which was photographed at Bervie around 1870.

The first North British locomotive to be used on the branch is reputed to have been No. 332, an 0-4-2 engine built in 1864 by S.W. Johnson for the Edinburgh & Glasgow Railway as their No. 86. After rebuilding by Holmes it was renumbered 1033 in 1909 and finally withdrawn in 1914. It is not known how long No. 332 ran at Bervie.[24]

For many years the branch engine was a Drummond 0-6-0 tank, NBR Class 'R', No. 241. This engine was built in January 1876 at Cowlairs and, in accordance with Drummond's practice at the time of naming engines after the locality where they worked, was originally named 'Roslin' for service on that branch. It was transferred to the Bervie Branch, presumably some time prior to Drummond's departure from the NBR, and renamed 'Bervie'. It probably did not carry this name for too long as the practice of naming engines was stopped when Holmes took over from Drummond as NBR Locomotive Superintendent in the summer of 1882. It was rebuilt by Reid in 1910 and renumbered 1299 in 1917, before being withdrawn in January 1925. It is not known when this engine left the branch – it is possible this was at the time of its rebuilding, around the time the Class 'M' 0-4-4 tanks were introduced.

GUARD'S DAILY JOURNAL FOR 12TH MAY 1902										
No. 560 J. Reid	**Timetable**	**Actual**		**Wagons Taken Up**		**Wagons Left Off**		**Wagons on Engine**		**Notes**
		Arr.	Dep.	Full	Empty	Full	Empty	Full	Empty	
Montrose	8.15am		8.30am	15	2					Shunt signals
St. Cyrus	8.35am	8.45am	8.50am			1	1	14	1	
Lauriston	8.43am	8.54am	8.57am			2		12	1	
Johnshaven	8.52am	9.04am	9.07am			3	1	9		
Gourdon	9.02am	9.13am	9.20am		1	3		6	1	
Bervie	9.33am	9.23am	9.40am	4	5	6	1	4	5	Late start, late arrival
Gourdon	9.38am	9.54am	9.58am				4	4	1	
Johnshaven										
Lauriston	10.00am									
St. Cyrus	10.05am	10.14am	10.20am					4	1	Shunting
Broomfield		10.28am	10.34am	1	2	1	1	4	2	
Montrose	10.24am	10.47am				4	2			
Montrose	11.25am		11.25am	10				10		
Lauriston	12.02am	11.45am	12.02pm			1		9		
Johnshaven	12.15pm	12.10pm	12.22pm			2		7		
Gourdon	12.25pm	12.28pm	12.40pm	3	1	3		7	1	
Bervie	12.30pm	12.45pm				7	1			
Bervie	1.44pm		2.05pm	5	2			5	2	Waiting train staff
Johnshaven	2.15pm	2.14pm	2.20pm	1				6	2	
Lauriston	2.27pm	2.29pm	2.32pm		3			6	5	
Broomfield	2.45pm	2.44pm	2.50pm				2	6	3	
Montrose	2.40pm	2.52pm				6	3			

Snow Plough

9.20am from Montrose to Inverbervie 29.12.61
Engine No. 64620; Driver G. Murray; Fireman A. Littlejohn

Owing to having difficulty coming from Johnshaven to St. Cyrus the previous day I asked the yard foreman at Montrose to reduce as a howling gale had been blowing all night and I surmised that this place would be full of snow blowing off the fields. My prophecy was right, we went bang into it tender first. We were standing knee deep in it before we stopped. The main road to Aberdeen which runs a field breadth from us was also blocked with lines of cars and lorries on both sides. My fireman walked over the field (which was bare) to the main road and got a lift from a car that had turned about. He came back with the Montrose Pilot No. 64786 (C. Ogg) (both his gauge glasses were broken) who when he saw us refused to come in and become stuck also, so Inspector, smiling by this time, had mustered twenty P.Way men with shovels to dig me out. The Pilot went back to Montrose to be relieved and returned about 4pm. By this time the brake van and fish vans were dug clear and the Pilot went to Lauriston with them. While they were away I was trying to loosen No. 64620 by reversing the lever back and forward with the steam full on. I had it moving about a yard each way when the Pilot returned. After some jerking we finally moved away back to Montrose just after dark. I developed a terrible head cold after that.

By George Murray. First published in the magazine of the Brechin Railway Preservation Society.

NBR Class 'M' 0-4-4 tank engine No. 475 (L&NER Class 'G9') worked the branch for a time. This engine was built under Reid by the North British Locomotive Company in October 1909 and became L&NER No. 9475 at the time of grouping. It was eventually withdrawn in November 1940. It may well be the case that the introduction of these Class 'M' tanks allowed the original branch engine, No. 241, to be taken out of service for rebuilding in 1910.[25]

The surviving guards' daily journals for 1894 and 1902 listed the following locomotives working goods trains on the branch: No's 409 (Wheatley 0-6-0 of 1872), 276 (Wheatley 0-6-0 of 1874), 207 (Hurst 0-6-0 of 1866) and 64 (Wheatley 0-6-0 of 1872) in 1894, and No's 560 (Drummond 0-6-0, later Class 'J34'), 410 (Wheatley 0-6-0 of 1872), and 160 (Holmes 0-6-0 of 1885), as well as No's 64 and 409, in 1902.[26]

Apart from these, other engines known to have been on the line are NBR 0-6-0 No. 267 (circa 1890), and NBR 0-6-0 No. 560 (L&NER Class 'J34') in 1898. NBR Class 'P' 0-4-4 tank engine No. 1334 (L&NER Class 'G8') is recorded on the 1921 shed list as being at Montrose and would almost certainly have worked the Bervie Branch passenger service. Also on the 1921 list, No's 1325 and 1338 were recorded at Dundee, so it is possible that these engines also did the odd turn on the branch although they were more likely used on the St Andrews and north of Fife services. NBR Class 'C' 0-6-0 (L&NER Class 'J36') No. 726 is listed on the same shed list as an Arbroath engine; this being so, it was probably the regular engine on the Arbroath–Montrose–Bervie daily goods at that time. NBR Class 'M' 4-4-2 tank engines (L&NER Class 'C15') also worked the branch; two in particular were No's 141 and 53 (L&NER No's 9141 and 9053, renumbered No's 7461 and 7471 in July 1946 – they were allocated BR numbers 67461 and 67471 but these were never carried). It appears these engines took over the branch duties from the Class 'G9's when they were withdrawn around 1940.

The last passenger train in 1951 was worked by 'J39' No. 64790.

Latterly the NBR Class 'S' 0-6-0 goods engines (L&NER Class 'J37') were used on goods trains and a number of these, including

NBR Class 'R' 0-6-0T No. 241 on the turntable at Bervie around 1910. The name 'Bervie' had been removed in the 1880s. The L&NER classification was 'J82'. *Allan Rodgers*

No's 64588, 64602, 64608, 64620 and 64624 are known to have been used. In addition, No. 64615 pulled the 1960 Scottish Rail Tour when it visited the branch on 16th June of that year and No. 64547 pulled the last special excursion, on 22nd May 1966.

The branch was also visited by diesel traction when English Electric Type 1 No. D8028 pulled the Easter Rail Tour on 22nd April 1962, and the last train was assisted by the Montrose 350hp shunter No. D3343.[27]

Notes

1. Reported in MMB1, p. 122 (1st Oct. 1865). Two locomotives could actually be present, provided they were coupled together. Porteous letter to Board of Trade dated 25th October 1865. Unfortunately the exchange of correspondence which would have been necessary to change to Train Staff and Ticket has not been preserved, so the actual date of introduction of the permanent method cannot be confirmed.
2. Although Col. Yolland of the Board of Trade Railway Inspectorate, in his report on Broomfield Junction in 1881, was quite specific that the Bervie line did not use a telegraph, clause 12 in the operating agreement with the SNER provided for the provision of an electric telegraph line; there is also an historic capital item of £238 for the '*erection of electric telegraph*' in the 1867 accounts, showing it was built. In the January 1868 Accounts, '*Electric Telegraph Services*' are in a separate section, together with '*clerks and messengers*' at Montrose, further suggesting that this was not signalling-related. Although Yolland does not mention ticket working with the staff, there would have been no point in providing fixed signals unless ticket working allowed more than one train on the branch.
3. The time interval would possibly have been determined by instructions in the Montrose & Bervie Rule Book, as in examples on other railways (e.g., the Cambrian Railway in Wales). Unfortunately no copy of the rule book has survived.
4. Yolland noted that the south distant signal at Lauriston needed raising and that the others needed to be painted.
5. It is quite possible (indeed likely, given the very limited use of the system when the line opened) that these signals were not interlocked until the resignalling of 1893. Caledonian Railway timetables in NRS (file BR/TT/S/54) exist for the whole of the 1866-81 period, and for most of the North British period from 1884 (file BR/TT/S/53).
6. The other major concern was the lack of continuous braking on trains on the line.
7. General Appendix to the Book of Rules & Regulations and to the Working Timetables, 1 March 1898 (NRS reference GD456/9/1). The section from Broomfield to Lauriston was operated under the Caledonian Railway Block Telegraph Regulations (Broomfield controlled the Caledonian line from Montrose [CR] to Dubton, and was a Caledonian Railway signal box). Tyer's Single Line Block and Train Staff was in operation from Lauriston to Bervie. Tickets on the Broomfield–Lauriston section were green, while those on the Lauriston–Bervie section were white.
8. General Appendix to the Book of Rules & Regulations and to the Working Timetables 1901 and 1922 both specify the less restrictive arrangement. It is assumed that the Annett's key would have been kept within the station masters' offices.
9. Oddly she was nominated as Miss K. Scott. Her name was Anna-Katherine, or 'Nan' to her friends.
10. Superintendent, Southern Scottish Area, L&NER to General Manager, 6th July 1925; NRS file LNE/8/778.
11. Engineer-in-Chief to General Manager, 19th August 1925; NRS file LNE/8/778.
12. Superintendent, Southern Scottish Area, L&NER to General Manager, 9th September 1925; NRS file LNE/8/778.
13. Superintendent, Southern Scottish Area, L&NER to General Manager, 23rd October 1925; NRS file LNE/8/778.
14. Superintendent, Southern Scottish Area, L&NER to General Manager, 13th March 1926; NRS file LNE/8/778.
15. General Manager, Southern Scottish Area, L&NER to Chief General Manager, 30th March 1926; NRS file LNE/8/778. The staff savings were estimated at two signalmen at Bervie and one at Lauriston, together with the station agent at Lauriston. In their place, a grade 1 porter at Lauriston and a grade 2 at Bervie were to be introduced. The saving on staff was £360 16s per annum.
16. Engineer-in-Chief to General Manager, 19th April 1927; NRS file LNE/8/778.
17. North British Railway General Appendix 1st March 1898.
18. This is confirmed by correspondence on out of class travel (NRS file BR/NBR/8/1532).
19. Allan G. Rodgers, 'The Montrose & Bervie Branch' in *North British Railway Study Group Journal*, No. 73 (Summer 1999), pp. 73/20-21. I am indebted to Allan Rodgers for advice on the method of operation of the branch as well as an update of the notes contained within his 1999 article.
20. *DC*, 3rd Nov. 1865, p. 4.
21. MMB1, pp. 205-6 (2nd Dec. 1867).
22. I am indebted to Jim MacIntosh of the Caledonian Railway Association for this detail. The CR minute books are not clear on whether two specific locomotives were allocated, or just any which were spare, though the specific complaints from the M&B Directors suggest that there was a regular performer.
23. MMB1, pp. 279-82 (5th Mar. 1869).
24. J. Thomas, *Forgotten Railways – Scotland*. The author is definite about this locomotive being the first used on the NBR Bervie line, but regrettably does not give his source.
25. Quoted from Rodgers, op. cit., p. 73/24 (amended by him 2014).
26. Bervie guard's journals for 1894 and 1902 (NRS file GD536/5966).
27. Abridged from Rodgers, op. cit., p. 73/24 (amended by him 2014).

No. 64624 awaits departure for Montrose at Bervie on a summer day in 1964. *Les Moffat*

Appendix 4: SNER-M&BR Working Agreement

Commenced, 1st October, 1863.

Terminates 30th September, 1873.

MEMORANDUM OF AGREEMENT

between the **Scottish North Eastern Railway Company**, on the first part, and the **Montrose and Bervie Railway Company**, on the second part.

The Companies above-named have agreed, and do hereby, in pursuance of the powers conferred upon them by the Montrose and Bervie Railway Act, 1860, contract and agree in manner follows, that is to say:—

First. The Contracting Companies have agreed, and do hereby agree, that the Scottish North Eastern Railway Company shall work by locomotive power the traffic of the line of the Montrose and Bervie Railway Company for the period of eight years from and after the 1st day of October, 1865, and in order thereto the following particulars have been agreed upon.

Second. That through rates and through booking shall be given between the Stations of the Montrose and Bervie Line and Stations on the Scottish North Eastern Railway Line, and subject to the approval of all other Railway Companies interested all Stations on other lines to which the Scottish North Eastern Railway Company book, the rates for which shall be fixed by the Scottish North Eastern Railway Company, except in the case of traffic other than Seaborn traffic, between Stations on the Montrose and Bervie Railway and Dubton, Bridge of Dun and Craigo Stations, the rates for which, as well as the rates for their own local traffic, shall be fixed by the Montrose and Bervie Company. The Montrose and Bervie Company shall receive the usual terminals on such through traffic in addition to their mileage proportion according to Clearing House Regulations in force for the time being.

Third. That the Scottish North Eastern Railway shall supply to the Montrose and Bervie Railway Company a 4-wheeled coupled engine of 16-inch cylinders, similar to the one that works the Montrose Branch, and shall uphold and work the same at the rate of 7d. per engine mile, but in no event shall the charge for said engine be less than £2 8s. per diem, and such payment shall be exclusive of charges for shunting, which shall be charged for according to the time at the rate of 5s. per hour; but no charge shall be made for shunting occupying less than five minutes at any one time, at any intermediate station, or 15 minutes at any terminal station.

Fourth. The Scottish North Eastern Company shall furnish to the Montrose and Bervie Company for the purpose of their local traffic twelve 6-ton wagons, or such other number as may be agreed on from time to time, and shall keep the same in good working order, for which Montrose and Bervie Company shall pay £10 per wagon per annum. For extra wagons of a like tonnage occasionally required for local traffic which the Scottish North Eastern Company may be able to supply without inconvenience to their own traffic, the Montrose and Bervie Company shall pay at the rate of 1s 6d per wagon for each time it is loaded, and also the usual charges if incurred for demurrage. Wagons for through traffic shall be supplied by the Scottish North Eastern Railway Company at the Clearing House mileage rates, with the usual charges for demurrage. These conditions, so far as they relate to occasional or to through traffic, shall apply to cattle trucks and horse boxes, in the same way as to wagons.

Fifth. Three passenger carriages, viz., one first class carriage capable of carrying 18 passengers, and two third class carriages, each capable of carrying 30 passengers, shall be furnished to the Montrose and Bervie Railway Company by the Scottish North Eastern Railway Company, together with a break van, the Scottish North Eastern Company upholding the same and the Montrose and Bervie Railway Company paying for each carriage and break van the sum of £12 10s. per annum. The Scottish North Eastern Railway Company will supply carriages for excursion trains on the Montrose and Bervie Railway at the rate of two shillings each for each journey to and from any Station on the Montrose and Bervie line, provided the excursion trains are not run on days in which the Scottish North Eastern Company are themselves running excursion trains. But on the Montrose holidays, the Scottish North Eastern Company shall furnish fifteen carriages for excursionists to the Montrose and Bervie line at the said rate of two shillings per double journey per carriage.

Sixth. The Montrose and Bervie Railway Company shall supply grease for the rolling stock employed on their line, with the exception of the engine, and the Scottish North Eastern Company shall furnish the same on the terms stated in Article 9 hereof, or, in the option of the Montrose and Bervie Company, the Scottish North Eastern Company shall supply the grease, charging the Montrose and Bervie Company therefor at the average rate which it costs them for greasing the rolling stock on their own line.

Seventh. The whole accounts connected with the traffic of Montrose and Bervie Railway Company shall be passed through the books of the Scottish North Eastern Railway Company, and shall be open inspection by the Secretary or other official appointed by the Directors of the Montrose and Bervie Railway Company, and abstracts thereof shall be furnished monthly to the Montrose and Bervie Railway Company. The Scottish North Eastern Railway Company shall pay all Clearing House expenses incurred in connection with the traffic of the Montrose and Bervie Railway Company. They shall advertise the trains on the Montrose and Bervie Railway in the same way as they advertise the trains on their own branch lines. Their Manager, or one of his assistants, shall attend a monthly meeting of the Board of Directors of the Montrose and Bervie Railway Company, and shall take a general charge of the traffic and servants of said Company, and the Superintendent of Way and Works of the Scottish North Eastern Railway Company shall superintend the way and works of the Montrose and Bervie Railway, and shall employ or dismiss such men as he thinks necessary, and shall once in each half-year go over and inspect the Montrose and Bervie Line, and make a report to the Board of Directors of the Montrose and Bervie Railway Company on the state of their line and works. For all services mentioned in this article, the Scottish North Eastern Railway Company shall be entitled to charge the Montrose and Bervie Railway Company at the rate of 7½ per cent, on the gross receipts of the Montrose and Bervie Railway Company: Provided always that nothing contained in this section shall in any way derogate from the stipulation contained in Section 14 hereof.

Eighth. The Montrose and Bervie Railway Company shall appoint and pay their own station agents and other servants, and such agents and servants shall conform to the regulations of the Scottish North Eastern Railway Company relating to the transmission of cash and all other matters relating to the conduct of the traffic, the accounts for which are to be passed through the books of the Scottish North Eastern Railway Company conform to the Seventh Article of this Agreement.

Ninth. If required by the Montrose and Bervie Railway Company, stores, including tickets and stationery, shall be supplied to them by the Scottish North Eastern Railway Company, deliverable at Montrose Station at the rate of 7½ per cent, above the price paid therefor by the latter Company, to cover the wages of store keeper, &c.

Tenth. The Montrose and Bervie Railway Company shall supply wagon sheets for their local traffic, the Scottish North Eastern Railway Company supplying all sheets for through traffic, and being entitled to charge the Montrose and Bervie Company 4d. for each sheet so supplied, together with the usual charges for demurrage.

Eleventh. Parcels shall not be booked through from or to Stations on the Montrose and Bervie Railway unless it is mutually agreed that they shall be so.

Twelfth. The Scottish North Eastern Railway Company shall erect a single needle telegraph with three instruments (one at Montrose and two on the line) along the line of the Montrose and Bervie Railway for the sum of £238, payable within one month after erection, and shall maintain the same in good working order for the sum of £20 per annum, the Montrose and Bervie Railway Company arranging and paying for the working of the instruments and carrying all stores and servants connected with the construction, maintenance or repair of the telegraph free of charge.

Thirteenth. All accounts between the Contracting Companies shall be settled monthly, the Scottish North Eastern Railway Company being entitled to retain from the cash in their hands, belonging to the Montrose and Bervie Railway Company, the various sums payable by them in connection with the working of the traffic.

Fourteenth. The Montrose and Bervie Railway Company shall be responsible for all accidents which may happen upon their line of Railway or at their Stations, and for all claims which may be made in connection with their traffic arising out of accidents and injury or detention on their own line, and between Montrose Station and the junction of the Montrose and Bervie Line.

Fifteenth. The general arrangement of the Montrose and Bervie Railway shall, except so far as affected by this Agreement, remain with the Directors of the Montrose and Bervie Railway Company.

Sixteenth. The Agreement contained in the Schedule annexed to the Montrose and Bervie Railway Act, 1860, shall not be affected by anything contained in this Agreement.

Seventeenth. In case of any difference of opinion between the Contracting Companies as to the intent and execution of this Agreement, all such questions shall be referred to the Chairman for the time being of the Companies respectively, such Referees to have the power to name an Umpire if necessary, whose decision shall be final and binding on the parties.

Eighteenth. The Contracting Companies bind and oblige themselves to fulfil the respective parts of this Agreement to each other under a penalty of £500 sterling, to be paid by the party failing to the party performing willing to perform, over and above performance, and both parties consent to the registration hereof, for preservation and for execution.

In witness whereof.

Dated 19th and 20th September, 1865.

Excursion trains were usually hauled by larger engines such as 'Scott' class L&NER 'D30' (NBR Class 'J') No. 62434 *Kettledrummle*, waiting to depart for Inverbervie from Montrose on 8th September 1948. *J.L. Stephenson*

Appendix 5: Montrose & Bervie Accounts 1865-1881

Year	Meeting Sequence	Half-year Ending	Revenue (£)	Working Expenses (£)	Operating Profit (£)	Operating Ratio (Exp/Rev) (%)	Wages (£)	Miles Run	Interest (£)	Profit (Loss) (£)	Dividend (%)
1865	12th	Jan 1866	770	595	175	77.3			247	(73)	0.00
			770	595	175	77.3			247		0.00
1866	13th	Jul 1866[1]	1,660	988	673	59.5			384	(152)	0.00
	14th	Jan 1867[2]	1,621	1,806	-185	111.4			264	(502)	0.00
			3,281	2,794	488	85.1			648		0.00
1867	15th	Jul 1867	1,716	1,343	373	78.3	242		431	(535)	0.00
	16th	Jan 1868	1,713	1,230	483	71.8	224		548	(622)	0.00
			3,429	2,573	856	75.0	466		979		0.00
1868	17th	Jul 1868	1,732	1,155	577	66.7	210	13,197	506	(633)	0.00
	18th	Jan 1869	1,689	1,141	548	67.6	212	13,288	428	(867)	0.00
			3,421	2,296	1,125	67.1	422	26,485	934		0.00
1869	19th	Jul 1869	1,781	1,120	661	62.9	198	13,169	408	(840)	0.00
	20th	Jan 1870	1,846	1,136	710	61.5	202	13,215	427	(796)	0.00
			3,627	2,256	1,371	62.2	400	26,384	835		0.00
1870	21st	Jul 1870	1,747	1,109	638	63.5	196	13,149	404	(761)	0.00
	22nd	Jan 1871	1,900	1,193	707	62.8	200	13,579	427	(675)	0.00
			3,647	2,302	1,345	63.1	396	26,728	831		0.00
1871	23rd	Jul 1871	1,792	1,113	679	62.1	200	13,188	437	(627)	0.00
	24th	Jan 1872	2,125	1,270	855	59.8	207	13,443	446	(396)	0.00
			3,917	2,383	1,534	60.8	407	26,631	883		0.00
1872	25th	Jul 1872	1,946	1,131	815	58.1	215	13,167	429	(189)	0.00
	26th	Jan 1873	2,029	1,336	693	65.8	220	13,201	419	(117)	0.00
			3,975	2,467	1,508	62.1	435	26,368	848		0.00
1873	27th	Jul 1873	2,091	1,374	717	65.7	212	13,126	420	(41)	0.00
	28th	Jan 1874	2,446	1,522	924	62.2	256	13,312	445	223	0.50
			4,537	2,896	1,641	63.8	468	26,438	865		0.50
1874	29th	Jul 1874	2,564	1,738	826	67.8	223	13,464	460	211	0.50
	30th	Jan 1875[3]	2,368	1,695	673	71.6	230	12,926	456		0.00
			4,932	3,433	1,499	69.6	453	26,390	916		0.50
1875	31st	Jul 1875	2,459	1,494	965	60.8	226	13,135	451	370	1.00
	32nd	Jan 1876	2,529	1,584	945	62.6	235	13,462	443	303	0.75
			4,988	3,078	1,910	61.7	461	26,597	894		1.75
1876	33rd	Jul 1876	2,474	1,433	1,041	57.9	238	13,282	446	408	1.00
	34th	Jan 1877[4]	2,446	1,795	651	73.4	246	13,039	446		0.00
			4,920	3,228	1,692	65.6	484	26,321	892		1.00
1877	35th	Jul 1877[5]	2,508	1,643	865	65.5	232	13,095	448		0.00
	36th	Jan 1878[6]	2,660	1,612	1,048	60.6	246	13,336	443		1.00
			5,168	3,255	1,913	63.0	478	26,431	891		1.00
1878	37th	Jul 1878	2,577	1,299	1,278	50.4	243	13,039	441	381	2.00
	38th	Jan 1879	2,453	1,618	835	66.0	239	12,933	436	460	1.00
			5,030	2,917	2,113	58.0	482	25,972	877		3.00
1879	39th	Jul 1879[7]	2,537	1,471	1,068	58.0	234	13,051	438		0.75
	40th	Jan 1880	2,419	1,524	895	63.0	236	13,078	440	321	0.75
			4,956	2,995	1,961	60.4	470	26,129	878		1.50
1880	41st	Jul 1880[8]	2,387	1,484	903	62.2	234	13,129	444	293	0.75
	42nd	Jan 1881	2,512	1,860	652	74.0	232	12,722	436		0.00
			4,899	3,344	1,555	68.3	466	25,851	880		0.75
1881	43rd	Jul 1881[9]	2,880	1,766	784	69.3	232		462		0.00
			2,550	1,766	784	69.3			462		0.00

Notes:
General: Working expenses exclude feu duties, taxes etc. Data from Montrose & Bervie printed accounts (BR/RAC/S/1/116), National Records of Scotland, and M&B Minute books (which contain the Jan. 1881 printed accounts and Jul. 1881 summary). Where there are blanks in the tables above, data is missing.
1 Revenue restated in 1867 from £1,603 due to reallocation of misc. revenues.
2 Including Montrose station charge.
3 Big fall in fish tonnage (-693tons) exported from Gourdon harbour and grain down 252tons.
4 Re-sleepering, storms and floods.
5 Gravel from Bervie beach.
6 M&B shares £2 10s.
7 Merchandise down. Fish exported from Gourdon harbour.
8 Shares £3 5s per £10 share.
9 Balance £562 to testimonials.
Total dividends paid amounted to £3,937 (5.62% of £70,000) and feu duties etc amounted to £4,707 (about 8.56% of the £55,000 invested by the three main landed proprietors).

The last day at St. Cyrus. The weather had cleared up for the second run and among the spectators was the last line Station Agent Charlie (Chic) Duncan, who can be seen standing on the tyre to the right. It was his day off and he lived in the station house on the right. The grounded coach behind the station building was probably a former NBR four-wheel, four-compartment First Class carriage, either by Drummond (1877-82) or by Holmes (1882-circa 1893). *Author*

Appendix 6: The Amalgamation Bill Proceedings

The Montrose & Bervie Amalgamation Bill was not heavily opposed, but the statements made during its Parliamentary passage are quite illuminating; they also throw some light on the aims and motivations of the promoters, as well as helping to explain the apparent satisfaction the shareholders derived from taking a 40% loss on their holdings.

In the preparation for the Parliamentary Bill, Counsel's opinion was sought from Lord Frazer, Dean of the Faculty of Advocates in Scotland, on a number of legal points relating to the agreements with the Caledonian Railway. Lord Frazer gave a very succinct (though in some cases exaggerated, as in the reference to the '*much frequented*' North Water Bridge station) overview of the difficulties facing the M&B:[1]

> *the existing arrangements, under which the Bervie Company carries on its operations, are of so burdensome a character, and leave so slender a margin after meeting all imperative charges, that the directors are unable on their own line to give due accommodation to the public. Their resources are so limited and the sources of revenue so exhausted by the pressure of their present agreements, that they can offer only the barest and most narrow accommodation to their customers. The whole of their trains are mixed, and passengers are constantly and at every station delayed during the removal and attaching of goods wagons. They cannot afford to run passenger trains only, nor can they supply all their stations with cranes for lifting heavy goods nor give adequate loading banks, or other conveniences at their stations. At one of their stopping places, much frequented by passengers, they can give no shelter.*
>
> *… The pressure of their working and other charges falls with extreme severity on their revenues, and not only leaves the most narrow margin for return to the shareholders, but cripples at every point the efforts of the Directors in the management and improvement of the line.*
>
> *Every charge within the control of the Directors has been cut down to the lowest figure consistent with a due regard to safety and necessary maintenance; but, forced as they are under present arrangements to meet an exhaustive and always increasing expenditure out of the limited revenue derivable from a small agricultural line only twelve miles long, it has become clearly evident that their line is too short to stand alone.*
>
> *The capital of the Company is £70,000 in shares and £23,000 in loans, of which latter £18,000 now exist. The revenue from traffic, after deducting £320 paid yearly to the Caledonian Company as tollage, has averaged £4975 for the five years ended 31st July 1880. The annual expenditure has averaged 71 per cent, on revenue. During the five prior years the revenue was £4347, and the percentage of expenditure 73.40.*
>
> *Out of the slender balance available after deducting fully 72 per cent, of expenses, the Bervie Company has had to provide the interest on £18,000 of mortgage debt, absorbing upwards of £900 per annum. Their bonds have borne interest at five per cent., being long past due; and it has been simply through the forbearance of the holders that the money secured by these bonds has been continued.*
>
> *It has resulted from these causes that the dividends received by the shareholders during the ten years ended 31st July 1880 have averaged 10s. 3d. per £100, and no more.*
>
> *The arrangements with the working Company are such that the financial position of the Bervie Company cannot be improved during their subsistence. The arrangements are twofold:—*
>
> *Under the Agreement scheduled to their Act 1860, the Bervie Company pay £320 per annum to the Caledonian Company for tollage, and £150 for the use of Montrose Station. These charges, though reduced below the figures which were originally charged, press very severely on the Bervie Company, and have only been justifiable at all as long as access into Montrose was available by no other route.*
>
> *Under a Working Agreement, made for eight years from 1st October 1865, and renewed for further period of like duration as from 1st October 1873, they hire locomotive power, rolling stock, and wagon covers from the working Company, who are entitled to specific payment for all these services, as also two and a half per cent, on the whole receipts for taking charge of the traffic and superintending the maintenance.*
>
> *The combined effect of these two Agreements is only too apparent from the straitened condition of the Bervie Company, who have from time to time represented with the utmost urgency the exigency of their position to the Caledonian Manager or Directors, but without obtaining any adequate relief.*
>
> *At the principal interview which the Bervie Chairman and Secretary had with the Caledonian officials, Mr Scott, on behalf of the Bervie Company, urged in the strongest terms that any renewal of the Agreement should be based on a percentage of traffic, which percentage should cover all services whatsoever. He pointed out the stringency of the arrangements then in force, and appealed to the working Company, who were then, as now, getting the whole traffic of the Bervie Company, to show some consideration to the latter.*
>
> *Mr Scott's arguments, however, were without any effect, for the sole alteration made by the Caledonian upon the renewed Agreement was a considerable increase in the rate by which locomotive power was to be supplied.*
>
> *… during their possession of the Bervie Railway the Caledonian Company made no outlay in ameliorating the condition of the Montrose Station with respect to the services required by the Bervie Company. A small uncovered platform was assigned to the Bervie trains, from which their passengers had to enter the carriages in rain and storm without shelter. This has been a standing grievance, solely resulting from the Caledonian making no outlay to meet the requirements of the Bervie traffic.*

Of course Lord Frazer was seeking to paint a picture demonstrating why the merger should go ahead, and in doing so, referred to the SNER and Caledonian Railway Amalgamation Act of 1866.

> *The Act of 1866 … points at the continuation of a railway to the north, passing by Montrose, Bervie, and Stonehaven. It provides for the extension or completion by the North British Railway Company of a line or lines of railway (of which a line between Montrose and Bervie is an essential part), viz., from Arbroath to Aberdeen by Montrose, Bervie, and Stonehaven …*
>
> *This prospective extension of the North British system has already been carried out as far as Montrose, but Section 140 contemplates the extension or completion to be accomplished by a Bill or Bills for a line or lines, and not as a thing to be done*

by a single operation. Such applications as are contemplated in Section 140 are to be made to Parliament within five ensuing sessions after 1866, but it will be recollected that the whole system of extended lines was in effect made dependent upon the completion of the Tay Bridge, and that Parliament in 1878 did not entertain the Caledonian Company's objection that the provisions of the Act of 1866 had not been literally carried out when the North British Company were promoting the joint ownership of the Dundee and Arbroath Railway. The North British Company therefore assume that in proposing to amalgamate the Montrose and Bervie Railway they are carrying out the spirit and intention of Parliament, as disclosed in Section 140 of the Act of 1866 ...

However it became clear that the possibility of an extension north of Bervie was being used as a bargaining chip for running powers over the Caledonian line to Aberdeen.

It having been thus intended that an extension ... should be adopted for carrying North-East Coast traffic to or from Aberdeen, and the parties promoting the Bill being mutually interested in such an arrangement, it does not seem that the Caledonian Company can have any reasonable ground for opposing a step so much in consonance with the scheme contemplated by Parliament in 1866, for connecting the North-East Coast system through Montrose and Bervie to the North. Such a method of carrying out the spirit of the Act is surely much more consistent than the making of a new line by Montrose and Bervie, which, as will be seen from the evidence, would be practically useless and unprofitable except for merely local purposes.

The Parliamentary hearing started on 4th May 1881 before W.H.B. Portman. Sir Edmund Beckett appeared for the North British and the M&B.[2] In his introduction, Beckett reiterated the problems which had always beset the M&B, as well as explaining why the NBR were interested in acquiring it.

The whole thing together has been very unprofitable. We have only paid for the last five or ten years, a dividend of the nominal amount of ½ per cent, sometimes a little more—2s. 6d., or some such thing—all our income is eaten up with the payment, first to the Caledonian company under this agreement, and secondly, to the people from whom we have to borrow money. And also I should mention that as is usual with small companies under difficulties, our working expenses are as high as from 71 to 73 per cent., and the result is that though we have an income which looks pretty fair, of £5,000 per year upon our capital of £70,000, our profits are practically only nominal.

Then comes the question of the terms that we get from the North British company, and as usual the large company have had to give a good deal for the small—more than it is worth at present; but in the hope that by making it a through line and working it better, the traffic will be greater; therefore we buy the shares at what might be called 60 per cent., which is a good thing for the small company, and we hope it will ultimately be not a bad thing for the North British company, though at present it will be a losing bargain for the North British company.

Once again the emphasis was placed on making the M&B a through line. Beckett also referred to s111 of the 1866 Act which provided that:

The moment the Montrose and Bervie Company becomes North British, then the Caledonian Company will have the right to run over it, as if it had been the North British Line in that neighbourhood in the year 1866.

The Caledonian would use those powers a few years later.

The principal witness was Hercules Scott, and in the first few questions he confirmed the effective ownership of the line.

Q6: Was the line promoted and the capital principally subscribed by parties locally interested in the line?—The greater portion of it. I may mention that the proprietors of three estates contributed £45,000 out of the whole capital of £70,000.

Q7: Then there was £15,000 which the Act gave power to the Caledonian Company to subscribe, that made up £60,000; but practically it was all found by the parties interested in the neighbourhood?—Yes, it was mainly found by my two brothers-in-law and myself, the proprietors of those three estates.

Q8: You and your brothers-in-law were practically the Railway Company?—We had the principal interest at the time.

The questions then turned to the SNER agreement.

Q32: Did you find that the expense of paying for it was so great that practically you were getting little or no revenue upon your line?—It was simply ruinous—we were paying something like 12 or 14 per cent, for the expense of the Montrose Station alone—on a traffic of about £3,400, we were paying something like £380 for the use of the Montrose Station alone.

Q33: I believe, as a matter of fact, your traffic is mainly third-class passengers from Bervie?—To a very large extent, I should say fifteen-sixteenths, or something like that, of our traffic is third class.

Scott was very forthright in describing the financial state of the M&B.

Q54: As to your present condition, what has been the dividend earned and paid upon the average by your Company since it was first of all incorporated?—Very meagre—for the last ten years we have paid about 10s. 3d. for £100.

Q55: About half per cent.?—Yes, upon the average of ten years. We have been as high as 2 per cent, for one half-year, and we ran at 1 per cent, for some two or three years, but the average of ten years has been 10s. 3d.

Q56: Your capital remains, I believe, as it was contemplated under the Bill, at £70,000; your borrowing powers were £23,000, and I think £18,000 of the borrowing powers still remain, at this date in the Company?— Yes that is so.

Q57: What have your average receipts been? They were £4,975 for the four years ending July, 1880, is not that so?—Within a few shillings of that for the last five years.

Q58: You cut down every charge within your own control, to the lowest possible limit?—We have economised and screwed at every point.

Q59: And notwithstanding that has your percentage of expenditure varied to between 71 and 73 per cent, of your total revenue?—I am sorry to say it has.

Scott then gave some interesting detail on the fish traffic before the questions returned to the question of the GNSR bonds.

Q61: And at present it is mainly an agricultural line?—Agricultural and we have fish traffic; but I would call it an agricultural line, though we have a considerable amount of fish traffic.

Q62: Does the fish come to Bervie?—It is caught on the coast.

Q63: Montrose is a great fishing station, is it not?—We have several excellent fishing stations; on my own property, where I have built an harbour, we have a considerable amount of fishing, and at Gourdon where they have a very good harbour indeed, there is a large amount of fishing and in short a good deal of fish is taken on the line.

Q64: The interest on your loans comes to £900 per annum?—It has run about that during the greater portion of our existence, but latterly our credit has been a little improved, and we have taken up a few thousands at a lower rate than 5 per cent.—we have £6,000 at 4½ per cent and even 4¼, but it has run generally about £900, the fact being that our bonds have been long overdue, and it has only been by the forbearance of the holders that we have not got into trouble with them.

Q65: Though they are overdue they have consented to hold them on? Yes.

Q66: I suppose you could not have redeemed them, if they had not?—The proprietors of those three estates that I have been speaking of, hold pretty largely the debentures, and everybody has been very forbearing to us, I am bound to say.

Scott then made it clear that he had indicated to the CR on renewal of the SNER agreement in 1873 that they were pushing the M&B into the hands of the NBR, and that as soon as the opportunity arose, he approached them.

Q74: Mr. LEDGARD: In the result, does it seem to you that the only chance that the Company have, is to amalgamate with the North British?—It appears to us our only chance, and if I may be allowed to state it, I distinctly pointed out at the interview that took place at Perth with the Caledonian Company, that that must be the effect; that we should do our best to preserve our organisation until better times came, and I pointed out that the North British Company had just got an Act which would bring them close to us, and that I should advise our shareholders to do their very best to keep in heart until that time; that time has accordingly come.

Q76: You approached the North British and the result is the Bill before the Committee?—Yes.

The terms of the NBR acquisition were laid out.

Q77: What are the terms upon which the North British Company consented to the amalgamation?—The North British Company are to give us £6 for the £10 shares; they are to take over our debentures; they are to take up our borrowed capital, and to make themselves liable for our feu duties payable to the proprietors. Those are the leading bases of the arrangements.

The questioning then turned to the motivations of the shareholders in building the line.

Q105: It is not likely that landed gentlemen would engage in a railway speculation, I presume your object was not so much to make a profit on your money as to improve your estate?—We acted both for the improvements of our estates, and for the general good which we believe we have very greatly promoted by our line.

Q106: No doubt you have; and I think promoted your own good. I do not mean in a dividend, but in the way of railway accommodation to your estate?—'Hope told a flattering tale.'

Q107: It must be some advantage to the estate to have a Railway in the neighbourhood?—No doubt of it.

Q108: And that advantage you retain and rather augment by having the Railway in the hands of a great Company which might work it better?—We think so, decidedly.

John Walker, General manager of the North British, gave some interesting answers on the motivation of his company.

Q248: I presume, if you acquire the Bervie line, you are willing to pay for it as agreed by the Bill?—Yes, we think the price between the parties was a fair one, and it was agreed to without much hesitation upon either side; and we look to the development of the traffic upon the line to repay us any little risk we run. The Bervie Company have not been in a position to spend a great deal of money during the last ten years for additional accommodation, and the traders have been deprived of facilities in forwarding traffic.

Q249: You look to the future development that you can give to the traffic to recoup you for the liberal price of £6 for £10?—The price appears liberal in the face of the price paid by the Bervie Company; but if the working expenses are 65 per cent, against what we should work at, namely 50 per cent., there is very little risk in the matter.

Much of the Lords hearing in June 1881[3] was taken up with renewed attempts by the CR to recover all of the £15,000 invested by the SNER, but with no more success. However at one point Scott was asked about his motives in investing in the line.

Q80: Both in your first subscription and in the addition you made to it afterwards, may I take it that your object was to do good to your own estate and neighbourhood, and not merely to invest money in the hope of getting a return upon those Montrose and Bervie shares?—The motives were mixed motives—the line undoubtedly would be a great convenience to the community, and it has proved so; and we hoped it would enhance the value of our estates, but I am afraid that as things have gone of late years we have scarcely realised what we hoped for.

NOTES

1. This and subsequent quotations in this section are taken from the North British & Montrose & Bervie Railways Amalgamation – Brief for the promoters.
2. House of Commons. Minutes of Proceedings before the Select Committee on Railway Bills on the North British and Montrose and Bervie Railway Companies' Bill (group 11), Wednesday, 4th May 1881. The proceedings on 9th May were taken up with the attempt by the CR to get £15,000 instead of £9,000 (NRS, file BR/PYB/S/1/569).
3. House of Lords. Minutes of Proceedings taken before the Select Committee of the House of Lords on the North British and Montrose and Bervie Railway Companies' Bill, Tuesday, 28th June 1881 (NRS, file BR/PYB/S/1/569).

ABOVE: Lauriston Castle, home of Alexander Porteous, as it is today. Most of the buildings have been restored, but the south-west range, seen on page 141, has been demolished. *William Newlands of Lauriston*

LEFT: Fireman's view of the line from the cab of Class 'J37' No. 64608 on 22nd February 1964. *Mike Stephen*

BELOW: On the last train, No. 64547 was crewed by Driver Mitchell and Fireman Soutar. *Kenneth Hay*

Appendix 7: Coaches, Carriers, Omnibuses and Buses Running through Bervie 1837-1950

Coach Services in 1837
Montrose to Aberdeen via Bervie and Stonehaven

	ROYAL MAIL DAILY	SWIFT SuX	NEW TIMES SuX
Montrose	0220e	[0530]	1300p
Johnshaven	0300	0630	1400
Bervie	0330	0700	1430
Stonehaven	0445	0800	1530
Aberdeen	[0530]	[1000]	[1730]
Aberdeen	1445	1600	0700
Stonehaven	1630	1800	0900
Bervie	1730	1930*	1000
Johnshaven	1800	2000	1100**
Montrose	1900e	[2100]	1130p

NOTES:
To/from: e Edinburgh;   p Perth.
*   time given in Pigot's guide is 1730.
**   time given in Pigot's guide. Probably should be 1030.
Times in square brackets are deduced.
Royal Mail started on 5th May 1797 from Edinburgh to Montrose, extending to Aberdeen on 1st August 1798.

Operators in the St. Cyrus–Bervie Area 1825-1903

1825 (Pigot)
MONTROSE
Carriers: Aberdeen: John Smart WO (return SO)
                     Alex Findlay SO (return ThO)
BERVIE
Foot post: Johnshaven: daily at 1230, returns same evening
Carriers: Aberdeen: Wm Walker ThO (return FO)
           Montrose: Jas Andrew and Jas Tindal TFO (return same day)
JOHNSHAVEN
Foot post: arrives 1400, departs 1600

1837 (Pigot)
MONTROSE
Carriers: Aberdeen: Archd Spark MO
                      John Smart ThO
           Bervie: John Andrew TFO
                      James Tindal FO
           Stonehaven: Alexander Watt SO
BERVIE
Carriers: Aberdeen: Archibald Spark from Andrew's MO
                      Wm Walker from Cowgate MThO
                      John Smart from Ship ThO
           Montrose: John Andrew and James Turnbull TFO
                      Archibald Spark from Andrew's WO
                      A. Watt from Salutation FO
                      John Smart from Ship SO
           Stonehaven: Alex Watt from Salutation SO

M	Monday	Th	Thursday	Su	Sunday
T	Tuesday	F	Friday	O	Only
W	Wednesday	S	Saturday	X	Except

JOHNSHAVEN
Carriers: Aberdeen: Alex Watt WO
           Montrose: Alexander Torry and Alexander Burness MWFO
           Stonehaven: Alex Watt WO
ST. CYRUS
Carriers: Montrose: Charles Waddie and Charles Edward TFO
STONEHAVEN
Carriers: Bervie: Wm Walker TFO from Mackies
           Johnshaven: Alex Watt WO David St

1847 (Watt's Angus & Mearns Directory)
MONTROSE
Carriers: Aberdeen: John Smart ThO morning (return SO night) from Lower Baltic St
                      Archibald Spark MO morning (return WO night) from Carnegie St
           Bervie: A. Mouatt TFO
                      James Tindal WSO from Red Lion, High St
           Johnshaven: Wm Watson MWFO from Black Horse
           St. Cyrus: D. Bruce Dly from White Horse

1877 (Worrall)
MONTROSE
Carriers: Bervie: John Allan FO
                      John Stewart TFO
           Johnshaven: Wm Watson TFO
           St. Cyrus: Jas Croll TFO
BERVIE
Coach: Stonehaven: Wm Whyte Crown Hotel 0800 TX
Carriers: Montrose: Jas Stewart TFO
JOHNSHAVEN
Carriers: Benholm: David Stephen and David Shield, daily
ST. CYRUS
Carriers: Montrose: Wm Watson TFO
                      James Croll TFO
STONEHAVEN
Omnibus: Bervie: Wm Whyte from Allardice St 1430 MWThSO, 1640 FO

1886 (Slater)
MONTROSE
Carriers: Bervie: John Sheret TFO
           Johnshaven: John Sheret WO
           St. Cyrus: John Croall FO
BERVIE
Letters: for Gourdon, Johnshaven 0630
Coach: Stonehaven: Whyte from Crown Hotel 0800 TX
Carriers: Johnshaven: Wm Watson TFO
           Montrose: John Sherrett TFO
ST. CYRUS
Carrier: Montrose: James Croll FO

1887-88 Lamburn's Forfarshire Directory
MONTROSE
Carriers: Bervie: John Sheret, North St, calls at shops TFO
           Johnshaven: John Sheret, calls at shops WO
           St. Cyrus: James Croall, Black Horse Inn FO

1903 (Slater)
Bervie
Crown Hotel licencee James Donald
Coach: Stonehaven: James Raitt 0830TFX
            Fordoun: (mail, carrying passengers) 1220 and 2000 daily
                          Conveyance MThSO 0715 and 1750
Carrier and agent: James Brown, Railway Stn
Stonehaven
Omnibus: Bervie: Raitt MWThSO

Scottish Motor Bus Timetable December 1938

Dundee to Aberdeen via Coast (extract)					
	S	M-F	M-S	Daily	Daily
Montrose	0712m		0812d	0912d hourly to	2312d
St. Cyrus	0729		0829	0929	2329
Inverbervie	0748	0815	0848	0948	2348
Stonehaven	0814a	0840s	0914a	1014a	0014s
	M-S	Daily		Daily	S
Stonehaven	0740a	0840	hourly to	2240a	2340a
Inverbervie	0806	0906		2306	0006
St. Cyrus	0825	0925		2325	0025
Montrose	0842d	0942d		2342m	0042m

To/from: a Aberdeen;   d Dundee;   m Montrose;   s Stonehaven

Glasgow–Forfar–Aberdeen (Limited Stop 15/6 to 30/9) Route 378			
	S	Su-F	S
Glasgow	0900	1000	1615
Montrose	1425	1525	2129
St. Cyrus	1439	1539	2143
Inverbervie	1458	1558	2202
Stonehaven	1523	1623	2227
Aberdeen	1600	1700	2304
	S	Su-F	S
Aberdeen	0900	1030	1645
Stonehaven	0937	1107	1722
Inverbervie	1002	1132	1747
St. Cyrus	1021	1151	1806
Montrose	1035	1205	1820
Glasgow	1602	1732	2332

Glasgow–Dundee–Aberdeen (Limited Stop) Route 281 and Edinburgh–Dundee–Aberdeen (Limited Stop) Route 320

Route 281	Daily		Route 320	Daily
Glasgow	0945		Edinburgh	0930
Montrose	1500		Montrose	1500
St. Cyrus			St. Cyrus	
Inverbervie	1530		Inverbervie	1530
Stonehaven	1555		Stonehaven	1555
Aberdeen	1630		Aberdeen	1630
	Daily			Daily
Aberdeen	1030		Aberdeen	1030
Stonehaven	1105		Stonehaven	1105
Inverbervie	1130		Inverbervie	1130
St. Cyrus			St. Cyrus	
Montrose	1200		Montrose	1200
Glasgow	1715		Edinburgh	1730

Scottish Motor Bus Timetable October 1950

Montrose–Johnshaven–Inverbervie Route 11H							
	M-F	M-F	S	S	S	S	S
Montrose	0800	1512	0800	1312	1612	1912	2112
St. Cyrus	0816	1528	0816	1328	1628	1928	2128
Johnshaven	0827	1539	0827	1339	1639	1939	2139
Inverbervie	0845	1557	0845	1357	1657	1957	2157
	M-F	M-F	S	S	S	S	S
Inverbervie	0857	1606	0857	1406	1706	2006	2206
Johnshaven	0915	1611	0915	1424	1724	2024	2224
St. Cyrus	0926	1624	0926	1435	1735	2035	2235
Montrose	0942	1651	0942	1451	1751	2051	2251

Gourdon–Inverbervie–Laurencekirk Route 43						
	M	M	S	S	S	S
Gourdon	1000	1545	1330	1530	2040	2240
Inverbervie	1010	1550	1340	1535	2050	2245
Laurencekirk	1045		1410		2120	
	M	M	S	S	S	S
Laurencekirk		1500		1630		2145
Inverbervie	0945	1535	1320	1505	2030	2230
Gourdon	0955	1540	1325	1510	2035	2235

Dundee–Aberdeen via Coast (extract) Route 11					
	M-S	Su		M-S	Su
Montrose	0742h	0942m	And hourly to	2242d	2142d
St. Cyrus	0759	0959		2259	2159
Inverbervie	0818	1015		2318	2218
Stonehaven	0844a	1040a		2344s	2244s
	M-S	Su		Mo-Sa	Su
Stonehaven	0640s	0940s	And hourly to	2140a	2140a
Inverbervie	0706	1006		2206	2206
St. Cyrus	0725	1025		2225	2225
Montrose	0742d	1042d		2242m	2242m

To/from: a Aberdeen;   h Arbroath;   d Dundee;   m Montrose;   s Stonehaven

Glasgow–Forfar–Aberdeen (Limited Stop 12/6 to 17/9) Route 14 now routed via Laurencekirk

Glasgow–Dundee–Aberdeen (Limited Stop 18/9 to 10/6/51) Route 15

Edinburgh–Dundee–Aberdeen (Limited Stop) Route 101

Route 15	Daily		Route 101	Daily
Glasgow	0945		Edinburgh	0930
Montrose	1500		Montrose	1500
St. Cyrus			St. Cyrus	
Inverbervie	1530		Inverbervie	1530
Stonehaven	1555		Stonehaven	1555
Aberdeen	1630		Aberdeen	1630
	Daily			Daily
Aberdeen	1030		Aberdeen	1030
Stonehaven	1105		Stonehaven	1105
Inverbervie	1130		Inverbervie	1130
St. Cyrus			St. Cyrus	
Montrose	1200		Montrose	1200
Glasgow	1715		Edinburgh	1730

Appendix 8: Bervie Line Fares – 1st May 1913

1st Single	Montrose	NW Bridge	St. Cyrus	Lauriston	Johnshaven	Birnie Rd	Gourdon	Bervie	Stonehaven	Aberdeen
Montrose		6d	11d	1/1d	1/5d	1/8d	2/-	2/2d	4/1d	6/9d
NW Bridge	6d		4d	6d	11d	-	1/5d	1/8d	4/8d	6/10d
St. Cyrus	11d	4d		2d	7d	-	1/1d	1/3d	5/1d	7/3d
Lauriston	1/1d	6d	2d		5d	-	11d	1/1d	5/3d	7/5d
Johnshaven	1/5d	11d	7d	5d		-	7d	9d	5/7d	7/9d
Birnie Rd	1/8d	-	-	-	-		-	-	-	-
Gourdon	2/-	1/5d	1/1d	11d	7d	-		2d	6/2d	8/4d
Bervie	2/2d	1/8d	1/3d	1/1d	9d	-	5d		6/4d	8/6d
Stonehaven	4/-	-	5/1d	5/3d	5/7d	-	6/2d	6/4d		2/8d
Aberdeen	6/9d	-	7/3d	7/5d	7/9d	-	8/4d	8/6d	2/8d	

1st Return	Montrose	NW Bridge	St. Cyrus	Lauriston	Johnshaven	Birnie Rd	Gourdon	Bervie	Stonehaven	Aberdeen
Montrose		10d	1/7d	1/10d	2/5d	2/6d	3/6d	3/9d	7/-	11/3d
NW Bridge	10d		7d	10d	1/7d	-	2/5d	2/10d	8/-	11/6d
St. Cyrus	1/7d	7d		3½d	1/-	-	1/10d	2/1d	8/8d	12/3d
Lauriston	1/10d	10d	3½d		9d	-	1/7d	1/10d	9/-	12/6d
Johnshaven	2/5d	1/7d	11d	9d		-	1/-	1/3d	9/6d	13/-
Birnie Rd	2/10d	-	-	-	-		-	-	-	-
Gourdon	3/6d	2/5d	1/10d	1/7d	1/-	-		3½d	10/6d	14/-
Bervie	3/9d	2/10d	2/1d	1/10d	1/3d	-	3½d		10/9d	14/3d
Stonehaven	7/-	-	8/8d	9/-	9/6d	-	10/6d	10/6d		4/-
Aberdeen	11/3d	-	12/3d	12/6d	13/-	-	14/-	14/3d	4/-	

3rd Single	Montrose	NW Bridge	St. Cyrus	Lauriston	Johnshaven	Birnie Rd	Gourdon	Bervie	Stonehaven	Aberdeen
Montrose		3d	5d	6d	8½d	10d	11½d	1/0½d	2/0½d	3/4½d
NW Bridge	3d		2d	3d	5d	-	8½d	9½d	2/3½d	3/4½d
St. Cyrus	5d	2d		1d	3d	-	6½d	7½d	2/5½d	3/6½d
Lauriston	6d	3d	1d		2d	-	5½d	6½d	2/6½d	3/7½d
Johnshaven	8½d	5d	3d	2d		-	3d	4d	2/9d	3/9½d
Birnie Rd	10d	-	-	-	-		-	-	-	-
Gourdon	11½d	8½d	6½d	5½d	3d	-		1d	3/-	4/1d
Bervie	1/0½d	9½d	7½d	6½d	4d	-	1½d		3/1d	4/2d
Stonehaven	2/0½d	-	2/5½d	2/6½d	2/9d	-	3/-d	3/1d		1/4d
Aberdeen	3/4½d	-	3/6½d	3/7½d	3/9½d	-	4/1d	4/2d	1/4d	

3rd Return	Montrose	NW Bridge	St. Cyrus	Lauriston	Johnshaven	Birnie Rd	Gourdon	Bervie	Stonehaven	Aberdeen
Montrose		6d	10d	1/-	1/5	1/6d	1/11d	2/1d	4/-	6/1d
NW Bridge	6d		4d	6d	10d	-	1/5d	1/7d	4/3d	6/1d
St. Cyrus	10d	4d		2d	6d	-	1/1d	1/3d	4/10d	6/8d
Lauriston	1/-	6d	2d		4d	-	11d	1/1d	5/-	6/11d
Johnshaven	1/5d	10d	6d	4d		-	6d	8d	5/5d	7/3d
Birnie Rd	1/6d	-	-	-	-		-	-	-	-
Gourdon	1/11d	1/5d	1/1d	11d	6d	-		2d	5/11d	7/10d
Bervie	2/-	1/7d	1/3d	1/1d	8d	-	2d		6/1d	7/10d
Stonehaven	4/-	-	4/10d	5/-	5/5d	-	5/11d	6/1d		2/2d
Aberdeen	6/5d	-	6/8d	6/11d	7/3d	-	7/10d	7/10d	2/2d	

Notes:
– Not every station had a fare to every other. Blanks are where no fare had been requested. For example, Birnie Road only had fares to and from Montrose, suggesting that these were fares utilized by the Scott family at Brotherton (Private) station.
– For comparative bus fares, see Table 11 in the text.

ABOVE: One of the regular Bervie Branch engines, Class 'J37' No. 64608, shunting on the main line south of Montrose station on 8th July 1964. The line in the foreground is the Montrose (NB) Harbour Branch.
Michael Mensing

LEFT: The last passenger train to Bervie arrives at Gourdon.
Kenneth Hay

BELOW: L&NER Class 'G9' 0-4-4 tank No. 9475 with a Brake Composite and a couple of vans on the 5.45pm from Inverbervie about half a mile north of St. Cyrus on Friday 18th April 1930.
K. Nunn, courtesy Bill Lynn

Appendix 9: Known Bervie Line Station Agents 1866-1966

BERVIE

Jarvis (1866-1874)
William Davidson (1877)
John Elliot (1886-1911)
Shand (1913-19)
Charlie Hunter (1920-31)
Shields (1932-34)
Guthrie (1953)

GOURDON

Milne (1871)[1]
John Elliot (1877-80)
Brown (1881-97)
Walter Douglas (1898-1903)
Wilson (1914-19)
Cameron (1920)
Watson (1921-25)
Robertson (1926-28)

JOHNSHAVEN

Ford (1866)
Caird (1866-67)[2]
John Smith (1868)[3]
George Thow (1877-83)[4]
Peter Braidwood (1884-90)
Lawson (1891-93)
Robert Ness (1903)
Charlie Hunter (1908-19)
McCallum (1920)
Cameron (1920)
Aitchison (1921-28)

LAURISTON

David Stewart (1882-1905)
Haxton (1906-24)
Low (1925-27)
Post withdrawn 1927

ST. CYRUS

James Mutch (1877-86)
George Murray (1896-1920)[5]
Bellamy (1921)
Mackay (1922-31)
McLean (1935-52)
Bill Dewar (1953-?)
Tom Armstrong (?-1961)
Charlie Duncan (1961-66)

LINE SUPERVISORS

Shields supervised all Bervie line stations 1932-34, and it is thought that McLean did so also 1935-52. In 1953 Guthrie oversaw Bervie and Gourdon, and Dewar was responsible for the other three stations. Armstrong and Dundan supervised the whole line.

NOTES

Dates given are when the individual was known to have been in post; it may be that some were posted at stations for longer (for example, Elliot at Gourdon).
1. Previous incumbent had been dismissed
2. Dismissed for dishonesty and plead guilty in court. Had been employed 5th August 1866-14th May 1867 (*DC*, 20th Sep. 1867, p. 3).
3. Absconded from his post in October 1868. Apprehended and charged with embezzlement in February 1869. He pled guilty and was sentenced to six months imprisonment (*Stonehaven Journal & Kincardineshire Advertiser*, 18th Feb. and 29th Apr 1869).
4. Thow dismissed.
5. Murray died in post.

ABOVE: Charlie Hunter was Passenger Agent at Bervie from 1920 to 1931. Here he is in 1926. *Brian H. Watt*

RIGHT: Two of the staff use the station barrow to harvest the tatties (potatoes). *Brian H. Watt*

Left: Charlie (Chic) Duncan was the last Station Agent on the Bervie line. He was previously based at Eyemouth, and continued as goods agent at Brechin after the Bervie line closed, though continuing to live in the St. Cyrus station house. His last posting was to Larbert. *Mrs Lily Duncan*

Right: It is not known who the porter at Gourdon was in June 1960, but he seems to have a large number of fish boxes to dispatch. The three gentlemen in the flat caps are presumably there to check that their consignments get on their way safely. *Norris Forrest*

Loading the train at Gourdon on 14th June 1957; the gentleman in the shirt and tie is possibly a supervisor. *Brian Hilton*

Appendix 10: Montrose & Bervie Railway Company Directors and Principal Shareholders

Hercules Scott (Chairman 1867-1881)

Hercules Scott, 6th Laird of Brotherton, was born on 14th June 1823, son of David Scott. His grandfather, also Hercules Scott, was Colonel of the 103rd Regiment and had been killed in action during the unsuccessful attack on Fort Erie in what was Upper Canada (now broadly southern Ontario) in 1814, during the American war of 1812-15. However, the family could trace its origins back to Uchtredus Filius Scoti, who witnessed the foundation charter of the Abbey of Holyrood House at Edinburgh in 1128.

Hercules was educated at Harrow School and Haileybury College, an establishment founded by the East India Company in 1806 as a school for 'writers' or clerks in the Company's service. Hercules was appointed to the Bengal Civil Service, before returning home because of what he later described as *'slight sunstroke'* in 1850. He then worked for a time as a banker in Manchester before marrying Anna Moon, daughter of a Liverpool cotton merchant, in 1857.

The Brotherton estate had originally been purchased by James Scott of Logie in 1670, and given to his son, Hercules (1659-1747), the first Laird. He was succeeded by his son, James (1719-1804), his nephew Hercules (1775-1814) and by Hercules' brother James (1776-1844). His brother David (1782-1859) was the fifth Laird and Hercules' father.

When Hercules succeeded to the Brotherton estate in 1859, he decided to replace the old castle. Hercules Scott was reputed to have said *'no one in Kincardineshire shall have a finer residence than the Brotherton Scotts, and no one shall pay higher rates!'*[1]

The old house has been described as:

an old capacious mansion forming three sides of a square. The walls in some places are about six feet in thickness. The older part on the East side has a circular turret at the back, which answers for a staircase inside. At the South East corner there is a flagstaff attached. It stands on a terrace, with beautiful terraced walled gardens in front, amid 'tall ancestral trees', and an extensive demesne. It is close on the sea coast ... and flanked on the west by a deep romantic wooded ravine, through which a murmuring streamlet meanders, and debouches into the beach at the foot of the garden grounds. It has a neat porter's lodge, and fine iron gates, at the turnpike roadside, about nine miles north-east of Montrose.[2]

The Scott family moved in to the new Brotherton house on 20th May 1868 amid *'great rejoicings'* according to the *Aberdeen Journal*, which described the building:

which for extent and design, may well be termed a castle, [it] occupies a site closely adjoining to that of the former House of Brotherton, and commands, both by sea and land, one of the most delightful prospects it is possible to conceive. The house is built in the castellated style from a design by [James] Matthews, Aberdeen.

The report continued:

Mr and Mrs Scott were met by a procession of the tenants on the estate, the feuars of Johnshaven, the Rifle Company Life Brigade, school children, and bands of music, &c, and drawn from the turnpike road to the castle in an open carriage by a number of gallant young fellows. On arrival, the Rev Mr Myers of Benholm, in a few eloquent words, welcomed Mr and Mrs Scott, and addresses were presented from the feuars by Mr Findlay, fishcurer, and by the 2d K.A.V., [2nd Kincardineshire Artillery Volunteers] by Lieut. Mitchell, to which Mr Scott made a feeling reply.[3]

Hercules Scott, circa 1890. Walter Blakeman collection

The interior of the house was equally grand:

It is constructed round a central hall, or 'salon' which rises to the full height of the building. The drawing rooms have ornamented plaster ceilings on which the initials 'HS' and 'AM' are intertwined amid thistles and roses. Much of the furniture was specially designed and gave its name to the Mahogany, Birch and Pine bedrooms. The domestic quarters were comprehensive and included a room set aside solely for storing vases and arranging flowers from the extensive gardens. In the yard there hangs a bell, used for summoning servants and for reminding guests when to change for dinner. Outhouses included several greenhouses, an ice-house and a pagoda-shaped game larder ...

It had its own laundry ... and its own gas-works, later converted for electricity. The Mains of Brotherton was run by a grieve [farm manager] complete with dairy, sawmill and blacksmith's shop.[4]

There was also a private halt on the M&B just outside the garden. A flight of wooden steps led up to a timber platform on the west side of the line about 100 yards north of the underbridge.

By this time the Scotts had four children: Hercules James (1860), Mary Isabella (1862), Helen (1863) and Edward Uchtred (1865). Anna Katherine was born on 10th June 1868 at Brotherton. Tragically, all but Anna Katherine died of diphtheria in late January and early February 1869, along with their nurse. One more daughter,

Top: Brotherton Castle in its heyday. The postcard was published by Montrose stationer J. Ward and probably dates from about 1890.
Author's collection

Above: A portrait of Nannie (left) and Rosie Scott. The elder sister, Nannie (Anna), eventually inherited the estate and lived at Brotherton until her death in 1948. Margaret Rose died in 1954.
Walter Blakeman collection

named appropriately Margaret Rose de Noel, was born on Christmas Day 1869.

Apart from his activities as Chairman of the Montrose & Bervie Railway, Hercules Scott took the obligations he felt as Laird of Brotherton seriously. He founded the Volunteers at Johnshaven in July 1859 and paid for an extension to the harbour at Johnshaven in 1884,[5] as well as for a new lifeboat station in 1891 to house the *Meanwell of Glenbervie* boat. In the same year he provided Johnshaven with drains and street lighting, the village becoming the first in the Mearns to have this facility.[6] When the Johnshaven water supply became contaminated, he paid for a bore hole on the Brotherton estates and supplied the water on nominal terms.[7] From 1872 to 1894 he was Chairman of the School Board, having previously been a Kincardineshire Commissioner of Supply and Roads Board Trustee, following his time as a Turnpike Trustee in succession to his father.

Even though the Scotts were Episcopalians (his father built St Mary's Church in Montrose), he supported the local Church of Scotland church at Benholm, where he is buried.

Anna Katherine became seventh Lady of Brotherton on Hercules' death on 31st May 1897, and lived there until her own death in July 1948. Thereafter the estate was bequeathed to her niece, Mrs Freda Gell, who sold it to Charles Alexander, a successful north-east road haulier and businessman. When Lathallan School in Fife (Charles Alexander's former school) was burnt down in 1949 he arranged for it to be housed at Brotherton, later selling them the house and grounds but retaining the farmland. The school is still based there today.

A fascinating insight into life at Brotherton during the Scott's residence is provided by M. Forsyth-Grant:[8]

Nan Scott gave the most lavish parties at Brotherton Castle, including Firework displays on 5th November, and magnificent Country Balls.

My first personal recollection of the largesse of Brotherton started with lavish Halloween Parties from 1925 onwards. Apples were strung in profusion in the Great Entrance Hall, and happy children [allowed] to eat them on the string. There were also magnificent 'side shows', not to mention 'big eats'.

To the end of her days Miss Scott lived in great Victorian splendour. Smith, a splendidly moustached chauffeur drove her Daimler. Hopkins was a superb butler of the old school. There were also footmen. 'Gamie' Findlay was the Gamekeeper, and lived in a house beside the Home Farm. There was also a 'Ground Officer' – today we would class him as a factor.

The Castle territory was vast. From Whitehouse Farm at Gourdon along the coast to near Den Finella, then inland half way to Garvock Hill, and back to Benholm. The estate incorporated many farms, and woods including the Muirton, and virtually all the land between Gourdon, St. Cyrus, over to Laurencekirk was held by relations.

King, in her *Short History of Brotherton and the Scott Family*, adds:

Before the last war [1939-45] five gardeners, five foresters and three gamekeepers kept the grounds in order, while in the castle there was a housekeeper, who acted as lady's maid, a butler, footman, hall-boy, cook, kitchen-maids and scullery-maids. After the advent of the motor car, two chauffeurs were also employed, and in the North Lodge there lived a gate-keeper.[9]

The Estate Book for Brotherton covering the 1890s has survived, and that records not only the family tree of the family and the list of tenants and servants (and their family details), but also the list of investments, liabilities and income of the family. It is notable how many of these investments were in railway companies. The net worth of the family in 1893, for example, was far more than the cost of the M&B and their annual income equivalent to five times the annual revenue of the line. That gives a measure of the wealth of the families involved.[10]

ALEXANDER PORTEOUS (CHAIRMAN 1860-1867)

Alexander Porteous of Lauriston Castle was born in 1797 and educated at Edinburgh University, marrying Helen Scott (Hercules Scott's sister) in 1851. He was the second-largest shareholder in the Montrose & Bervie Railway, after Farquhar of Hallgreen, Bervie. He was described as:

a native of Crieff, and sometime Merchant in the East Indies, where he amassed a large fortune. He purchased Lauriston from the trustees of Robert Lyall, Esq., in 1849 ... He is representative of the ancient family of Hawkshaw Castle, in Glen Fruid, Tweedsmuir, Peeblesshire ...

Mr Porteous has erected a number of splendid cottages in the Elizabethan style, on the turnpike roadside – and amongst the rest a school.

Mr Porteous purchased the estate of Lauriston for upwards of £50,000.[11]

Alexander Porteous resigned as Chairman of the company due to ill-health and after increasing losses by the railway during its early years, to be succeeded by Hercules Scott.

After his death in 1872, his son David Scott Porteous (1852-1931) became an M&B Director.

Lauriston Castle lies about two miles north of St. Cyrus. The castle was for sale in 1907 and a lavish sales booklet is held in the Local Studies Department of Aberdeen University Library. The property was described as follows:

The property ... embraces an area of 3,336 acres or thereby, of which 2,483 acres are arable, 479 pasture, 267 under plantation, and the rest houses, roads, waste ... The Estate is intersected by the Montrose and Bervie branch of the North British Railway, the Lauriston Station of which is on the property, and within three-quarters of a mile of the Mansion House.

The Mansion House consists of a mainly modern building, attached to the tower of the ancient Castle, and is approached from the high road by a wooded avenue of one-third of a mile in length. It stands on the rocky edge of a finely-timbered ravine, about 40 feet above the level of the small stream known as the Lauriston Burn, and at an elevation of about 300 feet above sea level. The old Castle is of some historic note, and is mentioned in various ancient Records, including the well-known ballad of the Battle of Harlaw. It was the former seat of the Scottish family of Straiton. The existing tower is believed to date from the fifteenth century. The ravine above mentioned, locally called the Den of Lauriston, extends for several hundred yards within

Lauriston Castle was equally grand. After a period when it was in some disrepair after being used by the military during the Second World War, more recently much of it has been sympathetically restored, although this section of the building was demolished. This photograph is from the 1907 sale brochure for the property. *University of Aberdeen*

the private grounds. Narrow and rocky immediately at the site of the house, where it is spanned by a picturesque single-arched stone bridge, it broadens lower down into more gently-sloping banks, overhung with beech woods. With its tastefully-laid-out paths, 'the Den' affords at all seasons a sheltered promenade, and in the summer is a spot of much beauty. In the woods bordering and overhanging it there is an extensive rookery.

The whole house is built of stone, having in the main block a ground floor and two upper stories, with the principal front facing south-east. It is well sheltered by the surrounding woods, and commands views of the sea from both south-east and south-west fronts. There is a spacious lawn, with lawn-tennis ground and bowling-green. The house contains Dining-Room, Drawing-Room, Smoking-Room, Library, and Business Rooms, besides Entrance Hall and Vestibule; 19 Bed and Dressing Rooms, Bath-Rooms; 5 Water-Closets, large Kitchen, Scullery, Pantry, Servants' Hall, and Housekeeper's Room, Brushing Room, and the usual offices. The Gardens are large and well stocked, and contain a Conservatory, 3 Vineries, Peach House, Stove and other Houses, including a Gardener's and Under Gardener's House. The Grounds are well laid out, and, including Policy Parks, extend to about 75 acres. There is a Lodge at the entrance gate, and also a Gamekeeper's House.

The Stables contain 10 Stalls and a Loose-box, 2 Coach-houses, Harness Room, Coachman's House, besides another House, with Byre and Cart-horse Stables, &c.[12]

During the twentieth century the house fell into disrepair, but has recently been sympathetically restored.

JAMES FARQUHAR (DIRECTOR 1860-1863)

James Farquhar was the second largest shareholder in the Montrose & Bervie Railway, but apart from being a Director for a short period, does not seem to have played a prominent role in the management of the company. One of the few reference to him in the Minute Book is when he objected to the location of the engine shed and turntable at Bervie as being too close to his house at Hallgreen.[13] He does not normally seem to have attended the half-yearly shareholders' meetings.

James Farquhar inherited Hallgreen in 1842, and was listed as one of the promoters of the Aberdeen Railway in 1844,[14] and both the Dundee & Forfar Junction Railway and the East of Scotland Junction Railway the following year.[15] On 29th April 1863 he married Diana Octavia, youngest daughter of David Scott of Brotherton, and Hercules Scott's sister.[16]

Hallgreen Castle from the sea. The railway would have passed just behind the photographer.
Margaret Gray

The Bervie locomotive shed was to be built behind the trees on the left on the shore, which explains Farquhar's concerns that his views would be impeded! *Margaret Gray*

Hallgreen Castle was described as:

a stronghold of the sixteenth century, remodelled in the Elizabethan style by the present proprietor, and situated on a rocky terrace on the coast, overlooking the sea, at the south end of a very romantic 'fairy den' (planted by the present laird), through which the coach-road winds its wavy course in a very unique manner, and alongside of which murmurs a streamlet of 'living waters,' with bridges thrown across; and below the one in front of the Castle, there is a gushing cascade. It stands about 300 paces south-west of the borough of Inverbervie.[17]

Farquhar was Provost of Bervie from 1859 to 1864 and when the M&B scheme was floated was able to persuade the Town Council that because of:

the great benefit which such a scheme … would prove to this Burgh – its inhabitants and all its interests, and being therefore desirous to encourage the undertaking, authorise the Treasurer to subscribe in behalf of the Burgh for Ten shares of £10 each.[18]

James Farquhar died in 1875, and his son became a Director of the company. An especially warm memorial in the Bervie Town Council Minutes recorded that he:

for a long series of years acted as Provost of the Burgh, and … by his many acts of liberality and kindness and the great interest he took in everything tending to the welfare of the Burgh endeared himself to the whole community, who felt that in him they had lost a generous and open-handed friend.[19]

Table A	Montrose & Bervie Railway Company Directors			
Director	**From**	**To**	**Notes**	
Alexander Porteous	1860	1872	Chairman 1860-66.	
Hercules Scott	1860	1881	Chairman 1867-81.	
James Farquhar	1860	1871		
William Forsyth-Grant	1860	1861		
David Mitchell	1860	1881	Main contractor for line. Served at Provost of Montrose for two terms. Owned Somerville & Co. manure works and Montrose Foundry. Was also a Director of the Dundee & Arbroath Railway. Died 1882.	
John Stephen	1860	1863	Died in office.	
Thomas Farquhar	1861	1865	Replaced W. Forsyth-Grant.	
Francis Paton	1864	1866	Replaced Stephen.	
John Duncan	1865	1866	GNSR interest.	
Frederick Forsyth-Grant	1866	1881	Replaced Duncan.	
William Mitchell	1871	1881	Replaced Farquhar.	
David Barclay	1873	1876	Replaced Porteous; died in office.	
David Scott Porteous	1875	1881	Replaced F. Forsyth-Grant.	
James Farquhar	1877	1881	Replaced Barclay.	
Patrick Dickson	1877	1881		

Notes:
There was a minimum of three and a maximum of six Directors.
There were six Directors from 1860 to 1866, five from 1867 to 1876 and six from 1876 to 1881.

James Grant Forsyth-Grant lived in this delightful neo-Gothic chateau just west of St. Cyrus. By the 1990s it was on the Royal Commission for the Ancient and Historic Monuments of Scotland's endangered list, being in very poor condition. The present owner of Ecclesgreig House is restoring it, and had replaced the 'witch's hat' turret roof by the date of this photograph in 2009.
Graeme Davidson

Notes

1. M. Forsyth-Grant, 'Recollections of Brotherton Castle, Lathallan School 1900-1999' in *Lathallan School Magazine* (Johnshaven, nd [c. 2000]).
2. D.M. Peter, *The Baronage of Angus and Mearns, comprising the genealogy of three hundred and sixty families – curious anecdotes – descriptions of clan tartans, badges, slogans, armoury, and seats – ancient sculptures, &c being a guide to the Tourist and Heraldic Artist* (Edinburgh, 1856), pp. 301-2.
3. *AJ*, 27th May 1868, p. 3.
4. P.M. King, *A Short History of Brotherton and the Scott Family* (Johnshaven, 1980).
5. *AJ*, 7th Jul. 1884, p. 4. The works took two years and were designed by Willet of Aberdeen, based on plans drawn up by John Rennie about 1800 for Colonel Hercules Scott.
6. Gas lighting was installed at Auchenblae in 1840, and Bervie in 1845 (Watt's Directory 1846-47 and www.bervie.net/history.php).
7. *ET*, 1st Apr. 1885, p. 3. Another example of his generosity was when he presented Constable Adam Murray of Johnshaven with a £5 note in appreciation of his efforts to catch an arsonist. He did this at the annual force inspection in Stonehaven to give Murray the greatest advantage (*ET*, 1st Aug. 1882, p. 4).
8. M. Forsyth-Grant, op. cit.
9. P.M. King, op. cit.
10. Estate Book of Brotherton, Walter Blakeman collection.
11. Peter, op. cit., pp. 275-6.

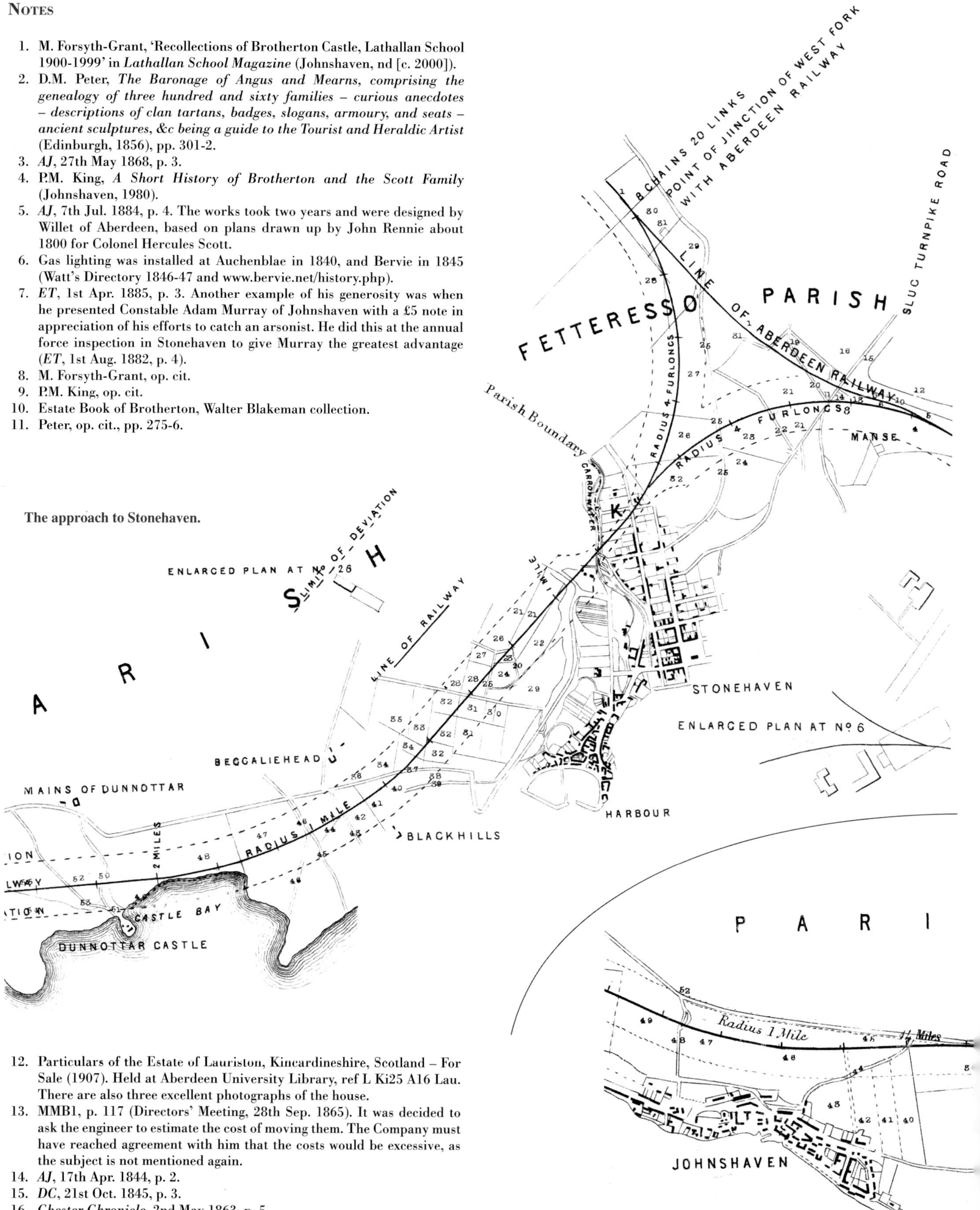

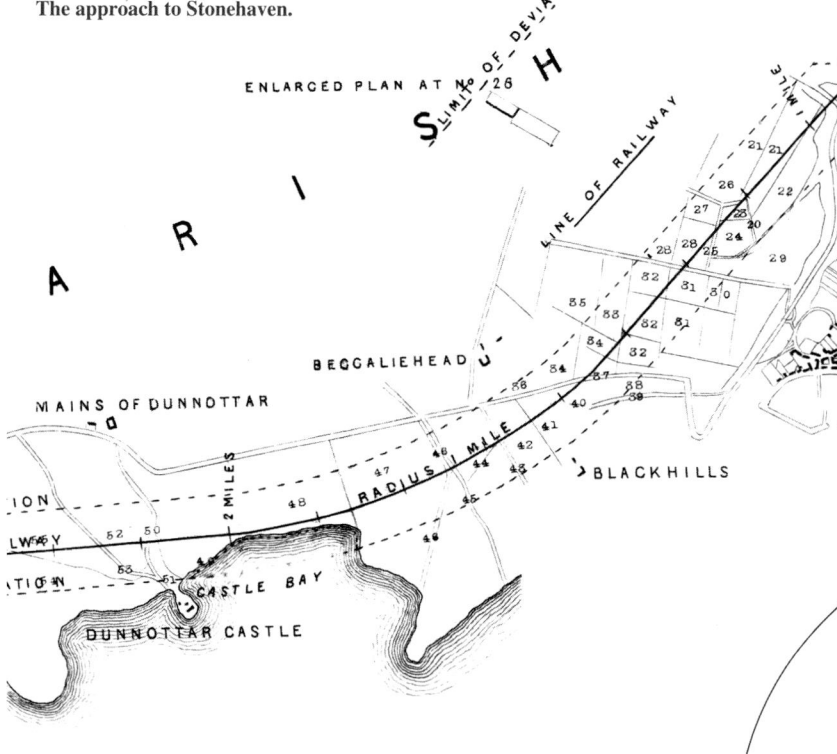

The approach to Stonehaven.

12. Particulars of the Estate of Lauriston, Kincardineshire, Scotland – For Sale (1907). Held at Aberdeen University Library, ref L Ki25 A16 Lau. There are also three excellent photographs of the house.
13. MMB1, p. 117 (Directors' Meeting, 28th Sep. 1865). It was decided to ask the engineer to estimate the cost of moving them. The Company must have reached agreement with him that the costs would be excessive, as the subject is not mentioned again.
14. *AJ*, 17th Apr. 1844, p. 2.
15. *DC*, 21st Oct. 1845, p. 3.
16. *Chester Chronicle*, 2nd May 1863, p. 5.
17. Peter, op. cit., p. 94.
18. Minute Books of Bervie Town Council, 1859, p. 192.
19. Minute Books of Bervie Town Council, 19th Mar. 1875.

Appendix 11: The Stonehaven Extension

The two extension schemes affecting Bervie were the East Coast of Scotland Junction Railway of 1845 and the 1862 Montrose and Bervie Extension. This appendix provides a brief description of where these railways would have run had they been built.

The East Coast of Scotland Junction Railway

This railway would have followed the later North British Railway alignment fairly closely from Arbroath to Montrose, and then the Montrose & Bervie alignment to the North Water Bridge. Here it would have taken a more easterly line close to the shore and, passing through a 400-yard tunnel at Milton Ness, would have followed the Bervie turnpike to Bervie (which it would have crossed just east of David Street) before passing round Kinghorny Head and following the shore to Stonehaven. The line would have passed within about 100 yards of Dunnottar Castle and then, after a viaduct over Invercarron, would have split on embankments for a triangular junction with the Aberdeen Railway south of the Slug Road. It is not clear why a triangular junction (that is, allowing trains from Bervie to head south) was required. Gradients would have been relatively benign, at a maximum of 1 in 100.

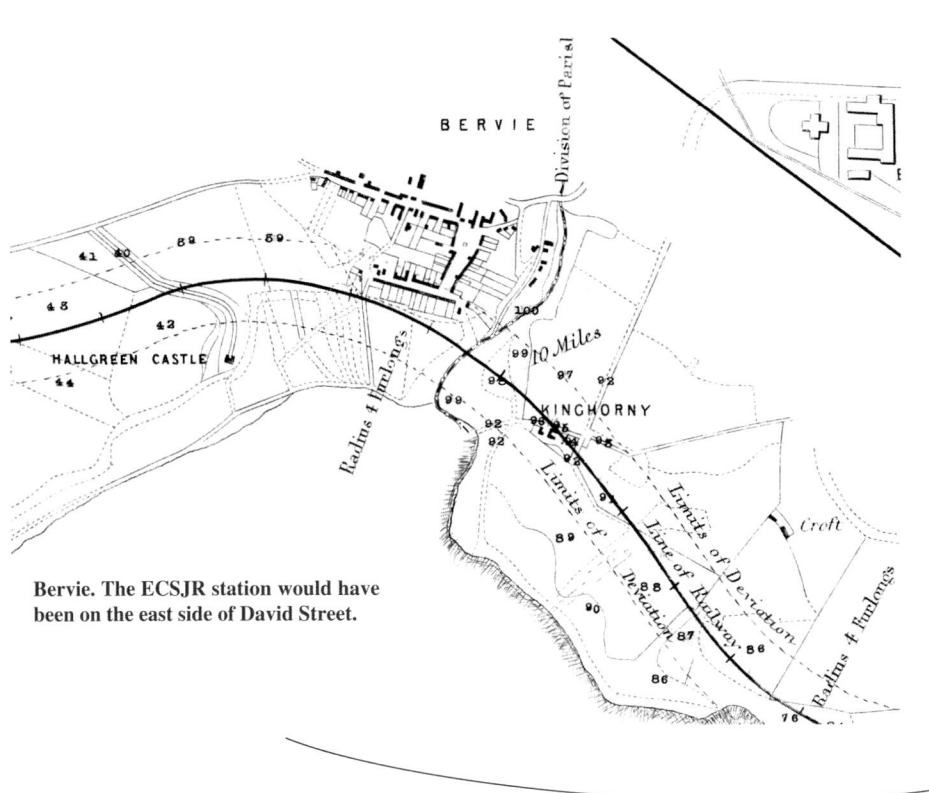

Bervie. The ECSJR station would have been on the east side of David Street.

The line of the ECSJR south of Bervie would have followed the turnpike road closely, and would have been at a higher level than the line actually built along the shore.

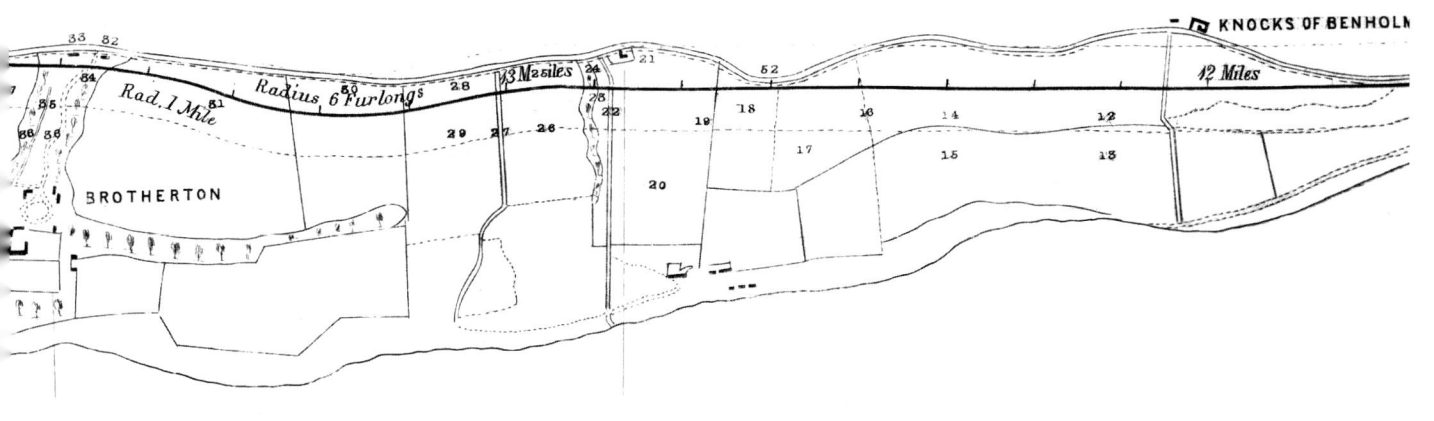

Kirkside deviation. The main works would have involved diverting the turnpike road.

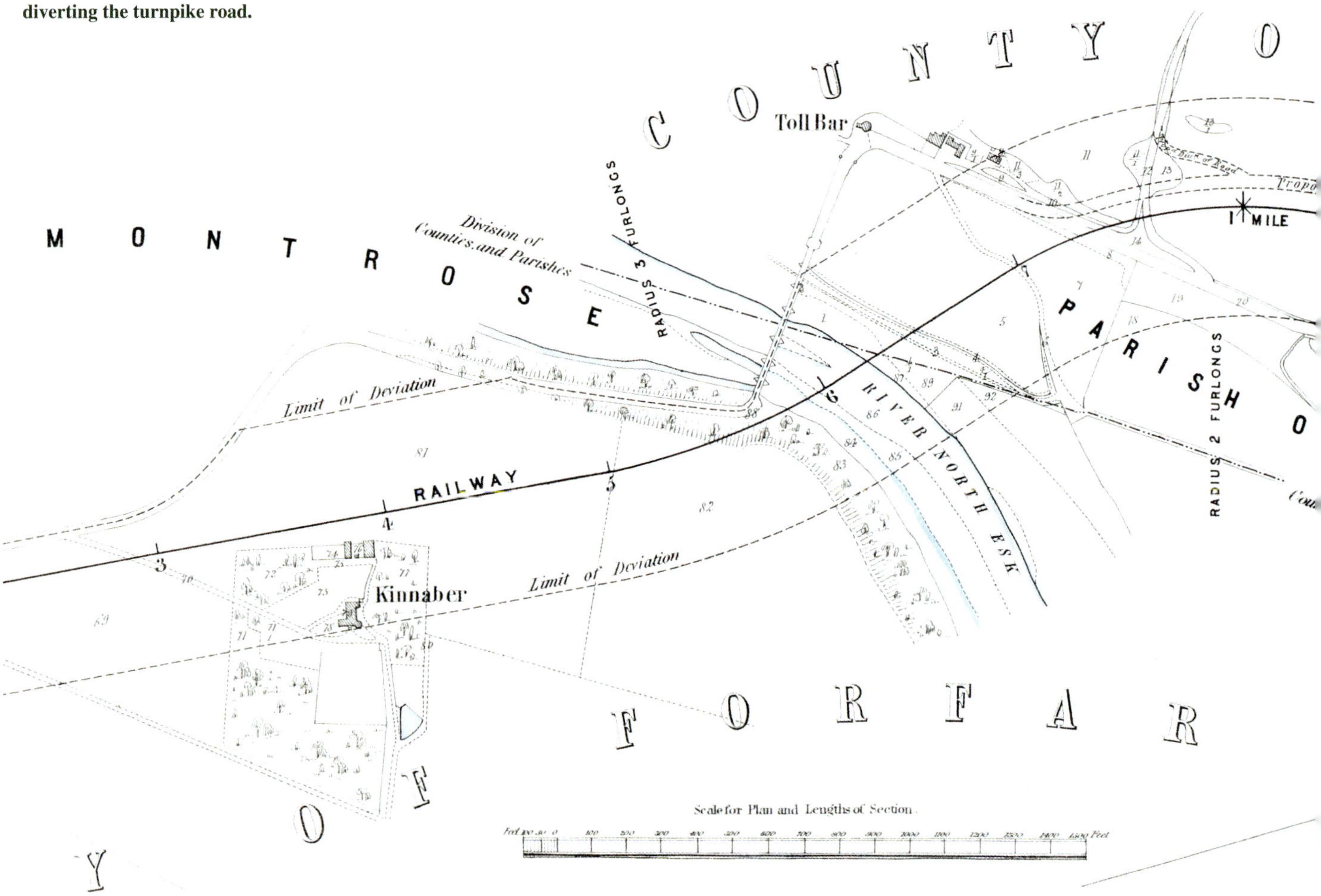

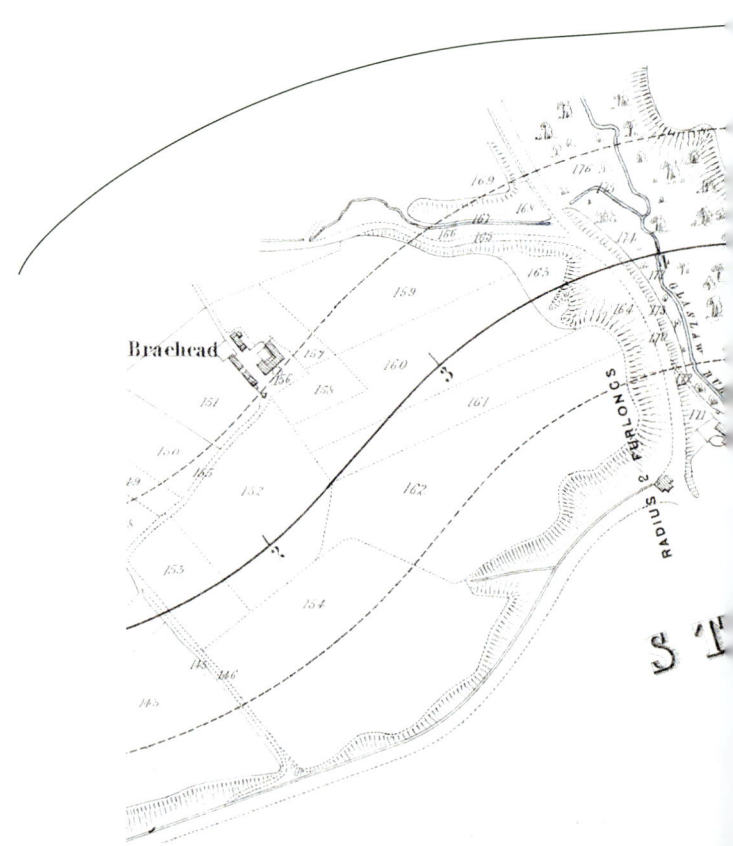

The Montrose & Bervie Extension

From Arbroath the railway would have once again largely followed the eventual North British alignment to Montrose. As the plans made clear, the Montrose & Bervie would be altered in three respects; there would be a deviation at Kirkside, between St. Cyrus and the North Water Bridge, which would have created a much easier curve, and would have involved a major realignment of the turnpike road. The gradient would still have been a relatively heavy 1 in 70, however. The second deviation would have been from Den Finella to Bervie, the line following closely the ECSJR alignment and the turnpike road, entering Bervie by a slightly more westerly alignment, with a station on the west side of David Street. The third amendment was of course the Stonehaven extension. This would have left Bervie on a 100-yard viaduct crossing the River Bervie, before curving round Kinghorny Head and then running on the east side of the turnpike road which it rejoined just north of Kinneff, having passed between Kinneff church and the village. Passing closely to the east of Fernyflatt Farm, it would have passed slightly more inland of Dunnottar Castle than the ECSJR scheme, and then swung round on a long embankment and viaduct to join the SNER just north of its Stonehaven station. There would have been a Stonehaven station on the line at the west side of the new town of Stonehaven.

APPENDICES

MONTROSE & BERVIE RY 1862.
SHEET No 9
KIRKSIDE DEVIATION.

The approach to Stonehaven would have once again involved a viaduct over the Carron River, and would have placed the junction with the SNER just north of Stonehaven Station. This plan would have implied an M&B station west of Arduthie Road at the top of Cameron Street.

Enlarged Plan of part of BERVIE to shew reference numbers.

The Bervie station of the M&B extension would have been just west of David Street and would have involved diverting the east end of the High Street. This location would have been a much more central site than that built, at the foot of Kirkburn.

Bibliography

Surveys and Reports

Wheel Carriage Tax Returns (NRS, Edinburgh)
Estate Book of Brotherton (held in private collection, Laurencekirk)
Local Reports of the Commissioners on the Municipal Corporations in Scotland (London, 1835)
Minutes of Proceedings before the Select Committee on Railway Bills on the North British and Montrose and Bervie Railway Companies' Bill (House of Commons)
Minutes of Proceedings taken before the Select Committee of the House of Lords on the North British and Montrose and Bervie Railway Companies' Bill Tuesday, 28th June, 1881
Minute Books of Bervie Town Council (Aberdeenshire Archives, Old Aberdeen)
Minute Books and Accounts of the Kincardineshire Turnpike Trusts 1796-1878 (Aberdeenshire Archives, Old Aberdeen)
Montrose and Bervie Railway references in The National Archive, Kew
Montrose and Bervie Railway references in the National Records of Scotland
Montrose and Bervie Minute Book No. 1
New Statistical Account of Scotland
Notices and Proceedings of the Northern (Scottish) Traffic Commissioners (Bus route licensing and fares)
North British Railway: General Appendix to the Book of Rules & Regulations and to the Working Timetables, 1898, 1901, 1922
Old Statistical Account of Scotland
Particulars of the Estate of Lauriston, Kincardineshire, Scotland – For Sale (1907). Held in Aberdeen University Library
Report of the Commissioners for Inquiring into Matters Relating to Public Roads in Scotland, 1859
Scottish Bus Timetable (SMT Group) Oct-Dec 1947

Guides and Directories

Angus & Mearns Directory & Almanac (1846)
Bon-Accord Directory (1840-41)
Groome, F.H., *Ordnance Gazetteer of Scotland: a survey of Scottish topography, statistical, biographical and historical* (London, 1882)
Inverbervie (The Royal Burgh of Inverbervie) etc., Kincardineshire. The Official Guide, (Cheltenham: E.J. Burrow and Co., 1934-)
Middleton, W.J., *Pictorial Kincardineshire* (Aberdeen, nd)
Post Office Directories for Aberdeen (1824-1912)
Pigot & Co's New Commercial Directory of Scotland ... (1825-26, 1837, 1878)
Slater's Royal National Commercial Directory and Topography of Scotland (1861, 1882, 1886, 1903)
Waldie's Guide: Stonehaven – a Guide to Town and District with Illustrations and Road Map (Stonehaven, c. 1935)
Wilson J.M., *The Gazetteer of Scotland* (Edinburgh, 1882)
Worrall's Directory of North East Scotland (1877)

FACING PAGE: No time was lost in lifting the track. This late 1966 view shows Gourdon with track gone, but with the footbridge intact. Over the next twenty years or so all the little wooden station buildings disappeared.
Author

Newspapers

(Aberdeen) *Evening Express*
Aberdeen Journal
Aberdeen Press & Journal
Caledonian Mercury (Edinburgh)
Chester Chronicle
Dundee Advertiser
Dundee Courier
(Dundee) *Evening Times*
(Dundee) *Northern Warder & Bi-Weekly Courier & Argus*
Dundee, Perth and Cupar Advertiser
Edinburgh Evening News
Edinburgh Gazette
Fife Herald
Glasgow Herald
Inverness Courier
London Daily News
Montrose, Arbroath & Brechin Reporter
Montrose Herald
Montrose Review
Montrose Standard
New Sporting Magazine
Otago Witness
Railway Herald
Sheffield Daily Telegraph
Stirling Observer
Yorkshire Gazette

Books and Articles

Stonehaven, Still Thriving, at www.Mearns.org.uk
Adams, D.G. *Johnshaven and Miltonhaven, a Social and Economic History* (Brechin, 1991)
Alexander W., *Northern Rural Life* (Aberdeen, 1879)
Anderson, J., *A General View of the Agriculture and Rural Economy of the County of Aberdeen (etc)* (Edinburgh. 1794)
Barron J., *The Northern Highlands in the Nineteenth Century* (Inverness, 1907)
Bremner, D., *Industries of Scotland: Their Rise, Progress and Present Condition* (Edinburgh, 1869)
Burness, I.J., *The Flax-spinning Industry of Inverbervie & District 1787-1992* (Inverbervie, 1994)
Cowan, S., *Perth, the Ancient Capital of Scotland: the Story of Perth from the Invasion of Agricola to the Passing of the Reform Bill* (Perth, 1904)
Day, T., 'Studies of the development of the turnpike roads and their associated engineering infrastructure in north-east Scotland 1780-1880' (unpublished PhD thesis, Aberdeen, 1992)
Douglas C., 'Enclosure and Agricultural Development in Scotland', in Economic History Society Conference Booklet 2004 (at http://www.ehs.org.uk/events/ehs-annual-conference-archive.html)
Duff, R.W., MP, *The Herring Fisheries of Scotland* (London, 1883)
Ferguson, N., *The Dundee & Newtyle Railway* (Oxford, 1995)
Ferguson, N., *The Arbroath and Forfar Railway* (Oxford, 2000)
Fletcher, F., *Directors, Dilemmas and Debt* (Aberdeen, 2010)
Forsyth-Grant, M., 'Recollections of Brotherton Castle, Lathallan School 1900-1999' in *Lathallan School Magazine* (Johnshaven, nd (c. 2000))

Fraser, D., *Portrait of a Parish* [Ecclesgreig and St. Cyrus] (Montrose, 1970)

Fraser, G.M., 'Aberdeen's Costly First Railway Project', in *Aberdeen Journal*, 20th February 1929

Gove, R., *The Story of the Royal Burgh* [Inverbervie] (Inverbervie, 1992)

Haldane, A.R.B., *The Drove Roads of Scotland* (Edinburgh, 1952)

Haldane, A.R.B., *Three Centuries of Scottish Posts* (Edinburgh, 1971)

Hay, G., *A History of Arbroath to the Present Time* (Arbroath, 1876)

Keith, Revd G.S., *A General View of the Agriculture of Aberdeenshire, Drawn Up under the Direction of the Board of Agriculture, and Illustrated with Plates* (London, 1811)

King P.M., *A Short History of Brotherton and the Scott Family* (Johnshaven, 1980)

Kinnear, G.H., *Cambridge County Geographies: Kincardineshire* (Cambridge, 1921, 2013)

Lindsay, J., *The Canals of Scotland* (Newton Abbott, 1968)

Lofts C., *Last Trains: Dr Beeching and the Death of Rural England.* (London, 2013)

Macdonald, J., 'On the Agriculture of the Counties of Forfar and Kincardine' in *Transactions of the Highland and Agricultural Society of Scotland*, Fourth series, Vol. XIII (Banff, 1881)

McIntosh, J. and A. Small, 'Road development in North-East Scotland 1746-1815: the Maritime Connection' in *Scottish Geographical Magazine*, Vol. 111, No. 3 (1995)

MacLeod, A.B., *The McIntosh Locomotives of the Caledonian Railway 1895-1914* (London, 1948)

Marshall, P., '1880s Picture shows Express Headcode and Reversed Route Indicator, in *Historic Model Railway Society Journal*, Vol. 13, No. 1 (Jul.-Sep. 1990)

Marshall, P., *The Railways of Dundee* (Witney, 1996)

Marshall, P., *Scottish Central Railway* (Witney, 1998)

Mitchell, J., *Angus and Mearns Remembrancer* (Montrose, 1830)

Mitchell, W.A., *Or was it yesterday?* (Aberdeen 1947)

Moore, K.L., 'Carrier Routes in the North-East of Scotland 1803-1914: Development and Change in a Service', in *Scottish Geographical Journal*, Vol. 119, part 4 (2003)

Mountfield, D., *The Coaching Age* (Hale, 1976)

Nichol, E., 'Early Days on the Montrose and Bervie Branch' in *North British Study Group Magazine*, issue 49

Nisbet, A.F., 'The Montrose & Bervie Railway' in *Backtrack*, Vol. 27, No. 11 (Nov. 2013)

Odlyzko, A., *Collective Hallucinations and Inefficient Markets: the British Railway Mania of the 1840s* (Minnesota, 2010) (preliminary version published on line at www.dtc.umn.edu/~odlyzco/doc/hallucinations.pdf)

Patrick, J., *The Coming of Turnpikes to Aberdeenshire* (Aberdeen, nd)

Peter, D.M., *The Baronage of Angus and Mearns, comprising the genealogy of three hundred and sixty families – curious anecdotes – descriptions of clan tartans, badges, slogans, armory, and seats – ancient sculptures, &c being a guide to the Tourist and Heraldic Artist* (Edinburgh, 1856)

Radford, P., *The Celebrated Captain Barclay: Sport, Money and Fame in Regency Britain* (London, 2001)

Ray, J., *A Compleat History of the Rebellion from the First Rise, in 1745 to its Total Suppression at the Glorious Battle of Culloden in April 1746* (Bristol, 1752)

Robertson C.J.A., *The Origins of the Scottish Railway System, 1722-1844* (Edinburgh, 1983). A sequel, *The Railway Mania and its Aftermath in Scotland, 1844-54* was planned, but the author died before he could complete it; the papers and unfinished chapters are in the University of St Andrews Special Collections

Robertson, G., *A General View of Kincardineshire; or the Mearns; drawn up and published by order of the Board of Agriculture* (London, 1810)

Rodgers, Allan G., 'The Montrose & Bervie Branch' in *North British Railway Study Group Journal*, No. 73 (Summer 1999)

Ross, D., *The Caledonian: Scotland's Imperial Railway – A History* (Catrine, 2013)

Ross, D., *The North British Railway* (Catrine, 2014)

Simpson, A.R.C., *Gourdon: a Brief History of the Village and its People, 1500-1800* (Aberdeen, 2005)

Smail, A., 'The Scottish Postal System in 1753 and 1759', in *Scots Magazine*, 1st Nov. 1899

Smith J.D. and D. Steven, *Fermfolk and Fisherfolk* (Aberdeen, 1989)

Smith, W.A.C. and P. Anderson, *An Illustrated History of Tayside's Railways: Dundee and Perth* (Clophill, Bedfordshire, 1997)

Stevenson, R., *A Memorial Relative to Opening the Great Valleys of Strathmore and Strathearn by means of a Railway or Canal, with Branches to the Sea from Perth, Arbroath, Montrose, Stonehaven and Aberdeen; Together with Observations on Interior Communications in General* (Edinburgh, 1820)

Stevenson, R., *Report Relative to Lines of the Railway, Surveyed from the Ports of Perth, Abroath, and Montrose into the Valley of Strathmore … in the Year 1826* (Edinburgh, 1827)

Thomas, J., *Forgotten Railways – Scotland* (Newton Abbott, 1981)

Vallance, H.A., 'The Montrose and Bervie Railway' in *The Railway Magazine*, Vol. 94, No. 576, Jul.-Aug. 1948

Vallance, H.A., *The Great North of Scotland Railway* (chapter 7: 'The Aberdeen Junction Controversy') (London, 1965)

Waterman, J.J., *The Coming of the Railway to Aberdeen in the 1840s* (Aberdeen, nd)

Waterman J.J., *Aberdeen and the Fishing Industry in the Eighteen Seventies* (Aberdeen, nd)

Whittaker, I.G., *Off Scotland: a Comprehensive Record of Maritime and Aviation Losses in Scottish Waters* (Edinburgh, 1998)

Wignall, C.J., *Complete British Railways Maps and Gazetteer from 1830-1981* (Oxford, 1981)

Zealand, G., *The Natural History of St. Cyrus* (chapter 8: 'Human History') (Edinburgh, 1980)

Maps

The National Library of Scotland has placed many of its historic maps online. A selection of those relevant to this book are:

Roy, *Military Survey of Scotland* (1747-1755)

Taylor, G. and A. Skinner, *A General Map of the Roads, Made Out of Actual Surveys Taken by Geo. Taylor and Andw. Skinner* (London, 1775)

Thomson, J., *Atlas of Scotland* (Edinburgh, 1832)

Ordnance Survey (various editions from 1864 onwards)

Video

A short video of the closure of the line was commissioned by Mary Officer in 1966, and this is now available as part of *Around Johnshaven – A Musical Tour of Benholm and Johnshaven* available from the Benholm & Johnshaven Heritage Society.